D0931103

NO KIDDING!

NO KIDDING!

Clown as Protagonist in Twentieth-Century Theater

Donald McManus

DELAWARE

Newark: University of Delaware Press
London: Associated University Presses

Associated University Presses
2010 Eastpark Boulevard
Cranbury, NJ 08512

Associated University Presses
Unit 304, The Chandlery
50 Westminster Bridge Road
London SE1 7QY, England

Associated University Presses
P.O. Box 338, Port Credit
Mississauga, Ontario
Canada L5G 4L8

The paper used in this publication meets the requirements of the American National Standard for Permanence of Paper for Printed Library Materials Z39.48-1984.

Library of Congress Cataloging-in-Publication Data

McManus, Donald Cameron, 1959–
No kidding! : clown as protagonist in twentieth-century theater / Donald Cameron McManus.
p.   cm.
Includes bibliographical references and index.
ISBN 0-87413-808-6 (alk. paper)
1. European drama—20th century—History and criticism.   2. Clowns in literature.   I. Title.
PN1650.C59 M38 2003
809.2'93527913—dc21   2003004112

PRINTED IN THE UNITED STATES OF AMERICA

Contents

Acknowledgments

THE AUTHOR WOULD LIKE TO THANK THE COMMITTEE ON GRANTS AT Franklin & Marshall College and the Horace H. Rackham School of Graduate Studies at University of Michigan for their support. Thanks are also due to John Russell Brown for his advice and friendship. Invaluable guidance also came from Leigh Woods, Bert Cardullo, Hubert Cohen, and Martin Walsh. I am grateful to Kurt Beattie, Bill Irwin, Larry Pisoni, Geoff Hoyle, and Joel Schechter for taking time to share their experience with me and allowing me to sit in on their rehearsals. Finally, I would like to thank Hilary Gopnik, without whose criticism and encouragement this project would have been impossible.

NO KIDDING!

1

Introduction:
Towards an Understanding of Clown

ADRIAN WETTACH (A. K. A. GROCK), WAS A SWISS CLOWN WHO RULED THE circuses and cabarets of Europe as "King of Clowns" until his death in 1959. Grock's audience included children, workers, politicians, artists, and intellectuals. As a punctuation to his routines he loved to yell "Sans blââgue!" [No Kidding!], indicating to his audience the potentially serious nature of his comic turns. "Sans blââgue!" was the trademark of a genuinely popular performer, but embedded in this comical utterance is the contradictory core of what made clown such an appealing character to modernist theater.

Most theatrical traditions have characters that we recognize as clowns. Playwright and performer Dario Fo has said that: "clowns can be found at all times and in all countries."[1] The very diversity of clown, however, makes a comprehensive definition a complicated matter. In fact, it has proven so difficult that most scholars and historians in the field have balked at trying to define clown at all, and confined themselves to describing character traits, or points of similarity from tradition to tradition. But the persistence of clown as a recognizable figure in virtually all traditions, suggests that some essential clown quality must exist and be worth exploring.

The popular perception of a clown is synonymous with laughter, but clown as adopted by twentieth-century artists, has more frequently been the means through which the contemporary tragic impulse has been expressed. Clown makes an ideal protagonist of twentieth-century theater because theatrical modernism was preoccupied with breaking the expectations of older genre systems and exposing the mechanism of art-making. If a character in twentieth-century theater looks like a clown and acts like a clown, but does not make us laugh, it is usually because our attention is being channeled in a new direction. What

11

was once a joke has now been presented as an insight, question, or commentary. Clown has become, in contemporary theater, a character from whom audiences can expect philosophizing, angst, or political criticism as much as physical comedy and fractured language. Clown's historical association as a comic character makes him instantly distinct from the protagonist in tragedies from earlier periods. The contradiction of having a traditionally comic character stand in for the tragic hero is complemented by the clown's inherently contradictory nature as a stage character.

Clown watchers generally agree that the clown seems to exist both inside and outside of the dramatic fiction, upon which the clown frequently comments as "the voice speaking from without and not from within the dramatic plot."[2] This blurring of the borders of mimetic space can usually be accounted for by one of two reasons. Either the clown is more aware of the fact that he or she is part of a theatrical illusion than the other characters, or he or she is too stupid to understand the rules governing the illusion being created. In other words, the clown is either too smart or too dumb.

The clown's genius, or stupidity, is more than just a character trait. It constitutes a distinct performance mode from that of the non-clown characters. Despite superficial differences from tradition to tradition, clown can be defined as a character with a peculiar status both inside and outside of the dramatic fiction. Clown achieves this special status, or alternate performance mode, by employing a different logic of performance practice from the other characters. While the behavior of normative characters is based on their emotional responses to the plot and other characters, the clown's behavior stems from an attempt to logically negotiate the arbitrary rules that govern the plot and characters.

A basic scenario for clown action involves the presentation of an obstacle that the audience recognizes as a simple problem, but which the clown, for reasons not always explained, cannot fathom. The American circus clown, Emmett Kelly, performed a routine in which he swept up the ring after an acrobatic or equestrian act. While sweeping, Kelly would notice the spotlight, not understand that it was operated by a technician somewhere in the rafters of the tent, and attempt to sweep it up. The spotlight would get smaller and smaller, teasing Kelly but never disappearing. Eventually, Kelly would sweep the light under the edge of a canvas drop cloth and the light would go out. A good clown act is usually resolved by means of the clown finding a solution to the problem at hand that takes the audience by surprise because it is either not the solution that they had envisioned or had not been presented as consistent with the theatrical convention being used. The solution can redefine the problem and the audience's relationship to the clown character.

Clown's defiance of normal rules of behavior, or physical logic, holds true even within the other-worldliness of a theatrical fiction. That is to say that rules to which the other characters in a drama adhere may not constrain the actions of the clown, just as the three rings of the modern circus need not constrain the action and antics of circus clowns who may appear in the guise of peanut vendors among the audience as well as performers within the confines of the rings.[3]

Even though the audience may acknowledge that the rules governing a given performance do not correspond to their own lives or environment, as in the case of the formal settings of circus rings and the proscenium arch, they accept these rules as a vital part of the illusion and recognize the disruption caused by the clown's action. This effect of disruption, or difference from the primary mimetic convention, is one of the key devices that allow clown to function both inside and outside of the theatrical fiction. Although clowns have varying costumes, makeups, dramatic, and social functions, their disruptive quality is constant from genre to genre.

The key feature uniting all clowns, therefore, is their ability, through skill or stupidity, to break the rules governing the fictional world. But in practice, this definition of clown becomes extremely complex. The rules governing the fictional world come in two distinct categories. There are the rules of performance, governing the mimetic conventions being used, and social rules, governing the cultural norms of the world being imitated on stage. The two phenomena affect each other because disruption of the mimetic conventions usually implies disruption of cultural norms, and the clown's difficulty with the cultural norm often leads to his disrupting the mimetic convention. Two examples of this from Shakespeare's plays are Dromio (from *The Comedy of Errors*), who begins to disrupt the mimetic convention when he confides in the audience after he has been alternately rewarded and beaten by his master, and Launce (from *The Two Gentlemen of Verona*), whose similar dialogue with the audience is prompted by his being forced to leave home.

Film clowns also contradict, or provide contrast to, the mimetic conventions established in the greater narrative. Buster Keaton steps

into a film within the film in *Sherlock Jr.* (1924) to create a duality
of mimetic space and break the essential rule of film watching, which
is that the viewer cannot affect the action. In later cinema, Woody
Allen used a reversal of the same device in his *The Purple Rose of
Cairo* and adaptations of this device in such films as *Zelig* (where the
documentary quality of newsreel films is distorted to tell the biography
of a fictional *übermensch*) and in *Annie Hall* (1977) (where Allen's
character is represented in an alternate mimetic mode—a cartoon—
for an entire scene).

While clowns are disruptive characters on the one hand, they also
act as a bridge between the mimetic world of the play, or show, and the
world of the audience. Clown as mimetic bridge is easiest to recognize
in plays where the clown frankly engages the audience by directing
his or her dialogue to them in such a way as to invite a response. In
Shakespeare's *The Taming of the Shrew* (1593), Petruchio turns to
the audience and asks them the frank question; "He that knows better
how to tame a shrew, Now let him speak—tis charity to show."[4] This
utterance provides space for a response in a way that Hamlet's "To be or
not to be; that is the question" does not. If an audience member answers
Hamlet's question, the scene is ruined, but if Petruchio is heckled, an
opportunity for creative clowning arises. Clearer still are instances
in which the clown physically disrupts the mimetic environment by
stepping into the audience and directly interacting with the crowd.[5]
In *The Knight of the Burning Pestle* (1613) for instance, Ralph and
his master's wife reverse the procedure by entering from the pit of
the theatre to interrupt the prologue of the play and assert their own
clownish ideas upon the performance. They establish solidarity with
the world of the audience by literally entering from the audience's
environment.

It is paradoxical that the character who is usually the most grotesque
is also able to transcend the mimetic structure of the performance and
thereby provide a link to the world of the audience. The audience
laughs at the "otherness" of the clown both because he is not like them
and because he is not like the normative characters in the fiction. But
because the audience is also unlike the normative characters, they
share with clown his outsider status. The audience may temporarily
accept the characters in the base culture of the play, the characters who
represent normalcy in the fictional world, but the audience, like the
clown, is always separate from that group. Clown's grotesque quality
therefore serves both to make the audience laugh and to create a bond
between audience and clown.

The essential "otherness" of clown accounts for the phenomenon of clowns being freakish or deformed in some way. Their "difference" lends credence to their naive ignorance of the laws of nature and man. When this inherent "difference" is not part of the performer's person he must take on some external sign in order to add it, hence the grotesque make-ups and masks that are associated with clown. The clown must stand apart from the heightened reality of the rest of the play or spectacle, even when it utilizes highly formal costume, make-up and speech to create its "normal" non-clown world.

Clown's paradoxical otherness, which in fact makes him similar to the audience, manifests itself in the superficial aspects of clown dress and makeup but extends, more importantly, to his behavior. The audience recognizes that clown not only looks different, but has a different approach to the world. Clown's contradictory approach to conventions, both mimetic and social, constitutes an alternate "way of doing" or a distinct "clown logic." The clown will always try to think through a given situation and either fail because of an hopeless inability to understand the rules, or succeed because of a limitless ability to invent new rules.

The contradictory impulse is a part of clown's performance logic and naturally implies a criticism of the nature of authority. Clown lends itself to political metaphor because the relationship of the clown to the structure of the mimetic world has its correlative in the power structure of the non-theatrical world. Although clown need not serve political ends, the essential nature of clownage is such that the political metaphor is inevitable if the dramatists or directors who turn to clown have a political motive. It is not surprising, therefore, that many of the twentieth-century artists who have been interested in clown have also been political artists.

The political use of clown as an iconoclastic, anti-authoritarian character has been emphasized by modern critics and theater people, but clown has been a voice for a reactionary, oppressive ethos, just as frequently as a voice for underprivileged proletarian culture. The most glaring example of this fact is the black-face minstrel shows of nineteenth-century America. These clown shows were both anti-authoritarian, satirizing the central government, and oppressively authoritarian in the presentation of racial stereo-types.[6] Despite the tendency to miscast clown as a natural fighter for the disenfranchised, there is an undeniable correlation between the relationship clown has to theatrical illusion and clown's potential as an instrument for political allusion. Theater as political metaphor with clown as *agent-provocateur* has contributed to clown's place at the forefront of twentieth-century theater.

No one in the contemporary theater better illustrates this tendency to claim a political function for clown than Dario Fo. Fo sees clowning as an artistic expression of the power struggle between classes in which there are clowns who represent the underclass, such as the zanni of commedia dell'arte, and those who represent the "bosses," such as Pantalone and Dottore. The clown's alternate logic for Fo is either an expression of class conscious revolt or an extreme application of the logic of the ruling class.

> Clowns, like minstrels and "comics," always deal with the same problem— hunger, be it hunger for food, for sex, or even for dignity, for identity, for power. The problem they invariably pose is—who's in command, who's the boss? In the world of clowns there are two alternatives: to be dominated, and then we have the eternal underdog, the victim, as in the *commedia dell'arte*, or else to dominate, which gives us the boss, the white clown or Louis, whom we already know. He is in charge of the game, he gives the orders, he issues the insults, he makes and unmakes at will, while various Tonys, the Augustes, the Pagliaccios live on their wits, occasionally rebelling but generally getting by as best they can. [7]

Semiotician Paul Bouissac describes the same division of clowns as Fo in his analysis of circus, clown acts.

> A clown act always has at least two participants, or, more to the point, a basic dichotomy in the status of the participants. Two strings of signs symbolize, respectively, the cultural norm and the absence of that norm, either as nature or as anticulture. [8]

The representatives of the cultural norm and its inverse are the two basic clown types of the circus, the White Clown and the Auguste.

Both Fo and Bouissac imply that the clown's relationship to the normative world and clown opposite has a direct reflection in the power structure of the non-theatrical world. Fo wants us to recognize the essential Clown—Auguste dichotomy in terms of class struggle, with Augustes representing anti-authoritarian, class-conscious values, and White Clowns representing pawns of the existing power structure. As has already been pointed out, the most successful, clown-driven theater of American history was the minstrel show and its musical theater legacy. Fo's attempt to characterize clowns throughout history as proletarian heroes is not born out by theatrical history in other countries either. The clowns of commedia dell'arte were irreverent and anti-authoritarian some of the time, but they just as frequently underscored the status quo as undermined the power structure. Clown logic does not have an essential meaning other than to contradict the environment in which the clown appears. The meaning is defined by the individual performer, context of the specific performance and reception of the audience. There are no essentially good clowns and essentially bad clowns, at least not in moral terms.

White Clown and Auguste do not represent a typology of clown so much as a theatrical dynamic, reflecting the relationship between any two clowns, their mimetic environment and the audience. This dynamic can be used to represent truths about the human psyche, social-poltical reality or even pseudo-religious spiritual planes, but it remains in essence a theatrical phenomenon to be adapted and interpreted.

Theater artists in the twentieth century, wanting to bring the revolution of aesthetic ideas that typifies modernism to the stage, often combined their impulse for formal innovation with political metaphor, combining revolution of one kind with revolution of another. In fact, the story of clown as protagonist of twentieth-century theater is one of artists being torn between clown's potential as a hero of avant-garde artmaking and as a hero of people's art. While most artists were somewhat interested in both artistic and social innovation, some artists were only interested in creating a new form of expression. One such artist was Paul Margueritte, who adapted an old commedia routine in 1888 and redefined clown as a central character of theatrical modernism by presenting the death of a clown in a new and different light.

2

Clown as Focus of Agon in Modernism

THE GENERAL THEORY OF CLOWN EXPLORED IN THE PREVIOUS CHAPTER describes the nature of clown in any era, but is particularly relevant to clown in modernism because the modernists were self-consciously interested in demonstrating the mechanics of art-making in an anti-illusionist fashion and breaking with traditional artistic genres. Clown was seized upon as a recognizable human figure who also transcends genre and artistic convention. Clown was a favorite image in impressionist, expressionist, and cubist painting. These images were drawn from the contemporary circus and music hall, but the most persistent images are those of Pierrot and Harlequin. Indeed, there is a direct connection between the clowns of *commedia dell'arte* and the birth of modernism in the theater.

The Italian improvised comedy, *commedia dell'arte*, was the only form of theater in history to be dominated by clowns throughout its existence. Yet even in this clown-based genre, the *zanni* (or knockabout clowns) were marked as different from the other, normative characters by their use of masks.

Although the *commedia dell'arte* troupes used their skill at improvisation in every genre, the *zanni* were the main attraction for the audiences and left the most significant legacy for later theatrical forms. *Commedia dell'arte* was a modular form of theater, so that the comic routines of the *zanni* were separable from the narratives in which they appeared.[1] Many of these separate comic routines, called *lazzi*, developed a stage life beyond the plays for which they were designed. The modular structure of *commedia* confined the clowning by the *zanni* to the margins of the plot but also leant the *lazzi* an autonomous existence. Some of these *lazzi* were mock tragic, providing comic mirroring of normative character behavior. The most enduring of these mock tragic routines was the "*lazzo* of suicide." The *lazzo* of suicide

18

makes an excellent basic routine for illustrating the difference between clown's function in traditional and modernist theatre.[2] The following is an excerpt from the suicide *lazzo* as it appeared in *Empereur dans la lune*.

Harlequin: Ah, I'm so wretched! The Doctor is going to marry Columbine to a farmer, and I'll have to live without her! No, I'd rather die! Let's make it a quick death. I will go to my room; I'll fix a rope to the ceiling, I'll kick the chair away, and there I'll be: Hung. (*Mimes being hung.*) That's it then off to the gallows. To the gallows? You must be kidding, don't even think of it. Killing yourself over a woman, that would be a silly thing to do (*He begins to debate with himself.*) Yes sir, but when a woman betrays a man, that's a terrible thing. Indeed but when you're hung, what then? No you'll be worse off then. If you want to take a part come along with me. Well no I'd rather not just the same. You won't go anyway. Oh yes, I'm going. No you're not. Yes! No! (*He takes out his bastone and hits himself.*) Voila! That's got rid of that. Now there is no-one to stop me from hanging myself. (Makes to go but suddenly stops.) But, no! Hanging is such an ordinary death. Let's see if we can come up with a more Harlequinesque death. (*Thinks a bit.*) I've got it! I'll block up my mouth and my nose, the air won't be able to get out and so I'll die. (*He tries but fails.*) No, the wind comes out the bottom. Damn it. Oh what trouble dying is. (*To the audience.*) Gentlemen, if someone would like to die to provide me with an example I'd be obliged. Aha! I've got it. I've read in stories that people have died laughing. Now that would be a witty death. I'm very ticklish. If someone tickled me long enough I'd die laughing. I'll tickle myself and then I'll die.[3]

Once Harlequin has tickled himself to death, the next scene is begun with Harlequin lying dead on the stage. However, he revives himself and returns to the normal world of the play as if nothing has happened. Harlequin's monologue can be extracted from the existing text and elaborated upon to suit the mood of the clown and audience. His suicide is a comic turn separate from the rest of the play. He can die a comic death without interrupting his function to the main plot and its normative characters. In keeping with the definition of clown proposed in chapter one, Harlequin can both die a silly death and defy the laws of life and death by coming back to life in the next scene. He also moves freely from one mimetic convention to another, speaking directly to the audience one moment, interacting with props the next and using both mime and verbal communication. When Harlequin turns to the audience in the written version and asks if someone would care to die as an example, it is obvious that a response from the audience is intended, with improvised comic riffing to follow. Biancolelli performed this routine with another character on stage egging him on and interacting with him.[4]

Harlequin's *lazzo* conforms to the tendency of clown explicated in chapter one but its marginal status within the play as a whole means that even in a clown-driven genre like *commedia* the clown's transgression of mimetic conventions, and by extension the social norms, tend to be fleeting, comic in nature, and ultimately reintegrated by play's end. Modernism changed this essentially conservative tendency by forcing the audience to focus more directly on the clown's contradictory nature.

In 1888, a young author named Paul Margueritte revisited the *lazzo* of suicide in order to write and perform a tragic pantomime that used Harlequin's clown technique. His effort resulted in a self-consciously modernist version of clown entitled *Pierrot assassin de sa femme*.

BIRTH OF THEATRICAL MODERNISM:
PIERROT ASSASSIN DE SA FEMME

Margueritte, when not advancing his career as a mime, was a novelist of the naturalist school. He had aligned himself with four other young writers who put their names to the *"manifeste des cinq,"* an article that chastised their mentor Émile Zola (1840–1902) for what they considered sentimental literary excess. André Antoine (1858–1943), founder of the Théâtre Libre and father of the naturalist movement in French Theatre, decided to stage an evening devoted to the authors who had voiced criticism of Zola. All of the pieces were grim, realistic vignettes with the exception of *Pierrot assassin de sa femme*, which was a grim, unrealistic vignette.

In addition to Margueritte's clown, *Pierrot assassin* included a secondary character, that of an undertaker's assistant. In the 1888 production, this role was played by Antoine himself. Antoine and his coterie audience were attempting to adopt a pseudo-scientific approach to theatrical representation. They were interested in the theatre as a kind of laboratory in which human behavior could be reproduced and analyzed.

Margueritte's play did more than move the clown's death to center stage, he put the focus on the clown's means of representing death.

Pierrot assassin is remarkably similar to the *lazzo* of suicide. Pierrot, like Harlequin, cannot bear to see Columbine, to whom he is married in Margueritte's version, with another man. In both plays, the clown tickles himself to death. Both Pierrot and Harlequin realize that their métier offers them the perfect, ironic (Harlequinesque) death, but Pierrot decides it is the perfect, ironic (Pierrotesque) murder weapon first. Margueritte has already committed the murder of Columbine before the play begins. During the course of the play he reenacts his crime for the audience. In retelling the earlier event, he passes from the mimetic mode to the diegetic mode. While telling the story he becomes infected with the terrible laughter with which he murdered Columbine and dies himself. He performs in the mimetic, present tense, and diegetic, past tense simultaneously. Here is a section of Margueritte's text in which he recreates for the audience how he came upon the idea of tickling his wife to death:

> But how am I going to do it? (*Because Pierrot, as somnambulant, reenacts his crime, and in his hallucination, the past becomes the present.*) Of course there's always the rope you pull it tight, snap it's all over! Yes but the tongue hanging out, the face turned horrible? No.—The knife? Or a sabre, A huge sabre? Slash through the heart . . . Yes! but the blood flows in torrents, it gushed out.—Whew I'll be damned . . . of course there's always the gun, bang! But the bang! would be heard. Nothing. I come up with nothing. (*He paces about solemnly and meditates. Accidentally he stumbles.*) Ouch that hurts! (*He rubs his foot.*) Ow! That hurts! It won't last long it's better now. (*He keeps rubbing and tickling his foot.*) Ah! Ah! That's funny! No! It makes you laugh. Ah! (*He suddenly lets go of his foot. He strikes his forehead.*) I've got it! (*Slyly.*) I've got it! I'll tickle my wife to death that's it![5]

Where Harlequin had used almost the same series of thoughts to arrive at a means of killing himself, Pierrot arrives at a means of committing murder, but which transforms into the means of a self-inflicted death as well. Although the two pieces read similarly, they play very differently.[6] Technically, both scenes call on the performer to divide himself. In Harlequin's *lazzo*, he divides himself in order to debate the pros and cons of suicide and arrive at a suitable method. The clown's technique is used to render the potentially tragic situation comically ridiculous. In Margueritte's version, the same technique is used, but with the opposite effect. Pierrot divides himself in order to portray Columbine's death at his hands. The horror of the murder is intensified because of the means of representing it.

Pierrot assassin is much longer and more complex than the *lazzo* of suicide, yet it is performed entirely without words.[7] When he reenacts the death of Columbine, he passes into a mode of representation in which the audience must interpret the action with even fewer clues. No longer is he simply a silent character who has committed a terrible crime. He transforms into a silent character who can conjure an invisible world for his audience. The more real that invisible, "past tense" world becomes, the more convincing the effect of Pierrot's present-tense, death through laughter.

Pierrot shifts from mimetic convention to mimetic convention in a similar manner to Harlequin, who also uses mime. Where another clown, such as Gherardi, might take the same situation and render it comic, Margueritte specifically avoided this reading. Both Harlequin and Pierrot reintegrate their two halves by the end of their respective scenes, but where Harlequin returns to his marginal role, serving the central characters of the play, Pierrot reintegrates himself in order to heighten the horror of the play. When he stops dividing himself, he has stopped "acting" for the audience. He no longer portrays Columbine, but becomes infected with the deathly laughter that he has already explicated when acting out the murder. The same physical action is endowed with different meaning when repeated as the suicide.

Margueritte performed his suicide *lazzo* with no alternate, core plot. The audience is never allowed to return to a more normal world in which they can forget about Pierrot's murder and suicide, nor do they return to a normative mimetic convention. The only other character is an undertaker who has helped Pierrot carry the body to the graveyard. Even Columbine is only evoked through Pierrot's reliving of his crime. Not only is the clown death moved to the center, doubled and final, but the clown behavior, his way of doing, is made significant to the audience. In fact Pierrot's way of doing, or clown logic, is the only significant element of *Pierrot assassin de sa femme*. It has no moral other than to disrupt the audience's expectations.

Margueritte said in his memoirs; "I recall the stir in the house when, both of us stumbling with drunkenness, and he holding me up, we surged in—the door thrown open with the blow of the fist-under a pallid ray of moonlight."[8] The audience was stunned by the performance because their reason for coming to the theater was to examine the reality of life. They were struck dumb by the grotesque character of Pierrot. The stark contrast between Margueritte's pantomime and the naturalist plays on the program that night must have made its effect all the more startling. Set against the backdrop of *Le Théâtre Libre's* self-conscious exploration into the methodology of representation, the modernist features of pantomime became more visible. The clown techniques, transformation of space and objects, and the use of various levels of representation, (confusion of mimetic and diegetic modes) were more novel, even shocking, than the death and murder of the story.

Pierrot assassin de sa femme was a crucial moment in the development of early twentieth-century theater in Europe. What had been a novelty form, popular pantomime, which the élite of the art world might condescend to admire, became in Margueritte's play the essence of a new aesthetic. Symbolist poet Stephane Mallarmé (1842–98), author of *Après-midi d'un faune*, developed an entire aesthetic treatise "Sketched at the Theater" based solely on Margueritte's pantomime.[9] Mallarmé suggested that pantomime reflected a greater truth than realist forms. Over 50 years later Jacques Derrida launched deconstruction by elaborating on Mallarmé's aesthetic formula in his essay "The Double Session" (1966). In this way, Margueritte's relevance to contemporary views of theater persist. Experiments with, and interest in, realism and naturalism would continue, and do to this day; but, from that evening at the *Théâtre Libre* in 1888 into the next century, the relationship between the grotesque aspect of theater, the "theater theatrical" as Meyerhold was to call it, and the representation of reality on stage, became an obsession for a new generation of actors, directors and writers.[10]

The naturalists who watched *Pierrot assassin de sa femme* thought they observed something as true as their scientism when Margueritte forced them to pay attention to the technique of representation itself, rather than the significance behind the technique. By moving the tragic clown from the margin to the center complete with his clown logic, Margueritte struck upon a formal innovation that was to be repeated over and over in the new century as a means of critiquing outmoded representational formulae.

Paris was the center for modernist experiments in all of the arts at the end of the nineteenth century. The revival of French pantomime, culminating in Margueritte's Pierrot, resonated with the anti-naturalist aesthetic of modernism. Naturalism sought to understand reality more accurately by eliminating theatricality and imitating life as directly as possible. When confronted with the passionate life force of clearly unreal, grotesque clown characters, the naturalists were forced to reassess their pseudo-scientific approach to the representation of reality on stage.

The craze for depicting clowns reached a fever pitch as the new century grew two decades old. Modernist developments in fine arts had an immediate effect on the theatre during this period. Painters, such as Renoir, Degas, Cezanne, Picasso, Klee, and Calder, made countless drawings, sketches, constructions and paintings evoking the image of clown. Indeed during a period of art history when figurative art was out of vogue, Pierrots and Harlequins were among the few consistent renderings of the human form. [11]

In music theater, clowns served as spokesmen for formal developments. *Pierrot Lunaire*, (1912) by Arnold Schoenberg (1874–1951) was written specifically to introduce a new kind of vocal music, which he called *sprechstimme*. This form of art singing, which imitates the spoken word, subsequently influenced Ferruccio Busoni (1866–1924) in his opera *Arlecchino* (1917). In this work Arlecchino is the only character who never sings and he provides an introductory curtain speech [12] to warn the audience of the adult nature of the play. [13]

Clowns were continually evoked by the opera and dance of the period, particularly in the work of Diaghilev, Fokine, Cocteau, and their circle. Diaghilev did more to promote modern music and visual art on the Paris stage than any other single figure of the *fin de siècle*. Stravinsky's ballet, *Petrushka* (1911), combined several modernist ideas including non-representational painting, especially cubism, and an approach to music and dance that gave precedence to rhythm through the plastic stage life of clown protagonists. A few years later, Stravinsky reinvented the Medieval vice as part of his *L'Histoire du soldat* (1922). [14] This work was one of the first pieces by an important European composer to use jazz rhythms. [15] Like Busoni's *Arlecchino*, it used spoken dialogue with music rather than arias. Rather than hang on to the traditions of the pantomime, as Margueritte had done with *Pierrot assassin*, the clown was liberated entirely from past forms during this period. Clown images in all the various incarnations, from circus, music hall, *commedia* and pantomime, were extracted from their original contexts and inserted for their value as icons of modernism.

3

Chasing and Gagging Clown: Early Modernism and the Development of French Mime

WITH CLOWN ESTABLISHED AS A CENTRAL IMAGE OF THE MODERNIST movement, young intellectuals were naturally drawn to living clowns who could be observed in their popular environment. The Fratellini Brothers, stars of the *Cirque Medrano* in Paris for over twenty years, more than any other popular artists of the period, fulfilled the modernist vision of clown. The Fratellini had a direct influence on modern theater, but not all modernists interpreted them in the same way.

Jacques Copeau (1879–1949), an actor, director, critic and educator was drawn to the Fratellini as a means of helping him to "renovate" theater. His research led to the rediscovery of *commedia dell'arte* and mime, which informed his own productions of Shakespeare and Molière, but, more significantly, became the staple of his training method for young actors. Jean Cocteau (1889–1963) a poet, dramatist, novelist, critic, painter and film director, recruited the Fratellini as performers to help create a modern theatrical form. This chapter explores the contrasting ways in which these two founding figures of modern theater interpreted and utilized the Fratellini clowns.

THE FRATELLINI BROTHERS

The Fratellini brothers came from an old circus family and had performed around the world, each of them having been born in a different country. During their wanderings across Europe, they refined and perfected their approach to clown and altered and adapted their characters over time. Their performances were much longer than traditional clown entrées, lasting up to twenty and thirty minutes, with clear internal development in which each brother was introduced in such a way that their individual entrance constituted a new scene. The context for the scenario would be introduced by Paul, (Scene 1), complicated by François, (Scene 2) and brought to a climax by Albert, (Scene 3). Their routines, or more accurately, playlets, always ended with the three brothers working together, usually playing music, representing the restoration of their clown family. The Fratellini self-consciously set out to adapt the White Clown-Auguste relationship by developing the character types for three performers in such a way that an infinite number of nuances on standard routines could be played out. As a trio, the Fratellini presented their own, balanced version of the Clown-Auguste dichotomy creating clown entrées that approached mini-theatrical presentations.

François was the White Clown, but he underplayed the aggressive quality of that character to suit the taste of the Paris audience. François' elaborate costumes were consistent with the White Clowns who had come before him such as Antonet and Footit, but where their costumes retained a late Romantic flavor in such details as embroidered roses and butterflies, François was more likely to sport geometric patterns accenting the cubist outline of the white clown costume.[1]

Paul would always begin their act. He wore almost no make-up and therefore warmed up the audience to give his brothers time to prepare. Paul's costume was consistent with that used by many Augustes, a slightly worn tuxedo, but his character was a novel combination of two previously antithetical types, the Auguste and the ringmaster (or, master of ceremonies).[2] As master of ceremonies for the show, Paul established the parameters of the event, but was thwarted by François, the White Clown. Paul was interpreted by critics as a parody of the bourgeois, down on his luck.[3] While Paul held the position as master of ceremonies, usually understood as one of authority, his Auguste character undermined this authority and won him the sympathy of the audience. He was no match for the suave and intelligent François.

Last to appear was always the youngest brother, Albert. Albert brought a new character to the clown dichotomy in the contre-Auguste. The contre-Auguste is a character so grotesque that even the Auguste is shocked by his lack of cultural refinement. Once Paul was established as the Auguste and François as the White Clown, Albert's entrance provided a butt for both of them. Born in Russia, his character owed much to the Russian tradition of clowning. He was an extremely grotesque Auguste with oversized shoes, a red nose and a series of frightful wigs. When Albert's grotesque contre-Auguste was inserted with Paul's Auguste-ringmaster and François' elegant, cubist White Clown, the narrative possibilities seemed endless. It was this quality of infinite variation that brought audiences back night after night to watch the same performers doing essentially the same routines.

In the eyes of the intellectuals of the early century, these performers seemed to hold the promise of Gordon Craig's *über-marionette*.[4] Jean Cocteau referred to the Fratellini as the "best mechanical puppets in the world."[5] Their performances were interpreted as magical events in which the performers transcended normal expectations by displaying an unexpected capacity to do anything required of them with grace and spontaneity: "They could act, dance, jump, fly, play twenty musical instruments and were masters of a hundred other métiers."[6]

The Fratellini Brothers were brought to Paris from Russia specifically to appeal to a high-brow clientele. The management of the Medrano circus realized that the working class audience was abandoning the circus in favor of other newer entertainments, especially films and music hall. The Fratellini specifically geared themselves, therefore, to an audience with intellectual and modernist tastes. Their costumes reflected cubist and futurist fashion in a self-conscious way. These fashions had drawn on clown and circus for inspiration and the circus was naturally returning the favor by reinterpreting itself to suit the audience who appreciated them.[7] The brothers took an avid interest in the intellectual aspect of their work and amassed a huge library of circus and clown memorabilia over their lifetime, including rare *commedia dell'arte texts*.

The literati of Paris would visit the Medrano Circus, imagining that they were discovering a naive kind of theater that captured the spirit of their modernist ideals. The Fratellini themselves, however, targeted their performances to this elite audience. Their act did not usually begin until 11:30 in the evening long after the children were in bed and the animal acts had also been put to sleep. The late evening time for their performances allowed the intelligentsia to come to the circus after the legitimate theaters and concert halls had closed.[8]

COCTEAU

Jean Cocteau interpreted the Fratellini as entirely modern performers. He had already experimented with *commedia* derived characters in his production of Eric Satie's *Parade* (1917) with sets and costumes by Picasso. Unhappy with the efforts of dancers pretending to be clowns in *Parade*, Cocteau ridiculed *commedia* in his essay *Coq et l'Arlequin*, (1918), a manifesto of modernist aesthetics. In this seminal essay, Cocteau criticized all romantic images of clown as well as foreign influences in French music and theater, urging his colleagues to eschew the past, characterized by Harlequin, in favor of the living forms found in circus and music hall.

Recognizing his mistake in staging romantic images of clown in *Parade*, Cocteau hired the Fratellini Brothers to perform the main roles in his stage extravaganza *Le Boeuf sur le toit* (1920) subtitled "The Nothing Doing Bar." The music was written by French composer Darius Milhaud (1892–1974) who became one of "the six" pillars of French modernism described in *Coq et l'Arlequin*.[9]

> Forgetting that I had written *Les Choephores* both public and critics agreed that I was a figure of fun and a showground musician . . . I, who hated anything comic and, in composing *Le Boeuf sur le toit*, had only aspired to create a merry, unpretentious divertissement, in memory of the Brazilian rhythms which had captured my imagination but had certainly never made me laugh![10]

The attraction of clown for Milhaud and Cocteau clearly has nothing to do with the power of comedy. Although Milhaud defends himself from the accusation of writing comic music this did not preclude writing music with clown in mind:

> I thought that the character of this music might make it suitable for the accompaniment to one of Charlie Chaplin's films. At this time the silent films were accompanied by fragments of classical music rendered by large or small orchestras or even a small piano according to the means available. Cocteau disapproved of my idea, and proposed that he should use it for a show, which he would undertake to put on.[11]

The "show" which Cocteau put on had a similar effect on its audience as Margueritte's *Pierrot assassin* had in 1882. While Margueritte's performance had the strange result of pointing out the truth of the grotesque to the naturalists, Cocteau's *Le Boeuf sur le toit* did much the same for dance theater, which was preoccupied with a natural physical expression in contradistinction to the perceived falseness of ballet. Cocteau developed a scenario that frustrated the dance rhythms created by Milhaud. While Milhaud's music alternates rhythmic figures with disconcerting frequency, Cocteau's scenario provided yet another disconnected rhythm. According to Milhaud:

> Jean had engaged the clowns from the Cirque Medrano and the Fratellini to play the various parts. They followed implicitly all the extremely precise orders he gave them as producer. Albert Fratellini, being an acrobat, could even dance on his hands around the policeman's head. In contrast with the lively tempo of the music, Jean made all of the movements slow, as in a slow-motion film. This conferred an unreal, almost dream-like atmosphere on the show. The huge masks lent peculiar distinction to all the gestures, and made the movement of hands and feet pass unperceived. [12]

Almost all the critics of the period commented on the disconcerting effect evoked between the tempo of the action and the music. Cocteau moved the show to London where it was presented at The Coliseum, a popular music hall. The Swiss clown Grock followed *Le Boeuf sur le toit* with his entrée, already successful with English audiences. The English press was perplexed by Cocteau's extravaganza. *The Times* belittled the performance as "a farce without a giggle, much less a laugh, a harlequinade with the tempo of an adagio instead of presto." [13]

Not all of the London critics were unimpressed, however. Leigh Henry of the *Musical Standard* was perhaps the most accurate in his appraisal of the show's significance. He also stressed the conflict between the physical action and the music.

> Cocteau . . . deliberately designed the movements to contradict the rhythmic movement of the music, thereby attaining a peculiarly grotesque quality, and a curiously irresistible comic effect. Spiritually the significance of *The Nothing Doing Bar* is important, in that it marks a departure from the sentimental cliché of the "halls," even as the music forms an example of the new musical tendency to get out into the fresh air, even if it be that of the streets. And though one may hear that the subject-matter may be designated as trivial by the solemn-minded, they are yet as important as the daisies immortalized in the Wordsworthian type of poem. [14]

Le Boeuf sur le toit was important because Cocteau used the Fratellini to make his audience rethink music theatre and dance. Once again, clown, with its tradition of challenging mimetic conventions, is used to restructure an established set of theatrical conventions.

Cocteau was not nostalgic for the *commedia dell'arte*, on the contrary, he viewed nostalgia as the enemy of modernism, declaring that

Harlequin was a foreign interloper in *"Coq et l'Arlequin."* He used the Fratellini to reorganize and restate a formal aesthetic rather than to deify clowns. Cocteau's experiment with clown contrasts with that of Jacques Copeau. Where Cocteau used clowns to contradict preconceptions about other genres, Jacques Copeau felt that they could form a basis for a new acting technique.

COPEAU

Jacques Copeau was the most influential director of his generation. Both in his theater, the *Vieux Columbier*, founded in 1913 and at his *École du Vieux Columbier*, founded in 1921, Copeau promoted a simplified, purer approach to theater that stressed the actor on an unencumbered stage (*tréteau nu*) and the sanctity of the dramatic text. In his *"Essai de rénovation dramatique,"* he promised to restore beauty to the stage. One of the principle means of achieving this goal, according to Copeau was by rediscovering a lost, naive approach to theater that he believed had existed with *commedia* actors.

Copeau was the first artist who looked to clowns, both tangible and mythical, as the building blocks of modern theater. The Fratellini were enlisted to help instill his young students with their spirit in the hopes that a new generation could rediscover the theater's popular spirit. Copeau's experiments and initiatives were to have a profound effect on twentieth-century theater and this legacy was to be no less significant for the future of clown. Two strains of modern clowning had their genesis at Copeau's school. The first of these was the rediscovery of *commedia* and the other was mime.

After Copeau formed his own company and theater school, he recruited young, idealistic actors who had exhibited talent but had not had enough contact with the boulevard theaters to pick up too many bad habits. Throughout his career, Copeau had an uncanny knack for drawing talented and resourceful men and women to him who would carry out his vision, almost as disciples to a prophet.

Some of Copeau's research into *commedia* had a practical effect on the productions of the company. Along with his partner, Suzanne Bing, Copeau researched pure movement and mask work in conjunction with work on text. This research led to a novel and a successful production (in 1914) of *Twelfth Night*, entitled *La Nuit des Rois* in Copeau and Bing's original translation. The production of *La Nuit des Rois* impressed audiences and critics with its simple approach to text and action which had grown directly out of experiments in improvisation inspired by observation of popular performers of the day such as the Fratellini Brothers. Louis Jouvet (1887–1951) played Aguecheek opposite Copeau's Malvolio and Suzanne Bing's Viola. Bing and Jouvet assisted Copeau in managing the school where they attempted to pass on their discoveries to a younger generation. Suzanne Bing was the single most important person in the daily operation of the theater school. Her work with masks and physical theater was the basis for much of the company's redefining of classic technique and also formative in the development of French mime through such young students as Étienne Decroux.

Copeau's approach to theater was literary, but he was committed to the idea that there was a lost form of drama, or dramatic presentation, and that actors in the past, even as recently as the nineteenth century, had been in command of skills that could be rediscovered. This idea is well expressed in Copeau's forward to the Fratellini Brothers' autobiography:

> What I call your pure style is technical perfection and especially muscular perfection in the service of a spontaneous and sincere feeling. What I call the "gentleness" in everything you do is the smile of your unsullied natures. In past ages, Antiquity, the Middle Ages, the Renaissance, that quality of "gentleness" was always accorded as supreme praise to the real actor, the one who, while amusing his contemporaries with his grimace, or enchanting them with his *lazzi*, never allowed his dignity as a man to waste away.

Later in the same preface, he pays the brothers what, for him, is the highest of compliments by saying that they are the true inheritors of the *commedia dell'arte*. Copeau interpreted the clown routines of the Fratellini as something basic, natural, and connected with a superior, ancient form of theater.

Copeau's veneration of text was criticized by subsequent visionaries such as Antonin Artaud (1896–1948) who complained that Copeau slavishly valorized language.[15] Copeau did include lessons in grammar at the Vieux Columbier but he was also one of the first directors to make liberal use of improvisation as a rehearsal tool. In fact, Copeau's interest in improvisation has been one of his most enduring gifts to theater pedagogy. His disciples, most notably his nephew, Michel Saint-Denis (1897–1971), spread the Copeau gospel to England, the United States and Canada, and with it the belief that improvisation was a fundamental tool for the development of young actors.[16] Copeau's approach

to the renovation of theater can therefore be seen as proceeding on
two apparently contradictory but actually complementary fronts. He
was at once focusing on the text and exploring non-verbal modes of
communication and artistic expression.

Because of clown's peculiar status as a character both inside and
outside of the text, and because he often corrupts language, he has
frequently been understood as the theatrical character most at odds
with language, or in some cases the character who makes language redundant. [17] For this reason clown is seen as an anti-literary character.
Copeau didn't share the belief that clown was incompatible with literary tradition, but he did separate the physical and verbal approaches
to theater.

Copeau confused the apparent naiveté of the clown characters with
their technique as performers. The clowns' ability to function outside
of the conventions then common in European theater was misinterpreted by Copeau as being an outgrowth of the purity at the core of
their technique instead of as a self conscious, structured theatrical
technique in itself. For Copeau, this naive quality was a spiritual matter, and the rediscovery of it would lead to a better understanding of
the great texts of the dramatic tradition.

Copeau continually referred to literary masters for evidence of lost
performance attributes. In 1916, he wrote in his notebook:

> In the time of this celebrated Spaniard (Lope de Rueda) all the properties
> of a theatrical manager were contained in a sack, and consisted of four
> white pelices trimmed with gilded leather, and four beards and wigs, with
> four staffs more or less. The plays were colloquies or eclogues between
> two or three shepherds and a shepherdess. They were set off by two or
> three *entremeses* (short farces or interludes), either that of the "Negress",
> the "Ruffian", the "Fool" or the "Biscayan", and these four characters
> and many others were acted by the said Lope with the greatest skill and
> propriety that one can imagine. [18]

Later in the same essay, Copeau declares that it is possible and in
fact necessary to "ape such early naiveté and penury." [19] Here, as in
his praise of the Fratellini Brothers, Copeau has in his mind's eye
a dynamic of performers who communicate with each other and the
audience at a very basic "pure" level.

When Copeau hired the Fratellini to teach at his theater school,
he had them instruct the young students in acrobatics and juggling,

leaving such intellectual topics as form and structure in acting technique to his son-in-law Jean Dasté. With all his admiration for the skill of the Fratellini, Copeau's attitude toward them was essentially patronizing. He greatly admired their improvisational ability, for instance, but the form of improvisation that his school developed, and that is still used in theater training around the world, serves an entirely different purpose from clowning. Rather than recognizing that clowns like the Fratellini based their improvisation on an understanding of structure and character as well as an acute sensitivity to the audience's perceptions of these aspects, improvisation in theater pedagogy, as developed by Copeau and his disciples, focuses on "freeing" students from their intellectual selves. Of Albert Fratellini, Copeau would tell his students "what an actor he would have made" implying that Albert's clowning prevented him from acting.[20]

As Copeau aged, he did not lose his belief in the potential of clown. His moral philosophy became more and more religious, however, and he simply continued to fit clown into his overall ethos as a kind of shadow of mankind before the fall. Haunted by past forms of theater, his vision of clown is something of an inverted version of the medieval clown concept. In Medieval theater the clown was usually a vice figure who represented the devil. To Copeau, clown's naïveté stemmed from an essential purity. Copeau's historicism differed in this respect from that of the futurists, such as Meyerhold, Marinetti and even Brecht who looked to clowns as anti-bourgeois heroes who would lift theater into a new age. Copeau's love of clown remained nostalgic and became more so as he aged.

Copeau strove to expand the possibilities of stage acting by incorporating the discipline and improvisatory energy of clown. While he did not see these experiments as anti-textual, the most significant contribution to the clown world from the Copeau years was the development of modern French mime. This genre of theater, also called corporeal mime, takes silence very seriously. In this sense it is, of course, anti-textual, at least as far as spoken text is concerned.

ARE MIMES CLOWNS?

Étienne Decroux, the man most responsible for the development of corporeal mime, said that "mime lives in the shadow of speech."[21] When mime is mixed with spoken text it will always be subservient,

according to Decroux. Fascinated by the relationship between movement and speech, Decroux forbade speech in his studio and refused
to acknowledge any speaking performer as a true mime. At the same
time Decroux had a great love of language and referred to himself as
a "grammarian of movement."[22] Having developed out of Copeau's
circle, Decroux was preoccupied with mime's relevance to acting in
general. Although he believed that all actors should master mime, Decroux strove to establish mime as an independent art form. But mime's
relationship to clown is as complex as its relationship to acting. An
entire generation of aspiring clowns went to Paris to study mime as the
foundation of their art.

Decroux's two most famous pupils were Marcel Marceau and Jean-
Louis Barrault. Marceau became the most famous exponent of mime
and linked mime with clown through his clown persona, "Bip." Barrault occasionally used his mime technique to play the clown. He portrayed Jean-Baptiste Deburau in the film *Les Enfants du Paradis*,
and played Touchstone in Copeau's production of *As You Like It* at
Charles Dullin's *Atelier* in 1939. But for the most part, Barrault applied his mime technique to tragic theater with little or no clown elements. Mime's contribution to contemporary clowning should not be
undervalued, yet there is clearly a distinction between mime as an independent art form and clown. Jean Dorcy, another student of L'École
du Vieux-Columbier, defines mime in contradistinction to clown:

> The most important figure, the poet, is that master of fantasy: the clown. In
> spite of his acrobatic skill and of all his evocative power, we do not consider
> him as a mime. His tricks and gags are limited to obvious comical situations,
> to accessories, and to the relation of objects. So the clown has knowingly
> reduced his field of action.[23]

It is surprising that the clown would be described as reducing his field
of action in comparison to the mime who will not admit language into
his performance. If the clown is not a mime, as Dorcy suggests, to what
extent can the mime claim to be a clown, and in what circumstances?

Clowns always destroy, or at least conflict with, the norm, whether
that norm is manifested in the world of the audience or in the purely
theatrical world of illusion. The clown might suggest a Utopia that lies
outside of the visible world of the play but the clown cannot exist within
such a world without losing his clown nature. Mime, stemming as it did
from Copeau's ideas and theater school, adopted much of his spiritual
rationale for theater's existence. When mime is used as a device to

conflict with or comment on the norm, then mime is a valid part of clown. When mime is used to create an incontestable, invisible world, then it becomes a convention unto itself.

Different genres of performance frequently adopt the external signs of clown characters, their makeup and costume and traditional relationships but idealize their existence. In such cases, the characters are not really clowns. They are simply dancers or actors who look superficially like clowns. Included in this category of *faux* clowns are the characters common in symbolist plays written during the *belle époque* into the 1920s, and the Christmas Pantos of the London stage, which presented clown characters who were usually west-end actors out for a frolic. These fantasy pieces cannot be considered the same type of application of clown as in circus and *commedia* or, as we shall see, in iconoclastic modernist plays.

However, the theater is currently enjoying a remarkable revival in clown and the performers who have spearheaded this revival owe a great deal to the legacy of French mime and, by extension, Copeau. Étienne Decroux attempted to define mime in his book *Paroles sur le mime* (1963).[24] His definition is preoccupied with differentiating his art form from Ballet and modern dance. The fact that Decroux viewed dancers as his main competition reminds us of the fact that clown-like characters had become a staple of dance repertoire and that mime had become a codified form belonging to high art.

The development of mime at the early part of the century coincided with the image of clown on film and particularly the silent clowning of Charles Chaplin. Chaplin was the most popular performer in the world and he was admired equally by the masses and elite, the intellectuals and modernists, including Copeau, Cocteau, Diaghilev, Nijinsky, and Meyerhold, as well as the French mimes, Decroux, Barrault, Marceau, and Lecoq.[25] Although the French mimes claimed to take their inspiration from clown and equate their art with the silent clowning of Chaplin, a stigma persists that mimes are those silent guys who are almost never funny, whereas clowns are guys who might be silent or not, but are always funny.

Although both strains of modern clowning, *commedia dell'arte* and mime, have their roots in Copeau's theatrical renewal of the 1920s and 1930s, it is undeniable that mime has given contemporary clowns the discipline with which they could perfect their skill, grow as artists and ultimately develop away from mime. Mime has become the grammar of modern clown.[26]

If the mime engages with animate objects he is not a pure mime in the French sense. Whether we call him a pantomimist, a silent actor, or a clown, the fact remains that when performers engage physically with tangible objects they use their technique in a different way than that of a strict mime such as Marceau, Decroux, or Lecoq. The distinction between mime and silent clowning becomes significant when one turns to a written piece such as Beckett's *Act Without Words*, which is specifically designated by Beckett as "a mime for one player." What does Beckett mean by mime? He clearly does not mean strict mime in the French tradition because *Act Without Words* is all about the silent player's encounter with a visible, tactile environment and props.[27]

Ever since Decroux, French mime has lured performers into an esoteric world of tragedy and spirituality, but it can be a productive tool for comedy as well. Mime is essentially different from clown in a subtle but important way. Mimes create an illusion through the body, whereas clown uses the body to contradict the sense of illusion created by the body of the play. While watching the mime we try to interpret his or her movements so as to determine what the surroundings are supposed to be and what the significance of the actions are. The mime's goal is to express clearly to the audience the details of the narrative. The audience's goal is to keep up with the mime. The mime's art implies an alternate world where imitations of things are not shown, only imagined. In this sense, mime is an essentially Platonic notion of mimesis. It is not surprising, therefore, that the prime mouthpieces for pure mime (Lecoq, Decroux, Marceau, and Barrault), although they love to quibble with each other, are all Platonic idealists, to the point of being messianic, when speaking of their art. This idealism originated with Copeau, who began by being attracted to the anarchic poetry of the Fratellini Brothers, but ultimately envisioned a theater that would include a family of clowns whose theatrical world would offer audiences a morally superior option to the crude reality of twentieth-century Europe.

CLOWN AND POPULAR CULTURE

The twentieth century began with naturalism as the dominant trend in theater. Although clown was used by artists seeking alternative forms to naturalism and realism, even these artists believed, or came to believe, that some "better" form of representation could be found and that clown might hold the answer to this quest. Cocteau, whose interest in theater was wholly aesthetic, avoided the tendency of reading clowns as somehow more "true" in their frank artifice. He used them as disruptive engines, and when they had served his purpose, he moved on to his next project. Copeau took clown more seriously than any other artist of the period. He tried to incorporate clown into a theater pedagogy so that the purity of artistic expression he perceived as their essence could be passed on to the younger generation. This led to a general interest in reviving the *commedia dell'arte and* the development of mime. Both of these genres continue to thrive, although strict French mime is so codified that it has become entirely divorced from clown.

The different uses of clown, typified by Cocteau and Copeau, were to be repeated throughout the century, as modernists reassessed their accomplishments. Both Copeau and Cocteau were drawn to clown because they recognized clown as belonging to popular theater. But the two visions of what that popular theater meant were quite different. To Cocteau, popular theater was of value because it was what contemporary audiences liked. The mass appeal of popular forms, such as clown and circus, was justification in itself. Cocteau wanted to harness the energy and vitality of popular forms and the excitement that their audience's brought with them in order to breathe life into the high art that was always in danger of stagnation. Circus, music hall, jazz and clown were all forms that the public already understood and accepted. These, therefore, provided a more direct language with which Cocteau could forge a modernist aesthetic.

Copeau saw the Fratellini as positive emblems of popular theater because they reflected an aspect of the mass culture that was, in essence, holy. Unlike bourgeois theater, which Copeau viewed as decadent and unhealthy, he interpreted the popular culture expressed by the Fratellini as positive for society. Popular culture in this sense is not simply what the mass audience enjoys, but what is good for them. Mime and *commedia* represent Copeau's legacy, but while both these forms continue to thrive today, they have lost their connection to popular culture and are now recognized as high art.

This tension between clowns as popular because they are enjoyed by many, and clowns as popular because they express what many *should* enjoy, resurfaces with each of the masters of modernism I examine in the following chapters.

4

Meyerhold's Transformation from Pierrot to Kapellmeister: *The Fairground Booth* and *Columbine's Scarf*

WHILE COPEAU AND COCTEAU WERE EXPERIMENTING WITH CLOWNS IN France, Vsevolod Meyerhold (1874–1940/3) was following a similar development in Russia. Meyerhold began his career under the tutelage of Nemirovich-Danchenko (1859–1943) and Konstantin Stanislavsky (1863–1938) at the Moscow Art Theater, where he was a founding member and had his professional acting debut in the role of Treplev in the 1898 production of *The Seagull* by Anton Chekhov (1860–1904). Meyerhold soon broke with the Moscow Art Theater, however, to pursue an anti-naturalist theatrical style that could harmonize with such non-representational art movements as futurism and constructivism. Meyerhold looked to clowns as a means of developing this new theatrical language, experimenting with *commedia* characters, circus and traditional Russian folk theater. As a director, teacher and theorist, Meyerhold became the most influential proponent for avant-garde theater in Russia. His acting technique, Biomechanics, is still taught at the St. Petersbourg Academy of Theater Arts, as well as other theater training schools in Europe and America today.[1]

Meyerhold began his research into clown performance as part of his own acting career when he undertook the role of Landowsky in *The Acrobats* (1903) by Austrian playwright Franz von Schönthan. The play portrayed the backstage life of a circus troupe in which Meyerhold's character, Landowsky, was a tragically incompetent circus clown, who shared much with Pierrot in costume, make-up and woebegone demeanor.[2] Until his portrayal of Landowsky, Meyerhold had played exclusively Chekhov roles in the naturalistic style he had learned from Stanislavsky.[3] Landowsky, a success with critics, began a phase of

Meyerhold's development that would see him play the role of the tragic Pierrot in his own production of *The Fairground Booth* (1906) and then in *Carnival* (1910) directed by Mikhail Fokine (1880–1940). If Pierrot seemed to be Meyerhold's *commedia*-based alter-ego during the early part of his career, he would eventually exchange the romantic anti-authoritarian mask for that of Dr. Dappertutto, a grotesque Kapellmeister derived from German poet-composer E. T. A. Hoffmann (1776–1822), *commedia dell'arte*, Skomorokhi,[4] and Slavic folklore. The antithesis of Pierrot, Dr. Dappertutto became Meyerhold's second alter-ego, which he used as a pseudonym to publish controversial essays and produce cabaret shows.

Meyerhold's experiments with clown developed into an artistic expression appropriate to the unfolding history of Russia. The marriage of his theater life to the political development of his country accounted for both the strength of his accomplishment and the limitations of his application of clown.

From the earliest union of clown and modern theater, two contradictory aspects of clown attracted dramatists and performers. One was the free-wheeling, anarchic quality that seemed to provide an antidote to realism and naturalism, but another aspect, equally attractive, was the physical prowess that clowns seemed always to possess. Their contradictory logic suggested a liberated stage character, while their physical prowess presented *auteur* directors with the ultimate utilitarian actor.

Meyerhold's theatrical vision developed from one in which the anti-authoritarian critique suggested by the White Clown-Auguste dichotomy was stressed, into one in which the utilitarian quality of clowns became the focus. It was during this later stage, that Meyerhold dropped the Auguste-like Pierrot persona that had characterized his early career as an actor-director and took on the persona of an authoritarian White Clown himself.

Two productions illustrate how Meyerhold developed from a director who used clown to liberate the actor's body, into a director who used clown to control the actor's body. The first was *The Fairground Booth*, produced in 1906 in collaboration with the poet-playwright Alexander Blok (1888–1921). This production, coming as it did directly after the 1905 revolution, was full of anarchic energy and contradictory, clown-logic. The performers on the stage literally burst from the theater space, breaking through set pieces, walls, windows and back-drops, challenging all modes of representation and, by implication, challenging social and political systems. Meyerhold's production of *Columbine's*

Scarf (1910) was superficially very much like *The Fairground Booth* because both plays used clown characters to enact a non-realist narrative. However, the two shows presented drastically different visions of clowns as modern theatrical characters. Where the clowns of *The Fairground Booth* retain their contradictory, anarchic quality, those of *Columbine's Scarf* are subdued and controlled by a concert-master.

THE FAIRGROUND BOOTH

Balaganchik [*The Fairground Booth*][5] was written by Alexander Blok (1880–1921) in close collaboration with Meyerhold for production in 1906.[6] Blok's intention was to satirize the symbolist poets and their mystical philosophy, with which he had been associated, but had become disillusioned.[7] Blok's discontent with the pretensions of contemporary Russian literature matched Meyerhold's discontent with the conventions of theatrical representation. At the time of his first production of *The Fairground Booth*, Meyerhold was developing a theatrical aesthetic based on the grotesque. According to Meyerhold, the grotesque could be defined as the result of the incompatible demands between form and content.[8] *The Fairground Booth* was a kind of thesis play on this concept of the grotesque that was expressed on the stage as the incompatible demands of the author's poetic vision and the human demands of the actors. Both Blok and Meyerhold recognized that the actors who are the least compatible to the demands of a text, are clowns.

In as much as it can be said to have a plot at all, *The Fairground Booth* is about a group of clowns who refuse to perform a play text as prescribed by the "Author" who appears as a character in the play. The cast of characters is made up of Pierrot who was played by Meyerhold himself, Columbine, Harlequin, Mystics, Chairman of the conclave of Mystics, three pairs of lovers and Author. Included also is a character named Clown who represents the circus tradition rather than the *commedia* derived Columbine, Pierrot, and Harlequin. A version of the traditional love triangle between Columbine, Pierrot, and Harlequin forms the basis of the main action. But this action is continually interrupted and, most importantly, seems to have nothing to do with the intentions of the character named "Author." Pierrot's foil in the play is, therefore, the Author rather than Harlequin. Author desperately tries to hang on to the idea of culture as he understands it.

In terms of the basic dichotomy of a clown act, Author corresponds to the M. C. or ringmaster of the circus world.

The Fairground Booth thwarts the audience's ability to draw meaning from it or even to construct a coherent fictitious world. The play does not stick to any particular generic expectations but rather transforms continually. At times it is broadly comic. Much of the play's comic drive comes from its satirical representation of Author. Author interrupts the action early on in the play to assure the audience that he wrote none of what the actors are performing.

> Author: Ladies and gentlemen! I apologize to you most humbly, but I must disclaim all responsibility! They are making a laughing stock of me! I wrote a perfectly realistic play, the essentials of which I consider it my duty to lay before you in a few words: what we are concerned with is the mutual love of two young hearts! A third personage places obstacles in their path, but eventually these obstacles are overcome and the loving pair are joined forever in holy matrimony! I never dressed my characters up like buffoons! without my permission they are staging some kind of ancient legend or other! I refuse to tolerate legends, myths or any other vulgar nonsense! Neither will I tolerate allegorical word-play: it is indecent to refer to a woman's braid as the scythe of death! It is a slander on the fair sex! Ladies and . . . *(A hand thrust out from behind the curtain grabs the Author by the collar. He disappears into the wings with a yell.)*[9]

Author reappears several times in the play and is yanked off-stage by unseen hands twice in mid-sentence. He desperately tries to reassert his will upon his creations, but everything conspires against him. He is like an artist who might prefer puppets, but is saddled with clowns who will not function in an orderly manner.

In Meyerhold's 1906 *mise en scène* for *The Fairground Booth*, each level of representation was clearly delineated by the physical playing space in a manner calculated to heighten the audience's awareness of different mimetic levels. Meyerhold wanted the audience to be sensitized to the mimetic space around them and the free movement of the clowns in and out of that space. Meyerhold described the setting, which he developed in close collaboration with designer Sapunov, in the following way:

> This booth has its own stage, curtain, prompter's box, and proscenium opening. Instead of being masked by the conventional border, the flies, together with all the ropes and wires, are visible to the audience; when the

entire set is hauled aloft in the booth the audience in the actual theatre
sees the whole process. In front of the booth the stage area adjacent to
the footlights is left free. It is here that the Author appears to serve as an
intermediary between the public and the events enacted within the booth.
The action begins at a signal on a big drum; music is heard and the audience
sees the prompter crawl into his box and light a candle. [10]

Meyerhold had not tried to produce anything with such clear meta-
theatrical aesthetics before this point in his career. The idea of exposing
the technical apparatus of theater magic was inspired by circus and
popular theater. Even the detail of the beginning of the action being
cued from the sound of a drum evokes the circus.

Meyerhold was fascinated with the circus and was on friendly terms
with more than one professional clown. Clowns, such as Vladimir
Durov (1864–1916) and his protegé Vitaly Lazarenko (1890–1939),
created political satire by juxtaposing fairly innocuous text with stage
action that heightened the political-satirical value of the text. [11] Rather
than having the physical action grow out of the text as one might expect
to find on the legitimate stage (in Chekhov plays, for instance), clown
action conflicts with, or comments on the text. In *The Fairground
Booth*, there is constant tension between the more obviously authorial
element of language and the "play" or physical action of the clowns.

The Fairground Booth is highly verbal, but there are also extended
mime sequences reminiscent of *Pierrot assassin de sa femme* or even
the Fratellini and *Le Boeuf sur le toit*. [12] Stylistically, Meyerhold and
Blok were putting ideas then current in the rest of Europe into a Russian context. Although the production predates Blok and Meyerhold's
overtly political, Bolshevik phase, it expresses both their discontent
with the art of the period and Russian politics and society.

The Auguste-White Clown dichotomy creates the central tension
in *The Fairground Booth*. The puppet-like characters in the play
correspond to White Clowns who attempt to uphold some kind of order
and structure while the *commedia*-derived Augustes are the ones who
refuse to cooperate.

There are instances in the text where characters are represented
in two-dimensional puppet form. These characters are the ones who
seem to be trying to carry out the Author's vision. The Mystics are
two-dimensional characters trapped behind a table as puppets would
be confined to an inner stage. They begin the play by trying to conjure Sophia, the Goddess worshipped by the symbolist cult Blok had

been a member of, but they misinterpret Columbine as Sophia. Also represented as a two dimensional figure is the "Medieval Lover":

> Large and thoughtful, he is all straight lines; on his head he wears a cardboard helmet; with an enormous wooden sword he is tracing a circle on the floor in front of his companion.

The two-dimensional nature of the Medieval lover is purposely juxtaposed with the plastic activity of Clown and Harlequin. In addition to this physical difference, the Lover demonstrates a lack of consciousness or understanding of the theatrical event, as in the following passage between the lovers:

> He: Do you understand the play in which we are playing not the least important role?
> She: (*Like a faint but distant echo.*) Role.
> He: Do you realize that the maskers have made this meeting wonderful?
> She: Wonderful.
> He: You must trust me then? O today you are lovelier than ever.
> She: Ever.

The Medieval Lover, or Knight in this sequence, although he is aware that he is a character in a play, is confused by the role he has to play. Like Author, he seems to seek order from the chaos, while his female counterpart can only parrot his words in the manner of a ventriloquist's dummy. Pierrot, Clown and Harlequin, on the other hand, break free of authorial control and the confines of the playing space as in the sequence directly following the Medieval lovers scene:

> *At this moment one of the clowns takes it into his head to play a prank. He runs up to the Lover and sticks out a long tongue at him. The Lover brings his heavy wooden sword down on the clown's head with all his might. The clown is doubled over the footlights, where he remains hanging. A stream of cranberry juice gushes from his head.*
> Clown: (*in a piercing yell*) Help! I'm bleeding cranberry juice!
> *Having dangled there for a while, he gets up and goes out.*[13]

Here, the two-dimensional world of the puppet-like lovers is interrupted by the plastic action of the clown. The Lover reacts with violence. Typical of a White Clown, the Lover attempts to reassert his perception of order through violent punishment of the Auguste. The

Lover's action is made redundant, however, when Clown, in his mock-death scene, droops himself over the footlights, physically merging two playing spaces and breaking the two dimensional scene that had been constructed by the medieval lovers. Like Harlequin in *The Emperor of the Moon*, this clown can simply walk off stage after his death with the full understanding that nothing has happened and that he will return in the next scene.

Death is a recurring image in *The Fairground Booth*. In addition to Clown's cranberry-juice death scene, Death is presented in the play as a character. By personifying death, Blok evokes both the Medieval theater and the apocalyptic mysticism practiced by the Symbolist movement, but effectively erases that image when Death turns out to be Columbine in disguise:

> Pierrot who appears as if from nowhere, walks slowly from one side of the stage to the other, stretching out his hand toward Death. As he approaches her, her face gradually comes to life. A flush mounts to the dead whiteness of her cheeks. The silver scythe is veiled by the morning mist. In the window recess, silhouetted against the dawn, stands a beautiful girl, her tranquil face lit by a gentle smile—Columbine. [14]

Meyerhold executed this scene in performance by presenting Columbine-Death as a two-dimensional cardboard doll. Characters who were portrayed as puppets are the mystics, the Medieval Lovers, and then Columbine in her final entrance as Death. This incarnation of Columbine is logically linked to the mystics, however. The fact that she appears as a cardboard cutout, just as they had been, implies that the Mystics and their Goddess are all false. Since it is revealed that this Goddess is, in fact, Columbine, this aspect of the *mise en scène* reinforces the idea that the transforming clown entity, the Auguste characters, thwart the expectations of the White Clown Author.

While Pierrot appears to be drawn to Death she is in fact his beloved Columbine. The Medieval lovers are associated with death because the Knight murders the clown who interrupts their scene. Both scenes turn out to be false, in the sense that Clown does not really die and Death is only Columbine in a new costume. Death, the ultimate Antagonist, is outmatched by the clown protagonists of *The Fairground Booth*, who either refuse to accept it, as in the case of Clown's cranberry-juice death scene, or co-opt Death's imagery to use as their own, as in the Pierrot-Columbine as Love and Death scene. Either way they make nonsense of the serious pretensions of Symbolism.

When Pierrot-Meyerhold reaches for Death she transforms back into the three dimensional Columbine, suggesting a possible vindication of the Author's romantic hope for his plot, but even this is frustrated when the set flies away leaving Author, a surrogate Blok, and Meyerhold in the guise of Pierrot, alone on the stage to end the play with a futile lament.

> Author: Ladies and gentlemen of the audience! My cause is not lost! My rights have been restored to me! As you see, all obstacles have been removed! The gentleman disappeared through the window! All that remains is for you to witness the joyful reunion of two loving hearts after prolonged separation! It has cost them a great deal of effort to overcome these obstacles, but now they are rewarded by being joined for eternity!
> *The Author goes to join the hands of Pierrot and Columbine. Suddenly the entire set flies up and disappears.* [15]

Harlequin had demonstrated the freedom of the clowns from Author's conventions by jumping through a window near the end of the play, demolishing part of the set and completely ruining the illusion. This sequence comes directly before the final disappearance of the entire set. The puppet-like, White Clown characters are equated with the set pieces and other flimsy elements of illusionist theatre. The Augustes are a different matter. They either make nonsense of the illusion, like Harlequin, or are oblivious to it like Pierrot. Of all the characters, only Author continues to try to control the event, but is controlled by it instead, tethered by a rope to the wings.

One year after writing *The Fairground Booth*, Blok wrote the following words, which could also serve to sum up his play: "Man is a man, not a puppet, not a pitiful creature doomed to decay, but a miraculous phoenix, surmounting the icy wind from infinite space. The wax melts, but life does not wane." [16] In *The Fairground Booth* Blok and Meyerhold put two opposing visions of humanity on stage together to collide. One vision is of man "doomed to decay," the other is of man as an infinitely transformable phoenix, confined by nothing, least of all the formal confines of a theater and a poet's text.

In an article in which Meyerhold expounded his concept of the grotesque entitled "Two Puppet Theatres," Meyerhold wrote:

> Art is incapable of conveying the sum of reality, that is, all concepts as they succeed one another in time. Art dismantles reality, depicting it now spatially, now temporally. For this reason, art consists either in images or

in the alternation of images: the first yields the spatial forms of art, the second—the temporal forms. The impossibility of embracing the totality of reality justifies the schematization of the real. The grotesque does not recognize the purely debased nor the purely exalted. The grotesque mixes opposites, consciously creating harsh incongruity and relying solely on its own originality. [17]

Meyerhold evokes an image of the theater as a contest between reality and art's version of reality. Meyerhold had faith in the theater as a genuine venue for social experiment. He believed in the theater as a place where different ideas about, or visions of, the world could exist together and enjoy play between them.

Just as *Pierrot assassin de sa femme* startled the naturalists out of their pseudo-scientific stupor, or Cocteau's *Le Boeuf sur le toit* worked against the expectations of his audience, who had developed too complacent an attitude toward modern music, cubist design and modern dance, *The Fairground Booth* served as a kind of critique of the sign system being used in both the naturalistic and symbolist Russian theater at the time of its presentation.

The Transformation of Meyerhold-Pierrot into Dr. Dappertutto: *Columbine's Scarf*

It was during a production of *Columbine's Scarf* in 1910 that Meyerhold began using the pseudonym Dr. Dappertutto (Dr. Everywhere). Meyerhold assumed this name in order to avoid a violation of his contract with the Imperial Theaters. The Director of the Imperial Theaters at this time was Telyakovsky who was aware of Meyerhold's extra-contractual employment and urged him to use a different name so that neither of them would have to answer problematic questions from the board of the Imperial Theaters. [18] Meyerhold was again playing the role of Pierrot when he transformed into Dr. Dappertutto.

Columbine's Scarf was based on a scenario written by Austrian dramatist Arthur Schnitzler (1869–1931), originally entitled *The Veil of Pierrette*. Schnitzler's play was only used as an outline for the pantomime produced by Meyerhold. As in *The Fairground Booth* the love triangle between Pierrot, Columbine, and Harlequin provides the essential plot.

The frivolous Columbine, betrothed to Harlequin, spends a last evening with her devoted Pierrot. As usual, she deceives him, swearing she loves him. Pierrot proposes a suicide pact and himself drinks poison. Columbine lacks courage to follow him and flees in terror to the wedding ball where the guests await her impatiently. The ball begins, then whilst an old fashioned quadrille is playing, Pierrot's flapping white sleeve is glimpsed first through the windows, then through the doors. The dances, now fast, now slow, turn into an awful nightmare, with strange Hoffmanesque characters whirling to the time of a huge-headed Kapellmeister, who sits on a high stool and conducts four weird musicians. Columbine's terror reaches such a high pitch that she can hide it no longer and she rushes back to Pierrot. Harlequin follows her and when he sees Pierrot's corpse he is convinced of his bride's infidelity. He forces her to dine before the corpse of the love stricken Pierrot. Then he leaves, bolting the door fast. In vain Columbine tries to escape from her prison, from the ghastly dead body. Gradually, she succumbs to madness; she whirls in a frenzied dance, then finally drains the deadly cup and falls lifeless beside Pierrot. [19]

The key element that differentiates this scenario from *The Fairground Booth* is the contrast between the Author and the Kapellmeister. [20] The grotesque Kapellmeister is analogous to the Author in *The Fairground Booth* except that, where Author is unable to exert his control, the Kapellmeister is all-powerful. The Kapellmeister and his band lead the action with their music. Once both Pierrot and Columbine die, the Kapellmeister runs off through the auditorium "acknowledging his manipulation of the tragedy."[21] Although the Kapellmeister is driven mad by the events of the play he is also successful in having exerted his control over those events. Where the Kapellmeister becomes tragically horrified by what he has done, Author from *The Fairground Booth* is comically impotent.

Columbine's Scarf was much closer to dance theater or even ballet than clown show. Undoubtedly, Meyerhold was influenced by choreographer Mikhail Fokine (1880–1940), for whom he had played Pierrot in the St. Petersburg production of *Carnival* in January of the same year. [22] Meyerhold played opposite the dancer Nijinsky (1890–1950) as Harlequin at the same theater where he was to produce *Columbine's Scarf* only ten months later. [23] Fokine as choreographer exerted a command over his performers that Meyerhold had never been able to achieve, or perhaps had not wanted to achieve. [24] Fokine's approach made a deep impression on Meyerhold whose idea of physical theater and pantomime was to move in an entirely new direction. One year

after these two performances, Meyerhold explained pantomime for his
students in the following way:

> In pantomime every single episode, each movement in each episode (its
> plastic modulations)—as well as the gestures of every character and the
> groupings of the ensemble—are determined precisely by the music, by its
> changes in tempo, its modulations, its overall structure. In pantomime the
> rhythm of the movements, gestures, and groupings synchronized precisely
> with the rhythms of the music; a performance may be regarded as perfect
> only if the rhythm of the music and the rhythm of the stage are perfectly
> synchronized.[25]

In this description, Meyerhold leaves behind the pretense that the
director is not in complete control of the pantomime as he sees it.
His model for the perfect director is similar to the Kapellmeister of
Columbine's Scarf. The clowns in *The Fairground Booth* defied restrictions set on them by Author or the expectations of the audience.
A sense of fun as well as grotesque anarchy was also maintained in
The Fairground Booth in a way that it was not in *Columbine's Scarf*.
Columbine's Scarf is a more straightforward Romantic scenario, presented with a new ardor to suit the anxiety of the period of its presenta-
tion. No longer is there a critique of theatrical representation; rather,
the mode is tragically glorified.

Perhaps nothing exemplifies Meyerhold's altered concept of
clowns in theater more clearly than his second production of *The
Fairground Booth* staged with members of Meyerhold's students in
1914. For this production (coming four years after his collaboration
with Fokine and his production of *Columbine's Scarf*) Meyerhold commissioned a new design by Yury Bondi. Unlike the original Sapunov
conception, the theater was designed to imitate a Greek classical theater
with a semicircular acting area for the majority of the action rather
than a circus ring with a showbooth as in 1906. The physical difference
of the playing space meant that the different characters all interacted
with the audience in the same mode. The varying levels of audience-
performer relationship were eliminated. As in *Columbine's Scarf*, a
generalized modernist aesthetic was promoted rather than a clown
show in which the very means of theatrical representation were challenged. Rather than playing Pierrot himself, Meyerhold instructed a
student to carry out his instructions in the manner of master to disciple.
His effort to communicate his idiosyncratic acting style to his cast was

purely academic without his leading by example. Blok witnessed the revival and was disappointed. In fact, his enthusiasm for Meyerhold was dampened by the restaging of his play. He complained that he was tired of "Meyerholdia" and now preferred "healthy realism, Stanislavsky, and musical drama."[26] Meyerhold's restaging of *The Fairground Booth* indicated the path he would follow for the remainder of his career. He retired from performing, never appearing as Pierrot after his 1910 performance in *Columbine's Scarf*. His early experiments with clown were to become still more codified through his acting method Biomechanics.

BIOMECHANICS

Just as Copeau's adoption of clown and *commedia* would lead to a codifying of clown energy and techniques to be used by mimes and modern French actors, Meyerhold's concept of Biomechanics would codify his earlier experiments with clown in *The Fairground Booth*. As late as 1914, Meyerhold still believed in the autonomous genius of actors:

> For the actor, the theatre is any stage he can construct for himself—without the assistance of a builder, wherever and whenever necessary, and as quickly as his skill will allow.[27]

By the 1920s, however, he was comfortable with reducing the actor's art to a formula:

$N = A1 + A2$

(where N = the actor; $A1$ = the artist who conceives the idea and issues the instructions necessary for its execution; $A2$ = the executant who executes the conception of $A1$)

The actor must train his material (the body), so that it is capable of executing instantaneously those tasks which are dictated externally (by the actor, the director).[28]

The autonomy of the actor, prized in Meyerhold's early essays and expressed artistically in his *The Fairground Booth*, is completely eradicated in the above formula in which the director's will is absolute. Where *The Fairground Booth* allowed for a by-play between Auguste and White Clowns, his later theory of Biomechanics reduced this dynamic to a form of gymnastic acting in which a company of highly-trained performers fulfill the physical vision of the director. The purpose of Biomechanics was to create "techniques for acting in non-illusionary theatre text constructed by a director as an author of a performance."[29] By becoming the author of the performance, Meyerhold stepped into the role of the Author satirized in *The Fairground Booth* and expressed dramatically as Kapellmeister in *Columbine's Scarf*. As the director of biomechanical actors, the Kapellmeister is even more clearly a puppet-master:

> In effect, these plays were "abstract" theatre, in which the actor, as an abstraction of the human element, was distinct from the other elements of the production. Thus, the actor sacrificed his individual artistic creation for that of a supermarionette in the hands of the producer.[30]

Meyerhold's development away from the autonomy of actors expressed by the contradictory stage action of clowns, to the disciplined action of puppets, was inspired by several theories of theater being debated during the period. Edward Gordon Craig, espoused a human puppet theater in his article *The Actor and the Über-marionette* (1918). Craig envisioned actors who could emulate puppets in order to eliminate the accidental quality that human emotion brought to performance. Long before Craig, German playwright Heinrich Von Kleist (1777–1811) put forward a similar argument in his *Über das Marionettentheater* (1810). According to Kleist, the conscious actor is flawed because he asserts a false center of gravity as the wellspring of movement whereas the non-sentient puppet never does this.[31] The puppet's lack of consciousness is what makes him a superior performer when compared with the human actor.

Kleist identifies a quality in puppets that clowns traditionally share. Both puppets and clowns use different centers of gravity in their physical action when compared with common actors. But the clown's center of gravity is not the result of a lack of human consciousness. Clowns use a logic that is different from the societal norm, thereby implying a different consciousness from the audience. Their alternate physicality (center of gravity) is a visual manifestation of this essential difference. The clown will purposely distort his center of gravity to create an illusion of being either imbalanced, or, overly concerned with stability. Frequently the clown's alternate center of gravity is an extension of his natural physical characteristics. Dwarves or hunchbacks, for instance, have clearly different centers of gravity from "normal" performers. Often clown teams are separated physically, with one being very fat and the other very thin.[32] In the circus these physical characteristics are emphasized through the make-up and costume. The White Clown's costume is symmetrical and his body posture demonstrates balance while his make-up contradicts this by being asymmetrical, yet neat. The Auguste is slovenly but symmetrical in make-up, yet imbalanced in costume and physical posture.

Assuming that the supposed superiority of puppets over actors described by Kleist, could be corrected through methodical training, Meyerhold, as well as many other directors and theorists of the period, set out to make Craig's vision of super-human, puppet-actors a reality. Meyerhold used the physical technique perfected by clowns, such as Lazarenko, who was famous for leaping incredible distances, as a building block to an acting theory that was essentially anti-clown in concept. Meyerhold took his early experiments with clown, improvisation and *commedia dell'arte* isolated certain physical characteristics and used them to create a grammar of movement. This grammar is similar to many other developments of the period, most notably Eurhythmics[33] and French Mime. Each of these movement systems attempted to solve the "problem" of human balance indicated by Kleist.[34]

Like Eurhythmics, Biomechanics separates physical action from text. But where clowns are separate from text due to a contrary logic that allows them to comment on the text, or convention of reality, Eurhythmics and Biomechanics are meant to express the essential truth behind the text.[35] Technically both corporeal mime and Biomechanics are built around the idea of a basic preparatory movement. In mime it is referred to as the "toc," in Biomechanics it is called "pre-acting."[36] In Biomechanics, the "dactyl" is the basic physical pose that must be mastered before all other movement occurs. Pre-acting is learned by striking the "dactyl" pose and visualizing the next movement phrase before executing it. This helps both the actor and audience to "read" the movement in relation to the text or dramatic situation. As the biomechanical actor becomes more proficient, he or she adds numerous other poses, some derived from drawings of *commedia* performers, and others derived from Asian theater, and martial arts.[37] The concept of "toc" (or pre-acting) is also relevant to clown technique, but it is applied to create the opposite effect. Clowns use the toc to slow down a motion or activity so that the audience has time to evaluate the clown's situation and what his next movement might entail. The toc as used by a clown is generally accompanied with misdirection in order that the audience will make the wrong guess about the next action.[38] Where Eurhythmics, mime, and Biomechanics all prepare the audience to accept the movement-action as harmonious with the text, music, or dramatic situation, clown prepares the audience to accept one movement-action and then contradicts that expectation.

In addition to the physical discipline of clowns, Meyerhold's concept of Biomechanics was also inspired by scientist Frederick Winslow Taylor (1856–1915), who developed a system for integrating workers with their machines to maximize productivity. Taylor believed that he had studied the most efficient means to carry out a given physical action and that his principles could be applied to any workplace. As Mel Gordon has said:

> In Meyerhold's constructivist vision of the theatre as factory and school-room—the use of the fastest and most efficient methods (Taylorism) to produce a predetermined audience reaction (reflexology)—we find a total emphasis on work output, i.e., the manufacture of effects in the spectator, creating a desired state of mind.[39]

This mechanization of humanity, which reads like a utopian version of the nightmarish work environment depicted in Chaplin's *Modern Times* had as its goal to create workers who were as effective as machines.[40]

As explained in Chapter 3, such techniques as puppetry, mime, dance, and Biomechanics, while not always belonging to the world of clown, can be used as tools by clowns to disrupt the mimetic conventions of the rest of the play but only when there is a normative context for contrast, or Auguste characters to balance the mechanized White Clowns. By the end of his career, Meyerhold had stopped encouraging his actors to use clown techniques to free them from representational formulae or as contradictory forms that created a grotesque aesthetic. Instead, Biomechanics became his new and superior formula.

5

Clown in Brecht's Theory of Acting:
Mann ist Mann as Anti-Tragedy

VERTRACKTE DIALEKTIK IST CLOWN LOGIC

BERTOLT BRECHT (1898–1956), ONE OF THE MOST INFLUENTIAL PLAY-
wrights and directors of the twentieth century, through plays, productions, and essays promoted a poetics for the modern age that would harmonize with his Marxist philosophy. This new poetics, broadly known
as "Epic Theater," like Meyerhold's concept of the "theater of the
grotesque," grew out of an interest in, and experiments with, clown
and popular theater. Brecht was friend to Soviet poet and dramatist
Sergei Tretiakov[1] and was aware of Meyerhold's achievements in the
Soviet Union, but his influences were so varied that it is difficult to
draw a direct line from the Russians to his own ideas.[2]

In the previous chapter (chapter 4), I argued that Meyerhold's exploration of clown devolved into a codified system of movement that
abandoned his clown-derived theory of the grotesque. Brechtian performance practice stayed much closer to Meyerhold's theory of the
grotesque, although this evinced itself in his playtexts less and less as
he matured. It is for this reason that *Mann ist Mann* (1926), a compar-
atively early play, has been chosen as the main focus of this chapter.
This play coincides with the formation of Brecht's early theories, as
well as his direct contact with clowns and cabaret performers. When
Brecht began writing *Mann ist Mann*, he had only just begun to study
Marxism and his theories of the theatre were only just developing the
concrete connection with political ideology that they were to have a few
years later.

A bias toward Brecht as playwright rather than theorist and director
was established early in English-language criticism, when John Willett
complained that "the [Berliner] Ensemble's productions get treated as

examples of a new theoretical approach, when they ought to be judged
primarily as realizations of the playwright's work."[3] This testy attitude
toward Brecht's performance theory stems from the fact that the theory
has been so misunderstood, as Willett himself argues elsewhere, and
because Brecht tended to add to the mystification of his ideas over
time rather than help clarify them.[4] But Brecht's mystification of
his theory was the result of constant attacks from Marxist literary
critics, chiefly Georg Lukács, who singled out Brecht as a formalist,
clearly opposed to the goals of Socialist Realism.[5] Ironically, the theory
behind Brecht's "formalism" was often rejected in the west because
of its apparent connection with Marxist-dialectical argument. In this
chapter, I take a close look at *Mann ist Mann* in order to demonstrate
that Brecht's theoretical concepts stem from his notion of *vertrackte
Dialektik* [perverse logic] which is at heart a related idea to "clown
logic."

The key phrases of Brecht's theory are Epic Theater, *Verfremdungseffekt*, and *Gestus*. Epic Theater is a general adjective for the
overall aesthetic approach and social purpose behind his theatre. Epic
Theater puts emphasis on the direct telling of a story in order to en-
courage the viewer to assess the situation explained in the narrative and
consider how it could be altered or adapted in different circumstances.
Central to this idea of alterability is the human being, "the object of
the inquiry."[6]

Verfremdungseffekt and *Gestus* are closely related in practice. *Verfremdungseffekt* (hereafter referred to as "V-effect") is easily understood when considered as part of clown technique. The clown continually breaks with mimetic conventions, thereby disturbing the effect of
illusion. Prior to the twentieth century, this effect was used as a means
of provoking laughter, or providing a parenthetic, satirical version
(burlesque) of a more serious, central action. Brecht simply adapted
clown technique, as did Margueritte before him, shifting its use away
from the comic mode and toward serious debate. In *Mann ist Mann*,
Brecht used this technique in both ways. At the beginning of the play,
the "V-effect" is part of the circus atmosphere and broad comedy of the
play. By the end of the play, it helps to focus the audience's attention
on the central debate of the narrative.

Gestus is the means of creating the "V-effect" through a contrary
physical action or an action that provides commentary on the spoken
text or implied situation. In practice it is created by externalizing the

motivations and sub-text of the characters. Brechtian characters, like all clowns, are not meant to be probed by the audience for hidden meanings or motives, rather, they display their motives by concentrating on economy of motion and striving for precision of action in order to show the audience the reason for their emotions and intent behind their actions as clearly as possible.

Brecht suggested that actors who want to master the new form of acting should practice transposition into the third person and transposition into the past.[7] Both of these devices have already been established as clown techniques from earlier chapters. Both Margueritte's Pierrot in *Pierrot assassin de sa femme* and Harlequin in "the *lazzo* of suicide" provide examples in which the clown passes into a different temporal mode, Pierrot into the past and Harlequin into the future, and both present themselves in the third person, Harlequin having a dialogue with himself and Pierrot "telling" a past event through purely physical means. Brecht's main devices can be explained as clown technique but he resisted using the term clown because of its connotation of the purely comic. As a result, he referred to "the actor Chaplin" as the model epic performer.[8]

CLOWN AS SOLDIER

Mann ist Mann is set in Kiplingesque Asia-India and tells the story of an Irish Dock worker, Galy Gay, who is shanghaied by three English soldiers who need him to play the part of their missing comrade, Jeraiah Jip, who has been trapped while robbing a Buddhist temple. The soldiers convince the weak-minded and weak-willed Gay that he will profit if he helps them by standing in for Jip. After the soldiers are unable to recover Jip from the temple, they decide that Gay must impersonate Jip permanently. They convince Gay to believe that he actually is the missing soldier. With the help of the canteen owner, Widow Begbick, the soldiers trick Gay into buying a phony elephant and selling it to Begbick, thereby committing several capital offenses. In order to solidify their hold on him, the soldier's pretend to execute Gay. Once he accepts that he has been shot, he transforms wholeheartedly into Jip. Having purged all human feeling in shedding his real identity, Galy Gay transforms into the perfect war machine. By the end of the play, Gay is a more efficient soldier than the three who were responsible for his transformation, or their commanding officer Sergeant Fairchild, a sadistic killer known as Bloody Five.

War is, in fact, the perfect context in which to stage a clown act because it is the most extreme example of a social situation where the arbitrary rule of law must be obeyed. The Auguste-White Clown dichotomy fits naturally into a battlefield situation. The Auguste character cannot adjust to the necessities of war. He cannot learn to march properly or carry a gun because his clown persona stops him from being able to understand, or physically comply with these activities in a normal way. The White Clown cannot carry out military tasks in an identifiably normal way either, but he, unlike the Auguste, will insist that he does understand the rules, or in this case the orders, and that they make sense. In *Mann ist Mann* Galy Gay is the Auguste character, and the soldiers who waylay him are the White Clowns with their Sergeant, Bloody Five, the authoritarian leader and Widow Begbick, the master of ceremonies (or, ringmaster) for the theatrical event.

There were several stage productions, with clown-like soldiers as protagonists, that had a direct influence on Brecht while he was developing the text for *Mann ist Mann*. One year before the première of *Mann ist Mann*, Alban Berg's (1885–1935) opera *Wozzek*, based on Georg Büchner's (1813–37) nineteenth-century play *Woyzeck*, had its première. The event caused a sensation throughout Germany. Brecht's second wife, and leading actress of the Berliner Ensemble, Helene Weigel (1900–71), was a performer in a production of *Woyzeck* in 1918. Berg was inspired to write the opera as a result of witnessing this very production of Büchner's play. The play has a darkly comic aspect to it that is subdued in the opera. Büchner reminds the audience of the theatrical setting of the story, providing a carnival-circus frame for much of the action in anticipation of Brecht's "Epic" devices.[9] While Berg's opera plays down the clown and circus aspects of Büchner's play, the music was so aggressively modern that it served a similar, disruptive function. Both versions of this story of a clown-like soldier who becomes homicidal had Epic Theater qualities.

Also appearing one year before *Mann ist Mann* was Igor Stravinsky's (1882–1971) *L'Histoire du soldat*. Again involving the story of a soldier, this piece presented innovative music derivative of American jazz with spoken text. The form of *L'Histoire du soldat* also provided a precedent to Epic Theater in several key ways.[10] The story is told as well as acted, and the music comments independently on the narrative. Stravinsky's piece has since become a staple of the contemporary clown repertoire.[11]

Brecht himself had no front line, military experience, but he served for a little over a month during World War I on the venereal disease ward of the military hospital in his home town of Augsberg.[12] He was discharged almost as soon as the war ended and never "witnessed terrible acts of brutality when he was a medical orderly" as has been suggested elsewhere.[13] Rather than being an artistic expression of Brecht's personal experience as a soldier, or of his pacifism, as has been claimed by critic and translator Eric Bentley, Galy Gay and his grotesque soldiers belong to a long line of warrior clowns.

The idea of a clown going to war has its roots in Greek comedy, tragedy and Satyr plays. The *commedia dell'arte* had Capitano Spavento who was a descendant of the braggart warrior from New Comedy. The captain of the *commedia* was often portrayed as a Spaniard. Since so much of Italy was under Spanish rule during the hey-day of *commedia*, Spanish soldiers were a natural target for popular comedy.[14] Arlecchino's slap-stick, or *bastone*, is a surrogate sword, both a reminder of the threat of military violence and Arlecchino's ineptitude as a potential soldier.

The tradition of clowns at war was continued by the great clowns of the silent-film era, most notably Charles Chaplin. Chaplin made two features about war, a short propaganda film to sell war bonds (1917), *Shoulder Arms* (1918) and *The Great Dictator* (1939). Of these films, *Shoulder Arms*, completed and released a few weeks before the armistice that ended World War I, was the most likely to have influenced Brecht.[15] There is little doubt that Brecht was influenced by Chaplin's artistry in his conception of Galy Gay.

BRECHT AND CHAPLIN

Brecht first saw Chaplin's films in 1921, when they were permitted to be shown in Germany for the first time. Luckily, we know the exact date that Brecht first came under Chaplin's spell because he recorded the event in his diary. On 29 October 1921, Brecht went to see Chaplin's short film from his Keystone period *The Face on the Barroom Floor*.

And then the teller of the story gets drunker and drunker, and his need to communicate ever stronger and more painful, so he asks for "a bit of that chalk you put on the tips of your billiard cues" and draws the loved one's portrait on the floor—only to produce a series of circles . . . Chaplin's face

is always impassive, as though waxed over, a single expressive twitch rips
it apart, very simple, strong, worried. A pallid clown's face complete with
thick moustache, long artist's hair and a clown's tricks: he messes up his
coat, sits on his palette, gives an agonised lurch, tackles a portrait by—of
all things—elaborating the backside. But nothing could be more moving,
it's unadulterated art.[16]

Brecht's reaction to this film is significant both to *Mann ist Mann*
and the theory of epic acting. Brecht stresses that the film is moving,
although Chaplin's performance is impassive and objective. He emphasizes the meta-theatrical aspect of the film. The fact that Chaplin
frames his film as a telling of a story caught Brecht's attention, and
he was to use similar devices in his own plays. In particular, the chalk
drawing device is an example of *Gestus* directly borrowed from Chaplin. Brecht incorporated a chalk drawing sequence into *Mann ist Mann*
reminiscent of *The Face on the Barroom Floor*. In Scene 5 of *Mann
ist Mann*, the soldiers return to the Pagoda in search of their comrade
and encounter Wang, the bonze[17] who has already discovered Jip and
knows full well that it was he and the other soldiers who robbed the
Pagoda:

> Wang: Permit your unworthy servant to draw four criminals with chalk. (*He
> draws on the door of the prayer box.*) One of them has a face, it is possible
> to tell who he is; the other three have no faces, they cannot be recognized.
> Now the man with the face has no money. Consequently he is not a thief. But
> those who have the money are without faces, consequently they cannot be
> known. That is, they cannot be known unless they are together. Once they
> are together, the three faceless men will grow faces, and stolen money will
> be found on them. You will never make me believe that a man who might be
> found here was your man.[18]

In both Chaplin's film and *Mann ist Mann*, the drawing is used to
expedite the telling of the story and direct the characters and audience
to a new truth about the situation. The scene, and Chaplin's film that
inspired it, both mix the telling of a story with the acting out of a
scene. The device is a variation on the technique examined earlier from
Pierrot assassin de sa femme and Harlequin's "*lazzo* of suicide." In
those cases, the clown technique were comic in one case and shocking
in the other. For Brecht, the effect of the clown technique *Gestus* is
neither comic nor shocking. By switching from one mode to another
the spectator is encouraged to view the entire story more objectively.

Wang uses a form of clown logic, or *vertrackte Dialektik*, to outwit the soldiers, turning the robbery of his temple into a tactical advantage.

FRATELLINI AND VALENTIN

The turning point in *Mann ist Mann* occurs when the three English soldiers concoct an elaborate scheme in order to convince Galy Gay to become Jip on a permanent basis. First, they convince him to buy an elephant and then lead him to believe that the elephant he has bought really belongs to the British army. Having been caught in possession of a stolen elephant, he is then shot. Once he has been shot, the path is clear for the old, weak Galy Gay to be replaced permanently. Two famous clown routines, one by the Fratellini Brothers and the other by Brecht's friend, the cabaret performer Karl Valentin (1882–1948), provide the basis for this turning point in *Mann ist Mann*. The Fratellini brothers performed an elaborate entrée in which Paul and Albert imitated an elephant while François tried to act as the animal trainer. [19]

In the beginning the "Elephants" was nothing but an entracte in which a clown-trainer worked with an animal made out of two men covered with a large sheet. One day the two pairs of legs started to quarrel during a show and the front legs delivered an impressive punch to the rear limbs. The comic effect was incalculable but the clown-trainer involved failed to take advantage of the situation. Furious, he fired his two assistants. The Fratellini got wind of the incident and converted the fight into the central attraction of their entrée. Nothing could be funnier than to see Paul and Albert squabbling in the animal skin while François, at the height of embarrassment, smiles to the public with the grace of a socialite who was just kicked in the backside. [20]

It is clear from this anecdote that such acts were commonplace in circuses and cabaret acts and that the Fratellini refined and enlarged upon a standard routine. [21] It is just such a routine that inspired the elephant auction section of *Mann ist Mann* complete with the quarreling elephant legs. [22]

Uriah: (*Whistles*) First number: The Elephant Deal. The machine gun unit which has been called The Scum hands over an elephant to the man who wants to have his name kept out of it. (*He leads the elephant forward by*

a rope.) Billy Humph, Champion of Bengal, Elephant in the service of the
British Empire etcetera!
Galy Gay: (*Catches sight of the elephant and is terrified.*) Is that the army
elephant?
Soldier: He has a bad cold, as you can see from his blanket. (*The elephant
urinates.*)
Galy Gay: The blanket isn't the worst of it. (*He walks around in some
consternation.*)
Begbick: I'm in the market for that elephant. When I was a child I wanted
an elephant as big as the Hindu Kush Range, but now that one will do.
Galy Gay: Well, Widow Begbick, if you really want this elephant, I'm its
owner.[23]

Galy Gay's willingness to believe in the elephant even though the
audience and other characters can clearly recognize that there is no
elephant is a perfect example of the "V-effect" easily recognizable in
this scene because of its comic nature. As in the Fratellini routine,
the soldiers under the elephant blanket begin to quarrel and run off
destroying the illusion entirely.

(*Polly inside Billy Humph, laughs loudly. Uriah hits him.*)
Uriah: Shut up Polly!
(*The front of the canvas slips, leaving Polly visible.*)
Polly: Damnation![24]

Where Brecht used the Fratellini clown act for the physicalization of
the elephant auction in *Mann ist Mann*, the complementary absurdity
of the exchange of money is provided by a Karl Valentin scenario.
The following is an excerpt involving Valentin and his partner Liesl
Karlstadt entitled *The Bird Seller* (1916–24):

Valentin: Here is the canary with the cage and here is the bill.
Karlstadt: That is all correct, but wait, where is the little darling? The cage
is empty. Where is the bird?
Valentin: It must be in there.
Karlstadt: What do you mean "must be in there?" It is not in there.
Valentin: That is impossible. Why would I bring an empty birdcage? . . .
Here is the bill. I want thirteen marks to pay for everything.
Karlstadt: What do you mean everything?
Valentin: The cage and the bird.
Karlstadt: The bird is not in there. I can't pay for something not received.
Valentin: Then I'll take the whole thing back with me.

Karlstadt: "Whole thing" is good. You can only take the cage, though. The bird is not inside.

Valentin: Madame, the bird must be inside. The bill says "Cage with bird." "Cage with bird," if you please. Therefore the cage must be with bird.

Karlstadt: I've never heard of anything so stupid. [25]

Valentin used a similar gag, centered around an exchange of money in his play *Grossfeuer* [*The Great Fire*] (c. 1922–24). Valentin's character sells an old fire engine to the corrupt Burgermeister of a village, but during the confusion of putting out the fire the expensive equipment ends up trapped inside the building. When the Burgermeister complains, Valentin replies "What's sold is sold," echoing both the bird seller and Galy Gay's line, "It's all one as long as you get paid." [26]

Just as Brecht was impressed by the way that Chaplin told a story in his film, *The Face on the Barroom Floor*, so he was influenced by Valentin's meta-theatrical style. In *The Great Fire*, Valentin explains to the Burgermeister exactly how the fire-engine got trapped in the burning building:

Commandant: There we were in front of the great fire with the busted fire engine. "Sonuvagoddamseacook," he yells, "the devil take the whole goddam engine." He had hardly uttered the last word when all around a cry could be heard: "The roof's caving in!" and in the next moment, Kaboom! (*A thunderous drum beat is heard from the orchestra.*) The Catastrophe had occurred.

Burgermeister: You told that so true to life that I really did hear a noise just now. [27]

In this scene, Valentin provides a clear example of the "V-effect." His Commandant tells the improbable story of the fire engine. The event of the fire engine being swallowed by the burning building is less important than the fact of the commandant's act of telling the story. The Burgermeister is so impressed by the story and the sound effect that he assumes it must be true. The veracity of the story told is equated with the event itself in the stupid Burgermeister's mind, but the audience can only understand this and appreciate the absurd gullibility of the Burgermeister if they can clearly recognize the theatricality of the sound effect. Hence the strangeness, or theatricality, of the sound makes the idea behind the joke clearer. Brecht used a similar device in *Mann ist Mann* for the execution scene when the soldiers inform Galy Gay that he must die.

Galy Gay: You can't do that to me.
Uriah: You'll find that we can, though. Listen carefully, my man: first
because you stole and sold a WD elephant—which is theft -, secondly
because you sold an elephant which was no elephant—which is fraud -, and
thirdly because you are unable to produce any kind of name or identity
document and may well be a spy—which is high treason. [28]

In this scene, Gay is condemned to death for stealing an elephant and
for selling a false elephant. As with Valentin's bird seller, the absurdity
of the situation does not prevent it from having its own internal logic.
The fact of the bill of sale overrides the fact of the empty birdcage, just
as Galy Gay's guilt for buying and selling the stolen elephant overrides
the fact that the elephant was false, even though the charge against him
acknowledges this and adds it to his list of crimes. The soldiers blindfold
him and prepare to pretend to shoot him. They count out "One!" and
then "Two!"; but before they reach three, Galy Gay interrupts:

Galy Gay: Whoah, don't say three or you'll regret it. If you shoot now you're
bound to hit me. Whoah! No, not yet. Listen to me. I confess! I confess I
don't know what has been happening to me. Believe me, and don't laugh:
I'm a man who doesn't know who he is. But I'm not Galy Gay, that much
I do know. I'm not the man who is supposed to be shot. Who am I though
because I've forgotten? [29]

Gay continues to beg for his life by claiming not to be himself after all,
when Uriah yells out "Three!":

Uriah: Fire!
(*Galy Gay lets out a scream.*)
Polly: Whoah! He fell of his own accord.
Uriah: (*Shouts*) Fire! So he can hear he's dead.
(*The soldiers fire into the air.*)
Uriah: Leave him there and get ready to move off.
(*Galy Gay is left lying as all the others exeunt*). [30]

Just as the Burgermeister believes the Commandant's story because of
the orchestral sound effect, so Galy Gay can only know that he is dead
when he hears the guns shoot into the air.

In short, simple plays, Karl Valentin managed to create a form of
theatre that pleased a broad cross-section of the public, while at the
same time pointing out the contradictions of German society in the

1920s. Brecht's friend from this period, Bernhard Reich described the influence that the clown had on the young Brecht:

> [He] enjoyed Valentin enormously, and I suspect he saw particular Valentin scenes so often because he was collecting observations and studying the plays as well as the acting technique of this extraordinary man. Here he may well have discovered that a simple and one dimensional (*einsleisig*) plot can get across an extremely complicated generalization to an audience, and that a small scene can stand for a big problem. He must have noted a basic difference between Valentin's performance and the commonly practiced form of acting. [31]

Brecht's cabaret days can be considered his first apprenticeship period. When in 1924 he went to work as one of the staff of directors and dramaturgs at the Deutsches Theater under the directorship of Max Reinhardt (1873–1943) his ideas had already been molded by his contact with street theater, cabaret and clowning. [32] Brecht openly credited Valentin for inspiring his concept of theater on several occasions. He was quoted once as saying that Valentin's play *The Christmas Tree Stand* "is, from a literary standpoint, a dramatic product of a high order, like all of Valentin's plays. It derives its inner structure as well as its production potential from the very basics of dramatic art."[33]

While Brecht was happy to point to Chaplin or Valentin as exemplars of the kind of acting and approach to theater that he wished to create, it seems obvious that Valentin's partner, Liesl Karlstadt, must have influenced him as well. *Mann ist Mann*, the play most clearly indebted to the Valentin-Karlstadt clown team, is also the first of Brecht's plays to have a significant woman's role.

BEGBICK AS RINGMASTER

During the early stage of Brecht's career he was searching for a style and in many ways an artistic personality. His early plays and poetry abound with images of transformation. He was fascinated with Liesl Karlstadt's transformational acting technique. This actress was as likely to appear as a man or a woman and her range seems to have exceeded even that of her more famous, male partner.

Brecht rarely credited Karlstadt in the same way that he did Valentin. He refers to Valentin directly in *The Messingkauf Dialogues* but only alludes to Karlstadt as "a popular woman comedian who used to pad herself and speak in a deep bass voice."[34] The very act of a woman playing a man's part constitutes a form of the "V-effect" according to Brecht, although, oddly, he never discusses the possibility of a man playing a woman's role. Karlstadt did more than just play men opposite Valentin; however, she played White Clown characters, such as bosses of factories, Orchestra leaders, Policemen and soldiers. Karlstadt was clearly the inspiration for Widow Begbick in *Mann ist Mann*. Begbick is the Ringmaster, or master of ceremonies of the entire theatrical event.

Begbick is the character who comes closest to speaking for the author, somewhat akin to Author from Blok's *The Fairground Booth*. That Brecht would choose a female character as his spokesperson is remarkable considering his attitude toward women around the time he wrote *Mann ist Mann*. The following poem from the period of Brecht's friendship with Valentin gives some idea of Brecht's misogynist tendency during his formative years:

> You know what a man is. He has a name.
> He walks in the street. He sits at the bar.
> You can look at his face, you can listen to his voice.
> A woman washed his shirt, a woman combs his hair.[35]

In this, and countless other poems, the individual worth of men is contrasted with the servile, often animalistic portrayal of women. A man is a man for two reasons: he has a name, and he is not a woman. And yet, in *Mann ist Mann* Widow Begbick points out the fallaciousness of this attitude:

> In this way I too had a name
> And those who heard that name in the city said "It's a good name"
> But one night I drank four glasses of schnapps
> And one morning I found chalked on my door
> A bad word.
> So don't speak your name so distinctly. What's the point?
> Considering that you are always using it to a different person.[36]

In the quotation above, Begbick prepares the way for the transformation of Galy Gay and Bloody Five, both of whom lose their names during the course of the play. At other times she breaks the mimetic illusion more clearly than any other characters. Even after the Fratellini-derived elephant scene, Begbick upstages the soldiers by stating what has been obvious to everyone, except Galy Gay: "What is going on? That's no elephant, it's just men and tarpaulin. The whole thing's phoney. Such a phoney elephant for my genuine money!"[37] When Widow Begbick breaks into song, or the other soldiers imitate the elephant, there is a strong sense that they are aware of themselves as characters in a play. Begbick has the most overtly meta-theatrical lines in the play, the strongest examples of the "V-effect." This is seen most clearly when, half way through the play, Widow Begbick refers to Brecht by name and alludes to the play's title in an "Interlude," also in verse, in which she synopsizes the main action of the rest of the play. [38]

> Herr Bertolt Brecht maintains that man equals man
> —A view that has been around since time began.
> But then Herr Brecht points out how far one can
> Manouevre and manipulate that man.
> Tonight you are going to see a man reassembled like a car
> Leaving all his individual components just as they are. [39]

Begbick's "Interlude" prepares the audience for the second half of the play through meta-theatrical reference to the author, making it clear that her character, at least at that juncture of the plot understands exactly what the play is about. The play is going to demonstrate that individuals can be changed, but the audience has no idea from Begbick's words whether they will be horrified or thrilled at the transformation of the individual.

In order to convince Galy Gay to transform himself permanently into their missing comrade, the English soldiers stage a funeral for him. The soldiers know that if Galy Gay looks into the coffin their plan will be thwarted because he will discover that it is empty. Gay does not have the courage to look in the coffin at his own funeral. Instead he chooses to accept that he has died and that, therefore he must not be himself, since he is still alive, so he will agree to become the person that they want him to be. Confusing as this scenario is, it is presented in the text as if it is perfectly logical and even elegant. This conversion of the apparently absurd into the acceptable is the other side of the "V-effect" which takes "characters and incidents from ordinary life, from our immediate surroundings, being familiar," and "alienates them" in order to "make them seem remarkable to us."[40] Conversely, the "V-effect" makes the unfamiliar seem commonplace. Brecht switches from prose to verse at the penultimate moment of Galy Gay's "recognition-suicide-rebirth" scene.

> Galy Gay: One man equals no man. Some one has to call him.
> Therefore
> I would gladly have looked into his chest
> As the heart clings to its parents.
> By what sign does Galy Gay know himself
> to be Galy Gay?
> Suppose his arm was cut off
> And he found it in the chink of a wall
> Would Galy Gay's eye know Galy Gay's arm
> And Galy Gay's foot cry out: This is the one!?[41]

The switch from prose to verse indicates a change in mode on the part of Gay. In each case from *Mann ist Mann* in which the character's lines stand out from the rest of the narrative either through song, verse or meta-theatrical direct address, the effect is much the same as Harlequin's *lazzo* of suicide from *Empereur dans la lune*. In this respect, these sequences are harmonious with previous forms of clowning and popular theatre and are straightforwardly adapted by Brecht for his purposes. But as with Pierrot from *Pierrot assassin de sa femme*, Galy Gay's transformation heightens the horror of the situation, rather than comically defusing it. He does not stop being a clown; instead, he becomes an aggressively modern, anti-comical version of clown.

Just as Galy Gay could be transformed from a dock worker into a soldier by learning that his name was not his essence, so the ultimate soldier is transformed into a eunuch, because he insists that his name *is* his essence. Sergeant Fairchild, nicknamed Bloody Five because he once murdered five prisoners in cold blood, loses confidence in himself when Widow Begbick and the soldiers humiliate him.

> Fairchild: Am I to lie down with you again, you Sodom?
> Begbick: If you want to, do.
> Fairchild: I do not want to! Get away from me! The eyes of this country are upon me. I used to be a big gun. My name is Bloody Five. The pages of the history books are criss-crossed with that name, in triplicate.
> Begbick: Then don't if you don't want to.
> Fairchild: Don't you realize that my manhood makes me weak when you sit there like that?
> Begbick: Then pluck out your manhood, my boy.
> Fairchild: No need to tell me twice. (*He goes out.*)
> Galy Gay: (*cries out after him*) Stop! Don't take any steps on account of your name! A name is an uncertain thing, you can't build on it.[42]

In the final line of this scene Galy Gay shows that he has learned from Widow Begbick the truth about the individuality of men while Fairchild takes Begbick's cue, not needing to be told twice, to exit and castrate himself. Begbick is the guide for both men's transformation, and is also the audience's rudder. In the final scene of the play, Gay becomes even more blood-thirsty than Fairchild. With Begbick's help, he fires a cannon at an enclave of "peasants, artisans and hard-working people" so as to liberate a mountain pass into Tibet. Although Gay has been transformed in spirit, he still knows nothing of warfare. He turns to Begbick as his tutor and, in imitation of Bloody Five's five murders, insists on shooting five cannon shots, massacring a thousand people.[43]

Begbick's character throughout the play is the ringmaster in the *Mann ist Mann* circus. At the beginning of the play, Galy Gay is a naive, Auguste character who, through the deception of the soldiers combined with Widow Begbick's tutelage, becomes an authoritarian White Clown more grotesque than Bloody Five. Galy Gay's transformation is balanced by Fairchild's. As Gay transforms into a White Clown, Fairchild transforms into the Auguste. The transformed, feminized Fairchild tries to stop Galy Gay from firing the cannon five times. He points his revolver at Gay but, because Fairchild is no longer the White Clown, Bloody Five, he cannot shoot. Fairchild, now the Auguste, is literally and figuratively impotent. His inaction at the end of the play implicates him in the death of the thousand souls, just as Gay's weakness during the first half of the play was as objectionable as his authoritarian, White Clown identity.

In *Mann ist Mann* the death of the clown protagonist is not literal but is, rather, a sleight of hand, or bit of stage magic of which Galy Gay is the innocent dupe. Gay's death is a simultaneous rebirth but of an entirely negative type. In fact rebirth, or reassembly as Brecht usually calls it, is the central idea of the play.

MANN IST MANN AS ANTI-TRAGEDY

At this point in his development, Brecht was seeking a modern expression of tragedy, or more properly, anti-tragedy that would be relevant to the modern political situation, as well as modern social life and science. In the middle of the execution scene from *Mann ist Mann*, just before the soldiers put the blindfold on Galy Gay, Brecht's stage directions indicate: *Galy Gay is led back and forth; he strides*

like the protagonist in a tragedy. Despite such indications, Brecht was
careful to qualify the tragic implications of his play.[44] One year after
the première of *Mann ist Mann*, Brecht expressed his exasperation
with the interpretation of Galy Gay's character as tragic:

> This contemporary, Galy Gay, surprising though it may seem, is very much
> against his case being turned into a tragedy; he gains something as a result of
> the mechanical infringement of his spiritual essence, and after the operation
> reports that he is in radiant health.[45]

It is clear that Brecht did not want his audience to mourn for Galy
Gay, to empathize with him, as they might for characters in classical
plays. In Brecht's theoretical writings he stresses the importance of
drama being suited to the new technological age.[46] Only two years
after the première of *Mann ist Mann* (and one year after the Berlin
production with Peter Lorre) Brecht wrote a short clown play as part
of *The Baden-Baden Lesson on Consent*, written for the Baden-Baden
music festival of 1929 and including an original score composed by Paul
Hindemith (1895–1963). This play is one of Brecht's "Learning Plays."
Three clowns provide an example of what happens when "some men
help another man."[47] One of the clowns is a giant named Mr. Smith
whom the other two "help" by disassembling him part by part. They
begin when Smith complains that his foot hurts. They help him by
sawing off his foot and giving him a stick to help him stand. After
removing his other limbs, they screw his head off and he falls over
backwards.

> Smith: Stop! Someone, put a hand on my brow.
> Clown 1: Where?
> Smith: Someone hold my hand.
> Clown 1: Which one?
> Clown 2: Are you feeling easier now, Mr. Smith?
> Smith: No, I'm not. There's a stone sticking into my back.
> Clown 2: Now really, Mr. Smith, you can't have everything.
> (*Both laugh loudly.*)
> (*End of Clown number.*)[48]

When one reads or views a production of *Mann ist Mann* it is tempting to think of the play as a pacifist piece. This is how translator Eric
Bentley, a conscientious objector during World War II, has interpreted
the play. But as we have seen, Brecht's ideas when he wrote it, and

statements about it made afterward, indicate that *Mann ist Mann* is
as much a justification of the dehumanizing of an individual as it is a
satire of imperialistic war making. In keeping with Brecht's concept of
Epic Theater, the play is contradictory. Gay's transformation is tragic,
yet glorious. As in the Baden-Baden clown show, *Mann ist Mann* attempts to demonstrate the necessity of man's reconstruction. Whether
we are morally offended by the events of the two plays (*Mann ist Mann*
and the Baden-Baden clown show) is less important than recognizing
that mankind is unprepared for the modern world without being re-
designed. The world must be recreated, according to Brecht, and man
must be altered to fit that world.

Galy Gay's death scene and subsequent transformation create a kind
of Brechtian *catharsis* that is *anti-catharsis*. The audience may feel
pity and they certainly feel fear, but cleansing is kept from them.
In classical tragedy, *catharsis* is related to the idea of purification.
Aristotle used the term *catharsis* in order to defend theatre from anti-
theatrical philosophers, mainly Plato, who warned that the emotions
raised watching tragedy had the potential to pollute the viewer. Aristotle's notion of *catharsis* is a rhetorical strategy to justify the pleasures
of theatre in "therapeutic terms."[49] If this notion of classical *catharsis*
is accurate, that catastrophe necessitates purification for normality
to be restored, then Brecht's strategy in creating a modernist tragedy
can be understood as designed to leave the audience polluted because
restoration of normality is exactly what he hopes to avoid. In *Mann ist
Mann*, it is the reintegration of the hero that strikes pity and fear rather
than the catastrophe, which is a false, clown death. The reintegration
of the hero is the catastrophe and *catharsis* in the traditional sense
of cleansing is deferred. Rather than the viewers purging themselves
as a result of witnessing the theatrical event, they are forced to admit
that the catastrophe, Galy Gay's transformation into a White Clown,
is necessary. The audience is left polluted. Any cleansing will have to
take place outside of the theater after the play is over. Cleansing can
only come through political action. Theatrical action is meant to spark
political action not provide the purification itself.

If we understand Galy Gay's transformation as a metamorphosis
from Auguste to White Clown he clearly becomes more authoritarian
than the other soldiers or even Bloody Five whom he outstrips in violent
action. As the play marches to its denouement, the comic mode is
superseded entirely by one of tension and escalating horror. Because
Brecht has convinced us that a man can be "reassembled," the audience

can envision Galy Gay transforming yet again. Should he face a still more horrific foe (i.e., Fascism) then he could be reconstituted as a counter-authority figure again, but with fighting potential! It is the very necessity of this horrific transformation that instills fear in the audience. The audience may wish to have the old Auguste-like Galy Gay back, but while this sentiment is felt, it is simultaneously contradicted because, when war eventually comes, the White Clown will be needed.[50]

Brecht's notes on the 1928 production, in which Peter Lorre played Galy Gay, indicate that they conceived of the role as consisting of four distinct masks. Brecht knew he wanted the final, soldier's mask to be a monster, but he also wanted one white-face mask. The problem was which phase of the character's development should the white face accompany? Lorre decided that it should be after the mock execution until the "reassembly" as the soldier. The third phase was painted white because, according to Brecht; "between fear of death and fear of life, he [Lorre] chose to treat the latter as the more profound."[51] Lorre was transformed into a grotesque puppet on stilts with a false nose, similar to the giant puppet from the Baden-Baden clown, for the finale in which he fires the cannon. He looked more like a clown than ever, resembling Chaplin in *Shoulder Arms*, but he had evolved beyond the language of known clowns altogether. At the end of *Mann ist Mann* Gay is a monstrous puppet of the war machine. Man does not equal man at all but, rather, man equals machine, or perhaps something less than machine; a mere cog or wheel.

6

Clown in Beckett's Theater:
Waiting for Godot, Act Without Words

WAS BECKETT'S THEATER ANTI-BRECHTIAN?

SAMUEL BECKETT (1906–90) HAD TRIED TO FORGE A CAREER AS A WRITER for several years, publishing his first story and essay in 1929, but he became an international figure from the success of *Waiting for Godot* in the early 1950s.[1] References to clowns and clown imagery permeated his earlier prose works; but, only when they reached the stage did Beckett's clowns capture the imagination of a generation. There can be little doubt that the reception, as well as the creation, of Beckett's stage works were influenced by the post-War mood. Just as *Mann ist Mann* was a product of the post-World War I era, the clowns who walked across a barren landscape in *Waiting for Godot*, or peered out at a wasted world in *Endgame*, reminded audiences of the tenuous relationship between contemporary man and the world that he had very recently almost extinguished.

In a series of plays, Beckett presents clown characters in a theatrical situation that directly contradicts Brecht's use of clown in *Mann ist Mann*. While Brecht's clown transforms into a man of action, or a mechanized man, Beckett's characters are presented in situations that offer them little positive action and their transformational qualities usually have little bearing on the social situation. *Mann ist Mann* suggests a model for reorganizing man as a useful tool for the collective by expurgating his individuality. Beckett suggests a model for reorganizing one's path to personal redemption, suggesting that social action is connected to individual moral character.[2]

In this chapter, I will demonstrate that, despite the apparent opposition, both Beckett's and Brecht's theaters were based on a quality of critical performing that had its roots in clown performance—what I have called "clown logic," and what Brecht called *Vertrackte Dialektik*. Beckett became famous when Brecht was nearing the end of his life. Absurdist theater seemed to point to a new direction for post-war theater, which had mostly been rediscovering naturalism. Brecht, although not part of the naturalism revival, interpreted the new, absurdist trend as an apolitical, nihilist movement that threatened the positivist approach to theater that he and others, such as French playwright and philosopher Jean Paul Sartre (1905–80) had sought to develop. Brecht wanted to write a play in response to *Godot*, which he saw as a step backward.[3] According to his surviving notes, the play that Brecht was planning would have given Vladimir (Didi) and Estragon (Gogo) specific historical context and shown that a passive response was not the only choice that they had, but Brecht never lived to write such a play.[4]

Brecht and Beckett have continued to be presented as polar opposites even as recently as Joel Schechter's *Durov's Pig* (1985). Schechter devotes an entire chapter to "Brecht against Beckett," concluding finally that Beckett's clowns were relics of a former theater forced onto the modern stage.[5] Schechter suggests that Beckett's tramps are not legitimate clowns because they do not share with Brecht's protagonists an awareness of the theatrical situation:

> Beckett's tramps are doubly divorced from their setting, as they are comic types from a past era . . . thrust onto a modern stage; and they cannot even see that they are on stage at all.[6]

But this statement is not borne out by the text of *Waiting for Godot* as the following example demonstrates:

> Vladimir: We're surrounded! (*Estragon makes a rush towards back.*) Imbecile! There's no way out there. (*He takes Estragon by the arm and drags him towards front. Gestures towards front.*) There! Not a soul in sight! Off you go! Quick! (*He pushes Estragon towards the auditorium. Estragon recoils in horror.*) You Won't? (*He contemplates auditorium.*) Well I can understand that.[7]

It is not that Beckett's clowns do not know that they are on a stage. They do. The difference is that they do not acknowledge that the audience represents a potential ally, as does Widow Begbick in *Mann ist Mann* or Harlequin in his *lazzo* of suicide.[8] Gogo's horror at venturing into the world of the audience has its parallel with Galy Gay's horror at facing life.[9] Gogo's horror is at real life rather than life as a stage character. Although Brecht may have been angered by the apparent lack of political conviction of *Waiting for Godot*, his own works contain much of the same preoccupation with individual human angst, albeit shrouded in a Socialist ideology.

CLOWN REFERENCES IN BECKETT'S FICTION AND DRAMA

As were Copeau, Meyerhold and Brecht before him, Beckett was inspired by popular performers, circus clowns and cabaret comics, as well as the silent film comedians Charles Chaplin and Buster Keaton. One of Beckett's collaborators, Richard Seaver, has acknowledged the importance of clown in all of Beckett's work: "like Chaplin—a tiny, vulnerable figure in a scarcely fathomable landscape—Beckett's characters, however dimly aware of the Void and all its terrors, are also clowns."[10]

Critic Normand Berlin, reflecting on the original New York production of *Waiting for Godot*, realized that much of his interpretation of that performance relied on his understanding of the visual references of the play:

> How could two men wearing bowlers, two men who were annoyed with one another and dependent on one another, one self-important, the other a little obtuse, how could two such men not remind me of Laurel and Hardy? How could I not see Buster Keaton when Gogo gazed in all directions with hands screening eyes? How could I not see Chaplin when those boots were displayed in that splayed way on center stage? How could I not be reminded of the Marx Brothers' hat routine in *Duck Soup* when Didi and Gogo play with their hats?[11]

Berlin's reaction to *Waiting for Godot* was typical of scholars, critics and the public who recognized the presence of clown in the action and dialogue of Beckett's characters. Vladimir and Estragon anticipate much of the critical response to the play when halfway through Act I, they have the following dialogue:

> Vladimir: Charming evening we're having.
> Estragon: Unforgettable.
> Vladimir: And it's not over.
> Estragon: Apparently not.

Vladimir: It's only beginning.
Estragon: It's awful:
Vladimir: Worse than the pantomime.
Estragon: The circus.
Vladimir: The music-hall.
Estragon: The circus. [12]

This dialogue so explicitly sets the play in a clown environment that critics could not help seizing on the circus analogy as an explanation of the play. But, recognizing that Beckett's characters resemble clowns does not in and of itself "decode" these complex plays any more than knowing that Gogo's name in an early draft was Levi, explains that Beckett intended him to represent the suffering of Jews during World War II, as Berlin goes on to imply in the same article. [13] When Berlin asks how he could keep from being reminded of Laurel and Hardy when watching Didi and Gogo, he is not merely responding to the fact that both pairs of characters wear bowler hats. He is responding to the fact that both teams are classic White Clown-Auguste pairings. One member of the team, Didi or Oliver Hardy, corresponding to the White Clown, continually looks for a logical explanation, insisting on some kind of order to whatever situation presents itself or some cultural information that he thinks he understands better than his Auguste partner. The other member of the team (either Gogo, or Stan Laurel, corresponding to the Auguste) understands neither the actual logic of a given situation nor his partner's efforts to explain it to him.

Herbert Berghof, who directed the original New York production of *Waiting for Godot* contrasted his production with the Miami première by focusing on the clown aspect of the play: "There was nothing fanciful or strange in it . . . In Miami the play was directed for style and crucifixion and I don't know what. I felt the play was comparable to clowning—the sublime clowning of Grock and the Fratellinis." [14] These comments could be seen as self serving because the director was trying to rationalize a production of the play with Broadway's leading clown, Bert Lahr, playing Gogo, but Berghof was not the first (or the last) to draw a parallel between Beckett's theater and the Fratellini Brothers. Jean Anouilh (1910–87), a self described "unserious, serious playwright," and early Beckett enthusiast, described *En Attendant Godot* as "Pascal's *Pensées* as played by the Fratellini clowns." [15]

One scene from *Waiting for Godot* that seems to reflect the Fratellini is the first entrance of Pozzo and Lucky:

Enter Pozzo and Lucky. Pozzo is the first to enter, followed by the rope
which is long enough to let him reach the middle of the stage before Pozzo
appears. Lucky caries a heavy bag, a folding stool, a picnic basket and a
greatcoat, Pozzo a whip.
Pozzo: (*off*): On! (*Crack of whip. Pozzo appears. They cross the stage.*
Lucky passes before Vladimir and Estragon and exit. Pozzo at the sight
of Vladimir and Estragon stops short. The rope tautens. Pozzo jerks at it
violently.) Back!
Noise of Lucky falling with all his baggage. [16]

This scene would evoke the Fratellini brothers to the Paris audience
especially considering the similarity between Pozzo's physical appearance and Paul Fratellini, whose faded tuxedo and top hat are reflected
in Pozzo's dress and general demeanor. Paul Fratellini was significant in clown history because he combined the qualities of the Auguste
and ringmaster. Pozzo also maintains some of the ringmaster's accou-
trements, with his whip and false authoritative tone.

Like the Fratellini act at the Medrano Circus, the characters in
Waiting for Godot are introduced one at a time and then interact as a
unit. With all four main characters acting in a broadly comic fashion
this scene conjures a circus ring more clearly than anything in the play
up to that point. It is also reminiscent of the elephant *entrée*, which
Brecht adapted in *Mann ist Mann*. [17] Despite the comic potential of this,
and other scenes in *Waiting for Godot*, the dark tone is never replaced
with the "Joy" that Copeau and others found so inspirational in the
Fratellini clowns. From what we know of the Fratellini's general style
of clowning, it was probably too sentimental (perhaps too "joyful")
to reflect the kind of clown relationship that Beckett felt would be
relevant to post-war audiences. Beckett did not romanticize the clown
performances of the Fratellini Brothers as Copeau had done. [18]

Vladimir and Estragon also reminded the European audience, including Herbert Berghof, of Grock, the Swiss Auguste. Grock had been
an enormous star in Paris, London, Germany and Spain from the early
part of the century until his retirement in 1954. He first worked with
a White Face partner in traditional circus entrées but later became
a cabaret performer, billing himself as "Grock and Partner." While
his act involved a great deal of silent clowning, tumbling, and musical
burlesque, he was also very verbal and made use of his skill as a linguist
to communicate with whatever audience he was appearing before. [19] His
trademark was the well-timed non-sequitur, such as "sans blââgue?"

[no kidding?] or "Nit Mö-ö-ö-glich" (from German, meaning impossible), but especially "pourquoa?" ["why?" with a drawl].[20] The inconvenient word "why" recurs frequently in *Waiting for Godot*, along with similar action-stopping questions and interjections, to create a verbal leitmotif for Didi and Gogo reminiscent of Grock's catch-phrases:

> Estragon: (*with exaggerated enthusiasm*). I find this really most extraordinarily interesting.
> Vladimir: One out of four. Of the other three two don't mention any thieves at all and the third says that both abused him.
> Estragon: Who?
> Vladimir: What?
> Estragon: What's this all about? Abused who?
> Vladimir: The Saviour.
> Estragon: Why?
> Vladimir: Because he wouldn't save them.
> Estragon: From hell?
> Vladimir: Imbecile! From death.
> Estragon: Well what of it?
> Vladimir: Then the two of them must have been damned.
> Estragon: And why not?
> Vladimir: But one of the four says that one of the two was saved.
> Estragon: Well? They don't agree and that's all there is to it.[21]

Despite the resonance that Didi, Gogo, Lucky, and Pozzo had with familiar clowns of the period such as the Fratellini and Grock, the most common specific clown reference in all of Beckett's work, both dramatic and prose fiction, is to Bim and Bom, an enormously popular Russian clown team who performed in Paris at the turn of the century, and later in Russia following the revolution. Bim and Bom specialized in political satire, eccentric dancing and music. The team had several changes in personnel over the years and many imitators who used the catchy names Bim and Bom.[22]

Beckett refers to the team of Bim and Bom in *More Pricks than Kicks* (1934) and later names the characters in *How It Is* (1962) Pim and Bom. Didi and Gogo also compare Pozzo and Lucky to Bim and Bom in an early draft of *Waiting for Godot*.[23] Similarly, Hamm and Clov refer to Bim and Bom in an early draft of *Endgame*.[24] In this earlier draft Hamm and Clov are not named but are referred to as "F" and "X." Each time that Beckett alludes to Bim and Bom he refers to a pair who are tied together, in the same way that a clown team are always associated as a unit, but who are both dependent upon and destructive to each other. Frequently in Beckett's work, the Bim-Bom unit is established, then reversed. In *How it Is*, for instance, Pim is initially the torturer of Bom, but in Part II the roles are reversed. The potential for Bim and Bom to trade places is made even more clear in Beckett's *What Where* (1984). This late play includes five characters: Bam, Bem, Bim, Bom, and Voice of Bam (V). The play consists of Bam questioning Bom, Bim and Bem as to their efficiency in giving each other "the works." The dialogue remains almost the same from scene to scene but with the roles reversing. Bom is initially cast as torturer, presumably of Bem, then Bim is cast in Bom's role but with Bom as the victim and finally Bem appears to give "the works" to Bim.

This reversal of roles is also used in *Godot*. Pozzo is in command the first time we see him but in Act II he has become blind, lost his authority, and even Didi and Gogo feel they can lord it over him. Lucky's rope, which was long enough in Act I to allow one of the pair to be half way across the stage when the other still had not entered, is much shorter in Act II. Beckett's stage direction, *"Rope as before, but much shorter, so that Pozzo may follow more easily."*[25] indicates that the shorter rope means that Pozzo must tighten his hold on Lucky because his previous power is diminished. At the same time, this change forces the audience to reinterpret Pozzo and Lucky's earlier relationship. Perhaps Lucky shortened the rope, as he alone can see to do it now, implying that he has been a much more active partner in his own subjugation than it seemed in Act I.

Beckett said of *Endgame*, "you must realize that Hamm and Clov are Didi and Gogo at a later date, at the end of their lives."[26] If we take Beckett's own word on the plays seriously, the main characters: Hamm, Clov, Didi, and Gogo are different variations of clown teams, different incarnations of Bim and Bom, or put in the language of the basic dichotomy of a clown act, with White Clown and Auguste and their relationship to an authority figure reminiscent of the ringmaster.

TRANSFORMING CLOWN PAIRS

The tendency for Beckett's characters to come in pairs makes comparison between them and the basic clown dichotomy more than usually straightforward.[27] All of Beckett's important characters have clown names and are described in clown terms. Hamm and Clov as well as

Krapp from *Krapp's Last Tape* share physical descriptions with Didi and Gogo that mark them as clowns. Krapp's description is particularly interesting because this play is the first of a series of shorter works that bear less obvious relation to clown than *Waiting for Godot* or *Endgame*. Beckett took great pains to describe Krapp's appearance, which clearly identifies Krapp as another incarnation of clown:

> Rusty black narrow trousers too short for him. Rusty black sleeveless waistcoat, four capacious pockets. Heavy silver watch and chain. Grimy white shirt open at neck, no collar. Surprising pair of white boots, size ten at least, very narrow and pointed. White face. Purple nose. Disordered grey hair. Unshaven. Very near-sighted (but unspectacled). Hard of hearing. Cracked voice. Distinctive intonation. Laborious walk.[28]

Didi and Gogo are differentiated from each other physically, and correspond to the two halves of the basic dichotomy in a number of other ways. Didi plays with his hat, searching it for the cause of some irritation; Gogo struggles with his boots. Didi remembers (and, tries to make sense of) biblical history. Didi tries to use his head, or at least has an idea of himself as someone who has a mind with which to think and connive; Gogo seems more elemental—he sits on the ground, sleeps in the gutter. Didi is clearly the White Clown; Gogo more of an Auguste. Didi is usually in the position of explaining a situation to Gogo, as in the scene quoted above concerning the thieves at the crucifixion. Their relationship changes somewhat in Act II, however, when Gogo "teaches" Didi to think more in his manner:

> Vladimir: When you seek you hear.
> Estragon: You do.
> Vladimir: That prevents you from finding.
> Estragon: It does.
> Vladimir: That prevents you from Thinking.
> Estragon: You think all the same.
> Vladimir: No, no impossible.
> Estragon: That's the idea, let's contradict each other.
> Vladimir: Impossible.
> Estragon: You think so?
> Vladimir: We're in no danger of ever thinking any more.
> Estragon: Then what are we complaining about?
> Vladimir: Thinking is not the worst.
> Estragon: Perhaps not but at least there's that.

Vladimir: That what?
Estragon: That's the idea, let's ask each other questions.[29]

Hamm and Clov continue the clown pairing with Hamm the White Clown enthroned in a wheelchair and, like Pozzo in Act II of *Godot*, blind. Hamm is a much more authoritarian White Clown than Didi. *Endgame* has a clown doubling in Nagg and Nell, but they do not intervene in the action of the protagonists in the same way that Lucky and Pozzo do. Nagg and Nell are a side bar commentary on the action of the main characters. Nagg and Nell represent an even more dysfunctional clown pair than Hamm and Clov. They are given space to do routines, but are prevented from achieving any clownish physical action because they are confined to ash cans. As a result, they are reduced to telling jokes:

> Nagg: I tell this story worse and worse. (*Pause. Raconteur's voice.*) Well, to make it short, the bluebells are blowing and he ballockses the buttonholes. (*Customer's voice.*) "God damn you to hell, Sir, no, it's indecent, there are limits! In six days, do you hear me, six days, God made the world. Yes sir, no less, Sir, the WORLD! And you are not bloody well capable of making me a pair of trousers in three months!" (*Tailor's voice, scandalized.*) "But my dear Sir, my dear Sir, look—(*Disdainful gesture, disgustedly.*)—at the world—(pause) and look—(*loving gesture, proudly*)—at my TROUSERS!"[30]

Nagg has told his story hundreds of times and for years and years. Despite his immovable state, and the fact that he tells it "worse and worse," he continues the struggle. He keeps performing. Nell, however, cannot even remember how to respond to a joke. She has stopped playing her part with Nagg as well as with Clov and Hamm. Nagg is forced to provide his own laughter and is interrupted by Hamm who whistles for Clov to lock the lids of the bins.

Nagg and Nell are a shadow of Hamm and Clov, who also seem to be fading. Hamm tries to position his chair as much in the middle of the stage as possible, like the slow, but all important king at the end of a chess match, simultaneously evoking Gloucester, Lear, and a vaudeville ham. Without Clov to continue to play with him, however, Hamm cannot continue. He depends upon Clov as his Auguste partner, audience and eyes.

Nagg's story refers to more than just his confused past as M C of some other show. The entire sequence serves to foreshadow the action of *Act*

Without Words I. Nagg's story is about a tailor. The mime in *Act Without Words I* uses tailor's scissors to cut his nails. And the tailor's scissors are connected to the mime's thought of suicide. After Nagg's story, Hamm, impatient with having relinquished the center of attention if not center stage for Nagg, whistles for Clov. Nagg immediately reacts by closing himself up in his bin, but Nell remains motionless, spitting out the word "desert!" when Clov feels her pulse before pushing her into the bin. Clov interprets her line as a direction for him to go into the desert. Nell, who is no longer a participant in the show, plants the idea of non-cooperation in Clov's mind, foreshadowing both the end of the play and the scenario for *Act Without Words*.

The repetition and development of clown characters in different circumstances with differing physical features and slightly different social dynamics is Beckett's version of the transformation of clown. Following Beckett's own statement that the different pairs of characters in his plays are re-statements of the same pair, it may follow that the mime in *Act Without Words I* is a representation of Clov after he has left Hamm. *Act Without Words I* was originally performed as a companion piece to *Endgame* when both plays were premièred in 1957.[31]

Act Without Words *I*

Beckett did not simply evoke clown characters in a superficial or romanticized fashion. He made use of their social roles, as expressed in the basic dichotomy, and in doing so created political plays.[32] If Beckett's plays do have a political significance, some ideology, or model of political activity must be implied, however obtusely the message may be delivered. In *Act Without Words I*, Beckett comes closest to articulating a political idea in the developing action of the mime.

Beckett's theater refers back to itself more obviously and more consistently, than any of the other modern masters I have examined.[33] The plays and productions of Brecht and Meyerhold were also self-referential, but the political, or extra-theatrical, references were stressed. Beckett, as we have seen with the example of the name change from Levi to Gogo, deflects the audience away from a coherent, non-theatrical reference. Beckett's reason for using this strategy did not stem from a lack of political convictions, but rather from an impulse to convey truth on stage. Beckett's truth, however, differed from the psychology and sociology of Naturalism and Realism, or the social-historical truths of Brechtian theater. Beckett limited truth to the stage itself. In other words, he wanted to force the audience to concentrate on the "true" situation of his fictional characters, divorced from specific non-theatrical references. *Act Without Words I* shows most clearly how Beckett limits the theatrical world in order to specify the situation and force the audience to confront the truth of the fiction. As with his other plays he chooses a clown (in this case the mime) as protagonist.

In Beckett's plays the clown protagonists repeatedly try to take their own lives and are frustrated. Didi and Gogo are willing to put off hanging themselves until another day when it will be more convenient. Hamm and Clov jostle towards death, the final move in their game, but never solve the problem of how to arrive at this last turn. In *Act Without Words I*, the off-stage fictional world taunts the mime with a rope. The mime's withdrawal is his only way of defeating the off-stage rope teaser, just as Nell's withdrawal from the Auguste-White Clown relationship with Nagg, allows her to escape through death. The strongest decision that the mime seems to make in the play, once it is clear that he cannot leave the desert that is the mimetic space, is his decision to kill himself. This decision process is conveyed to the audience through "takes" to the audience in which the mime "considers." As the audience realizes what the mime has in mind, so too does the off-stage presence and the means for suicide are also withdrawn from the mime:

He looks at his hands, looks around for scissors, sees them, goes and picks them up, starts to trim his nails, stops, reflects, runs his finger along blade of scissors, goes and lays them on small cube, turns aside, opens his collar, frees his neck and fingers it.

The small cube is pulled up and disappears in flies, carrying away rope and scissors.

He turns to take the scissors, sees what has happened.

He turns aside, reflects.

He goes and sits down on big cube.

The big cube is pulled from under him. He falls. The big cube is pulled up and disappears in the flies.

He remains lying on his side, face towards the auditorium, staring before him.

The carafe descends from the flies and comes to rest a few feet from his body.

He does not move.

Whistle from above.

He does not move.

The carafe descends further, dangles and plays about his face.
He does not move.[34]

The action of the play devolves away from involvement, or effort, on
the part of the clown-mime, even to kill himself.

Even if we consider the characters from the different plays as developments of the same characters, as Beckett has suggested that they are,
their situation changes little in comprehensible human terms, even if
drastic changes occur in formal theatrical terms. For instance, Beckett
takes a character who speaks in one play (Clov) and reintroduces him
as a character who is mute in the next one (as the mime in *Act Without
Words I*). The human situation of Clov and the mime are similarly hopeless, only Beckett's expression of it has changed. Unlike Harlequin in
Empereur dans la lune, the clown-mime of *Act Without Words* chooses
not to bridge the gap between different fictional worlds and between
fiction and the world of the audience. He seems to possess the clown's
traditional ability to transcend the world of mimesis, as we see through
his "takes" to the audience, but he refuses to enlist the aid of the audience in his dilemma. The clown-mime is trapped, and the little that
we know of the off-stage world, seems more aggressively hostile than
anything we see in the mimetic space.

Beckett's theater might seem to suggest an entirely new form of
mimesis. What action is being imitated or attempted? The action is
only that of a performance, or rather the reluctance to carry out a
performance. The mime wants to leave the stage and return to the non-
mimetic space, but the off-stage presence will not allow this option.
Perhaps the theatrical activity is a continuation of all life activity both
on and off-stage. This is not to argue that the "point" of Beckett's
theater is that the distinction between life and art is false. Beckett's
play, although extremely sophisticated, is still an illusion just like every
other example in this study. It is different from others because it is
entirely self-contained and about itself. Its meaning or purpose is no
more or less than what it is, a theatrical expression.

Beckett's form of theater is the most cut-off from a normative world,
least able to be defined and made understandable by that world, yet
it remains dependent upon the apparatus of traditional theater. The
simple fact that *Act Without Words* depends upon a clearly defined
playing area (distinct from the auditorium and the back-stage) reminds
us that although this form of theater may seem strange, it is still
dependent upon the shared reference of other theatrical experiences.

In *Act Without Words* we do not understand what the context is for the action and the mime cannot explain it to us because he's a mime. We know only that there is a logic behind the mime's actions and it is hidden with the off-stage presence. We also know that this "character" is cruel. The primary action of *Act Without Words* is between the mime and the unseen, off-stage tormentor, with the audience acting as onlooker.

Precedent for this gag can be found in countless clown routines. Two well-known examples are Emmett Kelly's (1898–1979) contest with the circus follow spot and the vaudeville cliché of the unseen hand operating the cane. In the first of these Kelly, the tramp clown, materializes cleaning up the circus ring and ends up in a duel with the follow spot, which both torments him and is finally controlled by him when he sweeps it away.[35] The vaudeville cliché of the off-stage hook or cane, which threatens to jerk a performer off-stage, derives from the competitive nature of this popular form. The audience's opinion of performers decided whether or not they were allowed to continue their act. If an act received a poor response they would be jerked off-stage by the hook or cane to the cruel laughter of the crowd. This same device was used in Blok's *The Fairground Booth*.[36] In that play the character of the Author is forced off-stage when he tries to reassert his will upon the performers. In *Endgame* there is another incarnation of this idea when Hamm cuts short Nagg's comic story and has him and Nell removed from effectiveness in the mimetic space by putting the lids on their cans. Still another good example of a variation on this old gag comes from one of Karl Valentin's sketches:

> *The Alpine Terzett* ends with the audience and the proprietor forcibly removing the performers from the podium. Valentin rushes back onto the stage after being given the hook and shouts at the audience the truth of the matter in a contradictory tone of reproach: "just remember this, you don't need us, we need you!"[37]

If we look at *Act Without Words* as an inversion of the clown conditions found in any of these analogous cases it becomes clear that while Beckett's play is a brilliant variation on an old theme, it still operates on the same mimetic principle. In Beckett's play, the cliché is turned on its head. Rather than a plucky and determined comedian who tries to avoid the cane, while simultaneously winning the love of the audience through direct appeal, the mime-clown in *Act Without Words* is violently forced to remain on-stage by the off-stage presence.

Whenever he tries to leave the stage, he is hurled back into the mimetic space in a direct reversal of the traditional situation.

This aspect of the play is articulated physically at the very beginning of the play:

> *Desert. Dazzling light.*
> *The man is flung backwards on stage from right wing.*
> *He falls, gets up immediately, dusts himself, turns aside,*
> *reflects.*
> *Whistle from right wing.*
> *He reflects, goes out right.*
> *Immediately flung back on stage he falls, gets up*
> *immediately, dusts himself, turns aside, reflects.*
> *Whistle from left wing.*
> *He reflects, goes towards left wing, hesitates, thinks*
> *better of it, halts, turns aside, reflects.* [38]

This introduction establishes that the mime has no recourse to the wings as an avenue of escape. Once the mime refuses to continue to try to exit, thereby frustrating the off-stage presence's opportunity to fling him back on-stage, the next strategy for teasing him is developed. The mime reconciles himself to living on the stage-desert and his interest is redirected towards making the most of a poor situation. The off-stage presence next tempts him with the comfort of shade from the "dazzling light":

> *A little tree descends from flies, lands. It has a single bough*
> *some three yards from ground and at its summit a meager tuft*
> *of palms casting at its foot a circle of shadow.*
> *He continues to reflect.*
> *Whistle from above.*
> *He turns, sees tree, reflects, goes to it sits down in its shadow.*
> *looks at his hands.*
> *A pair of tailor's scissors descends from flies, comes to rest*
> *before tree, a yard from ground.*
> *He continues to look at his hands.*
> *Whistle from above.*
> *He looks up, sees scissors, takes them and starts to trim his*
> *nails.*
> *The palms close like a parasol, the shadow disappears.*
> *He drops the scissors, reflects.* [39]

What the mime is thinking in the periods marked "He reflects" we cannot know for sure, although these "takes" are made less ambiguous when he considers suicide as an option. But as in any clown show, the audience is given ample time to think with the clown whose tempo is always slower than theirs. The action of using tailor's scissors for manicure scissors is standard circus clown material. This action allows the mime's attention to be diverted from his momentary contentment found under the shade of the tree which is then yanked away. Having withdrawn the shade, the off-stage presence moves to the main action of the play by tempting with water: "*A tiny water carafe, to which is attached a huge label inscribed WATER, descends from flies, comes to rest some three yards from the ground.*"[40] Most of the rest of the play consists of the mime's efforts to get the "tiny carafe" of water. The action could be summed up by a line from the early draft of *Endgame* when Hamm and Clov were named simply "x" and "f."

F: Well, there's always the Bom business.
X: Bom . . . Ah yes, that poor old woman who begs for a drop of water.
F: No, that's the Bim business.[41]

There are also direct ties to the final draft of *Endgame*, most notably the use of the whistle by Hamm to call Clov and the use of the whistle by the off-stage presence to torment the mime.

While *Endgame* is claustrophobically set indoors, *Act Without Words* is claustrophobically set in a desert. Is the outdoors suggested by *Endgame* and seen only by Clov the same space as the Desert in *Act Without Words*? If so then the mime's action can be understood as the fulfillment of Nell's terse expletive to Clov, "Desert!" Clov is terribly disturbed by her choice of protest at his cruelty in following Hamm's instructions. These lines directly follow Nagg's comic story. Nell and Nagg as a White Clown-Auguste team have been replaced by Hamm and Clov who will in turn, we may suppose, be replaced by another pair. Perhaps the mime in *Act Without Words* is the boy whom Clov has seen, or pretended to see, at the end of *Endgame*. In this case, the off-stage presence could be Clov who has taken on Hamm's authoritarian character. All of these are possible in the same way that "X" and "F" cannot remember which is Bim and which is Bom; hence the action of *Act Without Words* is the Bom business which is in fact the Bim business.

Act Without Words provides a corresponding punch line to Nagg's comic story. Beckett's play is like the tailor's pair of pants: compared to the world made by God, that of the audience, it is well made. Like the many clowns who are both victim and torturer, Bims who are Boms and Naggs who were Hamms, the audience identifies with both the mime and his tormentor. Although the audience may sympathize with the mime's suffering, intellectually, he is suffering for them as much as for the amusement of the off-stage "character." The audience's interest is the same as the torturer. They want to see a show—the off-stage presence wants the mime to remain on-stage. When the mime refuses to perform, by giving up his attempts to escape, the play is over.

It is precisely this final aspect of the play that carries the political implication of *Act Without Words*. The audience recognizes a kind of victory on the part of the mime in his withdrawal, his passive resistance. His action is the only form of protest open to him against his unseen tormentor but also puts the audience in the position of the tormentor more clearly than any other action of the play. When the mime withdraws from the action he thwarts the expectations of the audience and the unseen tormentor equally. Therefore the audience is forced to admit that their interests are implicated in the sadistic world of the off-stage character, whereas earlier in the play the members of the audience could distance themselves from the mime, laughing at his comedy, and the entire action.

The mime's withdrawal is doubly relevant when we consider the political significance of the play. Passive resistance, as a political expression, presents an option in direct contrast to the ideology of *Mann ist Mann*, which argues for a dismantling of mankind for better service. For Beckett, who lived through the occupation of France and had to make tough decisions about involving himself in a war when his personal inclination was toward pacifism, political action was not as clear cut a matter. [42] Since the war, passive resistance has become much more credible as a political action, perhaps more credible than armed revolution.

BECKETTIAN *GESTE*

Beckett became more and more interested in maintaining authorial control of his productions as he aged. In his later years, he explained his vision of theater as one where he could communicate directly to the audience: "The best possible play is one in which there are no actors, only the text. I'm trying to find a way to write one."[43] The plays that Beckett tried to write however, tended to reduce text as much as the place of the actor. Rather than writing texts that need interpreting by actors, Beckett wrote poetic scenarios that the performers must present physically. He limited all theatrical expression equally, reducing even clown to his (and her) most basic elements. "Writing, for Beckett, was not the illumination of things, but the amplification of the unspeakable rumor, the confused buzz of voice that circulates between things. It does not name the world, but rather casts rhythms against the verbal decor that one calls reality."[44] This "confused buzz" was Beckett's explication of clown logic, a Beckettian *geste*.

Through time, Beckett's plays contained less and less overt markers of clown. Other than the clown names Bim and Bom in *What Where* (1984), his characters do not have the physical attributes such as clown names, white faces, red noses, and ill-fitting clothing. The White Clown-Auguste pairings are obscured and the direct physical and verbal references to clown are eliminated, but clown logic remains at the heart of the dramaturgy nevertheless. As the plays become more and more precise and narrow, the author himself becomes the primary authority figure. Just as the character named Author represented the White Clown in Blok and Meyerhold's *Fairground Booth*, so Beckett's increasing confinement of his clowns made him a White Clown author.[45] Beckett continued to experiment with constraining his characters, providing an arbitrary logic against which his characters must struggle. The exactness of the stage directions exerted upon the performer the same kind of physical demands as the clown stunts and pratfalls would in a more traditional clown play. The clowns are in conflict with the environment invented by Beckett. The environment itself is clearly atypical, and so the character, paradoxically, seems more familiar to the audience.

A character such as Mouth from *Not I*, for instance, seems as divorced from clown as any stage character ever invented, yet on another level she is simply an inversion of the mime from *Act Without Words*. The mime only moves and does not speak, while Mouth speaks but does not move. He is tormented physically by an unseen force, while she is observed by an non-speaking auditor. The primary performer in both cases uses a limited form of expression, which is at the same time physically demanding. His and her effort to communicate to the other character, and the audience, reasserts the basic clown dichotomy with the author and audience increasingly implicated in the White Clown role. The minimalist plays help to focus on Beckett's *geste* an idiosyncratic form of *Gestus* or "clown logic," the integration of clown technique into a poetic, dramatic form.

Another example of this phenomenon can be seen in the short, silent film, entitled simply, *Film* (1964). Beckett insisted on casting Buster Keaton as "O," the film's main character, over the reservations of director Alan Schneider. When it came time to shoot *Film*, Keaton did everything that Beckett and Schneider asked of him even though the action of the scenario seems arbitrary. Keaton's craft as a clown allowed him to create an exhausting physical action which, for him, had no logical or psychological motive. *Film* is moving precisely because Keaton meticulously carries out the apparently unjustified physical action, interspersed with some direct looks to the camera, reminiscent of the mime in *Act Without Words*. Keaton always maintained that he never knew "what the hell was going on."[46] Even though, by Keaton's own admission, the action of *Film* was incoherent to him, the result of his clown-logical approach to action (to carry it through whether it made sense to him or not) was that Keaton's humanity shone through. He looks more alive because of the very pointlessness of his action. Beckett understood this aspect of clown and simply utilized Keaton's ability without the gags. And yet, Beckett intended for *Film* to be "comic and unreal. "O" should invite laughter throughout by his way of moving."[47] The core of this clown-man ("O"), according to Beckett's notes, is his awareness of self despite lack of awareness of anything else:

> All extraneous perception suppressed, animal, human, divine, self-perception maintains in being. Search of non-being in flight from extraneous perception breaking down in inescapability of self-perception. No truth value attaches to above, regarded as of merely structural and dramatic convenience.[48]

Clown *sans* gags, or social context, looks profound simply because we instill the characters with our own sense of the profound. Beckett's shorter, very constrained plays, clarify what attracted him to clowns in the first place. Clown is divorced from other stage characters and is also different from the experience of the audience, yet clowns remain clearly human. The more strictly Beckett forces his clowns to act, the more restricted they appear, yet their inherent human quality becomes intensified. This essential paradox forms the basis for all of Beckett's plays, but he puts this aspect to the test more extremely, the more he limits the environment of the play.

Brecht's theory of performance was his most cogent expression of what he learned from clown while Beckett worked clown theory into his dramaturgy and expressed it through the text in such a way that even a non-clown performer will use clown logic when carrying out the specified words and action. Beckett never expressed a theory of theater or performance comparable to that of Brecht, but he took an active hand in the production of his works and frequently directed them himself in the later stages of his life. At the beginning of Act II of *Waiting for Godot*, Didi enters and performs a brief pantomime before singing the first text of the act. The text Beckett gives him to sing is as follows:

> A dog came in—
> (*Having begun too high he stops, clears his throat, resumes.*)
> A dog came in the kitchen
> And stole a crust of bread.
> Then cook up with the ladle
> And beat him till he was dead.
> Then all the dogs came running
> And dug the dog a tomb—
> (He stops, broods, resumes.)
> Then all the dogs came running
> And dug the dog a tomb
> And wrote upon the tombstone
> For the eyes of dogs to come:
> A dog came in the kitchen
> etc. [49]

Some critics have pointed to this song as an example of Beckettian circularity, but while it is yet another example of Beckett's fondness for repetition, the song itself is a traditional children's nursery rhyme. [50] Brecht mentions the same song as part of a list of training devices for actors as early as 1930. [51] The dog song variations have continued to be a standard actor-training device at the Berliner Ensemble to this day. [52] What to Brecht was a device to help actors develop the kind of acting style which would allow them to perform his plays "gestically," to Beckett was part of the play itself.

7

Clown in Giorgio Strehler's Theater

GIORGIO STREHLER'S (1921–97) PRODUCTION OF SHAKESPEARE'S *KING Lear* (hereafter referred to as *Re Lear*) at the Piccolo Teatro of Milan in 1972, was influenced by Beckett's plays and like them drew on clown tradition for its cast of characters. Both Lear and his Fool were portrayed as clowns and the entire *mise en scène* relied upon a circus metaphor. Recalling the effort made earlier in the century, especially by Meyerhold in Russia, to combine the spectacle of circus with the art of theater, Strehler's *Re Lear* was set in a circus ring with tent ropes barely visible around the perimeter of the acting area. Strehler's first allegiance was to Brecht and this presented certain problems with regard to an entire section of the modernist repertoire particularly the plays of Ionesco, Genet, and Beckett. Strehler waited until well after Brecht's death and until after the death of his partner, Piccolo Teatro co-founder, Paolo Grassi (1919–1981), to stage his first Beckett play, *Happy Days* in 1982.

Paolo Grassi was a committed Socialist who disliked Beckett's theater and, until his death, the Piccolo rarely staged works from the absurdist repertoire.[1] As noted in Chapter 6, post-war European theater became divided along political-aesthetic lines broadly defined as politically committed Brechtian theater, and apolitical, nihilistic, and "absurdist" theater with Beckett's *Waiting for Godot* as its standard bearer. In his book *Per un teatro umano*, Strehler recounts that he asked Brecht's opinion about the apparent abyss between the contemporary avant-garde and Brechtian theater:

> I spoke with Brecht about this particular problem: of Beckett's theatre and especially *Waiting for Godot*. And Brecht agreed with me about the sincerity

and poetic value of Beckett. He told me: "I've also thought about presenting it. In a different style, however. In the style of dialectical criticism. In a completely different style from how it is usually presented." And I agreed with him.[2]

Strehler's sympathy with the avant garde aesthetic was tempered by his affinity for theater with a clear social purpose. As reflected in his account of his conversation with Brecht, however, he found a common ground between the two modes of expression by stressing what Brecht called "dialectical criticism." This stress on dialectic had its clearest expression in Strehler's use and development of clowns who were always presented in clearly opposed units as in the basic clown dichotomy. Strehler recognized that despite their stylistic differences Beckett and Brecht both derived much of their dramaturgy from an opposition of characters that had its clearest manifestation in clown-based personae.

Strehler's accomplishment in *Re Lear* was that he effectively managed to merge Brechtian dramaturgy and Beckettian metaphysics while maintaining the closest possible connection to Shakespeare's text. *Re Lear* effectively combined the aggressive Brechtian clowning, which would make Shakespeare's play relevant in contemporary political terms, with the timeless moral questions raised by Beckett's clowns.

Strehler was one of the last major European directors to work closely with Brecht on an important production. He visited Brecht in Berlin while planning a production of *The Threepenny Opera*, and Brecht visited Strehler's rehearsals for the same production in Milan in 1955. Despite stylistic differences, Brecht seems to have embraced Strehler as he rarely did other directors. Brecht died while the show was in production so that there was no possibility for further direct collaboration between the two men.

The major stylistic element that Strehler adopted from Brecht was an emphasis on theater as narrative and meta-theater. Meta-theater in Strehler's dramaturgy is less an "alienation" device with a didactic political motive, than an aesthetic foundation. All of his productions have had a meta-theatrical frame and in most cases referred clearly to a theatrical past. As his career progressed this theatrical past was increasingly autobiographical, as seen in self-referential elements in the productions of *Re Lear* and, more especially, *La Tempesta* where Strehler associates Prospero with both the author, Shakespeare, and himself as the director.[3]

Strehler has defined his métier as that of a story teller. "I am a teller of stories. I must tell them. If you take away my theater, the actors and the lights, I will go on telling stories alone with no props as long as there is someone to listen."[4] His emphasis on the narrative function of the director's art is partly due to Brecht's influence, but Strehler himself qualifies Brecht's theoretical statements:

> Brecht had his theory and his ideology, he certainly asserted something and believed in something. But his expression is aesthetic. It is as free as poetry. Therefore it is fair to deviate independently, even conflict.[5]

Elsewhere Strehler characterizes theories in general as "not useless but of little value."[6] From these and other comments it would appear that Strehler views himself as a practical theater man who is uncomfortable with theorizing. Yet, at other times he has made it clear that theoretical issues have been at the heart of his theater practice throughout his career:

> Representation, theatrical representation and the mystery connected with it has been and remains the great theme of my entire life. It still challenges me, eludes me and makes it difficult for me to apprehend definitive answers to the questions it endlessly suggests.[7]

Strehler's attitude toward theoretical issues of representation is, therefore, mixed. They interest him but he becomes frustrated if theoretical discourse strays too far from the rehearsal room where, for instance, he insists that Brecht's obscure examples from the pages of *The Short Organum* were made "extremely clear, simple and convincing" by the master and have served him every day since.[8]

Clown offered Strehler a theatrical device through which he could express his own theory of theatrical representation through the practice of theater. He absorbed this way of proceeding primarily from his research into *commedia dell'arte*, the plays of Goldoni, the inspiration of Copeau and Brecht's dialectical approach to acting.

STREHLER AND CLOWN

From the earliest phase of his career, Strehler was interested in the role of clown in drama and was instrumental in the development of contemporary *commedia*. His interest in clown was not confined to historicism, however, but was an extension of his concept of theater as storytelling and meta-theater as a basic dramaturgical device. Strehler has used clowns in his *mise en scène* again and again because of their ability to transcend mimetic conventions. Because Strehler has always thought of theater as an extension of story telling, the disruptive nature of clown has helped accentuate this aspect of his style. In a sense, the clowns in Strehler's theater have acted as surrogate narrators for the director himself. Like Beckett who identified himself with the clowns he created, Strehler's clowns step out literally from his *mise en scène* to communicate Strehler's point of view or remind the audience of who is telling the story.

Strehler's interest in clown began in earnest in 1947, the founding year of the Piccolo Teatro, when he and Paolo Grassi began researching *commedia dell'arte* for their production of *Servitore di due padroni* (1745) by Carlo Goldoni (1709–93). This research involved Amleto and Donato Sartori, the Bolognese craftsmen who recreated the lost art of Italian mask-making. But recreating the genuine leather masks was only the beginning. The actors of the company also had to learn to use them:

> With Jacques Lecoq, Dario Fo and Marisa Flach, Strehler spent long nights working the mask to see how the chin and neck should be interposed, how the head should be inclined, and how the voice, intonation, speech rhythms might emerge. At the same time the Piccolo actors began physical exercises designed not only to enable them to do acrobatics, but also to be able to put themselves in a state of internal justification for doing them. [9]

Along with Brecht, Goldoni represented an anchor for Strehler's research in the theater. [10] If Strehler had not achieved anything else in his career as a director, his popularization of Goldoni as a major playwright would assure his place in Italian theatrical history. Before World War II, Goldoni was popular with low budget touring repertory companies and their working class audiences, but did not receive the respect of mainstream theaters or academics. Even amongst artists who were drawn to clowning and *commedia*, Goldoni was less popular than was Carlo Gozzi (1720–1806) whose aggressively absurd aesthetic seemed to have more in common with the anti-naturalist avant-garde. Generally, Goldoni was looked upon as a kind of second rate Italian Molière. In referring to Goldoni's prejudice against the masks of the *commedia dell'arte*, for instance, Duchartre says:

> He had neither vitality, force, nor art enough in his peculiar talent to enable him to stylize his characters. He dashed off his plays with the nonchalance of a Neapolitan street-singer twanging his guitar. His over-facility gave his work a fragile charm which has stood the test of time but badly. The masks of Pulcinella and Harlequin will always signify something vital and intense, for they are sculptured by both art and time to a semblance of humanity.[11]

Strehler's production of *Arlecchino, servitore di due padroni* almost single handedly altered this view. The production was so successful that Strehler restaged it six times and succeeded in putting Goldoni's peculiar talent back into the repertoire of all other major European theaters.

Strehler's *Arlecchino* is in many ways a scholarly compilation of two Goldoni plays: *Il servitore di due padroni* and *Il teatro comico* (1750). *Il teatro comico* was Goldoni's most didactic dramatic creation. In it he argued for a reform of the theater by means of the form of theater. In effect, Goldoni dramatized his theory of comedy. The meta-theatrical sequences in Strehler's production of *Arlecchino* have their genesis in *Il teatro comico*. The main character in *Il teatro comico* is the capocomico, an early Italian incarnation of the director, whom Strehler inserted into his version of *Arlecchino*, appearing on the fringes of the acting area, paraphrasing lines from *Il teatro comico*, and periodically interfering with the central action.

The production of *Arlecchino* was built on a base of research stemming from the historical context of the original text and performance demands. Strehler changed the name of the central character from Truffaldino, as it was in Goldoni's original, to Arlecchino, a recognizable popular character who provided a link between the contemporary audience and the experiment in rediscovering *commedia* style that was a cornerstone of the production. The Strehler production tells a particular story distinct from, but bound to, Goldoni's text and it placed the action in both theatrical and political history. In this way, Strehler also highlighted the contradictions of Goldoni's text in which the bourgeois characters have superior values, but the proletarian clowns are presented as more productive and imaginative members of society. Strehler's version of Goldoni borrows a dose of Brechtian dramaturgy,

creating proletarian heroes out of the clowns Arlecchino and Smeraldina. The following lines by Smeraldina were delivered presentationally
to the audience in the manner of a feminist call to arms:

> I say as the old proverb says: we get the curses and you all get the crackers.
> Women are the famous adulterers while men have as many affairs as they
> can. The women get talked about but about the men nobody says a thing. We
> get criticized, and you all go scott free. Do you know why? Because the laws
> were all made by men; if they had been made by women everything would
> be the other way around. If it were up to me I'd make all the unfaithful
> men carry the branch of a tree in their hands, and I know that all our cities
> would become forests. [12]

When I saw this scene in rehearsal at the Piccolo Teatro in 1990,
the actress playing Smeraldina was encouraged to pause after the line
"Sapete perchè?" as if she was waiting for a response from the audience.
Eventually she began repeating the word *perchè* three or four times,
pausing longer after each repetition until she got her response from
the audience. Her repetition of this single word created a minor piece
of theater unto itself, similar to a Beckett play with the Grock-like
repetition of that one word: Perchè? After allowing the young actress
to exhaust herself in this enterprise, Strehler casually told her that she
was beginning to get the idea of the scene. Strehler followed this tirade
from Smeraldina by paraphrasing Goldoni's *Il teatro comico*. He had
the capocomico turn to the prompter and tell him to cut Smeraldina's
lines from the next performance.

Strehler credits three men as his *maestri*, Copeau, Jouvet, and
Brecht.[13] All three of these *maestri* were preoccupied with clown, as
has been discussed in previous chapters. *Il servitore di due padroni*
provides a good example of how these different *maestri* manifest themselves in Strehler's process. One aspect of the story that Strehler tells
in a production such as *Arlecchino* is rooted in the past and the world of
the author and his original creative invention. To tell this story Strehler
borrows the research methods derived from Copeau. To tell the story
effectively to an audience that might not be as sensitive to this research
as the intellectuals or elite, he draws on the "humility" of Jouvet. To
tell a story that is relevant to the present he draws on Brecht's political
commitment to a useful theater. These three aspects of Strehler's story
telling, and his *mise en scène*, manifest themselves in his use of stage
space. The nature of the stage space is made clear by the physical action
of Arlecchino from area to area.

A clear duality of narrative space is created by retaining the vis-
ibility of the actors when they leave the stage as characters in the
comedy. When they exit the narrative space of the play, the actors
become ambiguous characters that represent both themselves as actors and the eighteenth-century *commedia* actors performing the play.
They all cease to be the named characters from the story when they
leave the playing area, with the exception of Arlecchino. Arlecchino is
the only member of the core characters who is free to pass from space
to space maintaining his clown persona. In this way, the clown becomes
of prime importance because he not only bridges the physical areas of
the theater but also the aspects of the social situation that those areas
imply. While the actors who play the lovers, for instance, become contemporary characters when they leave the eighteenth-century acting
space, Arlecchino remains a clown for all periods. Strehler's decision
to change the character name from Truffaldino to the archetypal Arlecchino and insert that magical word-name into the title of the play
signaled to the audience before they even entered the theatre that clown
had been reborn. The fact that this message was received is reflected
in Jan Kott's (1914–) celebrated essay *"King Lear* or *Endgame,"* in
which the Piccolo production of *Arlecchino servitore di due padroni*
was used to explain to his reader what a clown was.[14]

CLOWN REVISITED IN *RE LEAR*

After *Arlecchino servitore di due padroni*, which quickly became
a signature piece for Strehler and the Piccolo Teatro, the next major
phase in Strehler's development was marked by *Re Lear*. This production was significant because it brought a professional crisis of Strehler's
life to a close, marking as it did his return to the Piccolo Teatro after a
self-imposed exile of six years. The reasons for his departure from the
theater he had co-founded are relevant to a full understanding of his
production of *Re Lear* and his use of clown at this time. Self-reference
and biographical aspects of his productions would come to be a central
element of his style after *Re Lear* in which he used Shakespeare's text
to communicate his own doubts.

During a period of student unrest in the late 1960s, *la contestazione*,
all aspects of life came under attack from the younger, restless generation. Strehler, much to his surprise, was targeted as one of the establishment figures against whom the students voiced their discontent.
The Piccolo Teatro was picketed and Strehler's resignation demanded.

He shocked the city, and probably the protesters more than anyone, by promptly quitting:

> The contestazione taught me a terrible lesson: one wakes up one morning and discovers that one is right wing, considered conservative by everyone, while the night before you felt that you were left wing and one of the avant-garde. [15]

After leaving the Piccolo, Strehler set out to reassert his political identity. He produced mostly political plays by Brecht and Peter Weiss (1916–82) and made an effort to reach a new working class audience with these productions, but on the whole his work while away from the Piccolo failed to map out a significant new direction.

Upon returning to the Piccolo and beginning work on *Re Lear* he started a new phase of his career by self-consciously utilizing his earlier exploration of clown with Goldoni's comedies. [16] Not wanting to confuse Shakespeare's tragedy with the Italian clowns of *commedia dell'arte*, however, he chose an entirely different style of clown for *Re Lear*. The production was set in a circus ring with Lear and his Fool both portrayed as circus clowns. Lear is the authoritarian White Clown and the Fool is the Auguste, yet the Fool also plays the role of instructor in clown logic to the King, who holds the titular power of authority.

The Fool's costume in *Re Lear* was patterned after the costume worn by Swiss clown Grock. Strehler's Grock-Fool is also reminiscent of Beckett's clowns because, like Didi and Gogo, *il Fool* repeats words in a Grock-like manner, creating verbal *gestes*. [17] The clearest example of this came on the heath where the Fool repeated "*Zio mio*" [uncle] whenever a lesson in clown logic was about to be, or had been, learned by Lear. Each repetition of this phrase was slightly different in character, inflection and implied significance in the same way that Smeraldina had been required to repeat *perchè* over and over again at the rehearsal of *Arlecchino servitore di due padroni*. Over this adaptation of Beckettian *geste*, Strehler superimposed a more Brechtian form of "V-effect" by casting a young woman in the Fool's role and had the same actress, Ottavia Piccolo, also play Cordelia.

Although *Lear* offers a director an opportunity to comment on political power, which Brecht's technique is ideal for revealing, the metaphysical questions it raises require a less material approach to dialectic. The dramaturg for *Re Lear*, Agostino Lombardo, [18] acknowledged the connection between Strehler's *Re Lear* and Beckettian theater and especially the influence of Jan Kott who drew attention to similarities between *King Lear* and *Endgame* in his book *Shakespeare Our Contemporary* (1964). [19] But Lombardo takes pains to point out that Beckett's theater does not explain Shakespeare's play, that there is a danger in seeing *Lear* as entirely "contemporary" and that Strehler and his team wanted to strike a balance between the historical fact of Shakespeare's text and the relevance of Lear's story to a post-Beckettian audience. Strehler was influenced by Kott's analysis inasmuch as he recognized the opportunity that *Lear* offered him to realize some of the poetic expression he admired in Beckett. *Re Lear*, however, also serves as a critique of Kott's reading of the play and the connections Kott makes between *Lear*, *Endgame*, and *Act Without Words*.

As in Kott's analysis of the play, Lear's experience in Strehler's production is one of a gradual awareness of the darkness in the world he has inhabited. Strehler, who always designs his own light plot, made darkness a tangible reality in the circus motif, where the lighting is extremely sparse except when spotlights are used for intense and physically specific moments of the production. [20] As in Beckett's *Act Without Words*, *Re Lear* had an off-stage reality that the audience was never given the privilege of witnessing firsthand, yet the *mise en scène* implied that the Fool could come and go as she pleased. The periphery of the acting area in *Re Lear*, when it was visible, was clearly defined as a circus tent with ropes anchoring a canvas awning. This awning delimited the perimeter of the acting space. The effect of this image was that even when the stage was well lit, the circus tent motif reminded the audience that their vision was being defined, hemmed in and constrained.

While most of the characters seemed to be struggling through the thick darkness of the circus space, the Fool popped in and out as if by magic. Not the magic of a fairy or a Merlin, but the stage magic of the unexpected spotlight that revealed a character where previously there was only darkness. Strehler described his concept for the setting of the production: "A place that is empty and tiring: desolate. A tragic surface, muddy, primordial, in which we walk and tire. Where one's feet sink in and where one is made filthy when one falls."[21] Where all of the other characters are caught in the mud and advance only slowly through a tiring and tragic substance, the Fool is allowed to appear and disappear like a circus star doing a clown entrée. Frequently, she trips lightly along the perimeter of the ring balancing with a tiny umbrella so as not to allow herself to be bogged down in the mud that makes others filthy.

In Strehler's production, there was no ambiguity as to the parallel character of the Fool and Cordelia because they were both played by the same actress. Although Strehler refers to the Fool as female in his notes for the production, he makes it clear that he does not think of her as feminine *per se*, but rather as a clown whose sexuality is not fixed in the same manner as normal characters: "Like a mask she is poly-valent, without age, I would say without gender."[22] Strehler explains the multi-modal, or "poly-valent," to use Strehler's own word, capacity of the Fool in the following way:

> To me there can be no question as to whether the fool is young or old or whatever, or happy or sad, or half mad or not. She is an oral-physical-mimetic entity who performs a specific function. Here it is to contradict (which is a characteristic of a clown relationship to their "masters"), to comment, to demystify etc. Above all she must be anonymous, physically malleable, be able to sing, dance and move mimetically with agility and assurance. . . . The Fool is continually inside and outside of the tragedy, she has a gestural legitimacy in the scene and out of the scene—as an intermediary figure between the stage-actors and the stalls-audience.[23]

These comments make Strehler's understanding of clown logic clear. The clown's purpose is to contradict, and this contrary spirit extends from the social realm, in which the servant contradicts the master, to the realm of the performance itself where the clown is not confined by the mimetic conventions of the play but is "inside and outside of the tragedy." Strehler appeals directly to original performances of *Lear* to rationalize the doubling of Cordelia and the Fool by suggesting that Robert Armin (c. 1568–c. 1611) may have played both parts at the Globe. Working his creative imagination on the question of the Elizabethan audience's response to a doubled Cordelia-Fool, Strehler maintains that the psychological linking of the characters was so strong that the audience must have acknowledged it, at least on a subconscious level:

> Did the public recognize Fool as Cordelia and in the end Cordelia as Fool? They probably only recognized a few things, a vocal quality, some essential characteristic and nothing more, the characters are so distant. But they must have recognized an impalpable, mysterious *link*.[24]

This "mysterious link" was made concrete in Strehler's version. When Lear says at the end of the play; "My poor fool is hanged" the audience at the Piccolo could only conclude that Lear was referring to both characters at once because of the doubled role, with a heightened awareness of the possibility of this impossible truth. In Strehler's notes for this scene he describes Lear as "furiously clasping her to his heart, while her arms hang inertly by her side, swinging rhythmically."[25] Strehler intended this gesture to evoke a "broken puppet" with a face "white in death," "bianco bianco," so as to match Lear's bleached out clown face.[26]

The union of Cordelia and the Fool allows the Fool to remain with Lear even after he (or she) mysteriously disappears. Strehler suggests that Shakespeare might even have intended the Fool to follow Lear silently throughout the end of the play.[27] Early in the rehearsal process Strehler experimented with this idea by having the Fool follow Lear everywhere, imitating all of his gestures and actions as "Lear's shadow."[28] This proved useful only as a rehearsal exercise, however, as Strehler searched for a more subtle expression of the omnipresence of the Fool:

> The fact is that the Fool is only of service to the negative character Lear, so as to comment on that negativity. He can no longer be of service once Lear's personality emerges out of the darkness and is reborn, becomes the opposite of what he was. . . . But then it isn't possible, or at least it doesn't seem possible here that the fool must disappear. He is no longer needed as he was, but rather, in a new form and with a new substance. And so we have Cordelia.[29]

Strehler's rhetoric echoes Kott's closing words from "King Lear or Endgame":

> The Fool appears on the stage when Lear's fall is only beginning. He disappears by the end of Act III. His last words are: "And I'll go to bed at noon." He will not be seen or heard again. A clown is not needed any more. King Lear has gone through the school of clown's philosophy.[30]

Strehler's production, and his rehearsal notes, serve as a response to this statement of Kott's. Strehler insists that just because the Fool says nothing more, it does not follow that he disappears. More importantly, Strehler rejects the idea that once the Fool has no more text that therefore "a clown is not needed any more."

Lear's death scene, as staged by Strehler, is analogous to Harlequin's "*lazzo* of suicide" which has had a counterpart in each of the previous chapters. In Strehler's version, Lear appears powerful and very much alive when he carries Cordelia into the ring. Lear's death is the result of a deliberate choice on his part to join Cordelia and the Fool in death. It is a positive action comparable to Harlequin's decision to take his life, and in contrast to the Mime's realization that suicide will not work, or cannot be achieved, in *Act Without Words*.

There are, in fact, two "*lazzi* of suicide" in *Re Lear*, and their treatment marks another telling difference between Kott's reading and Strehler's production. Jan Kott drew a parallel between *Act Without Words* and *Lear* in his analysis of Gloucester's suicide scene:

> The blind Gloucester who has climbed a non-existent height and fallen over on flat boards, is a clown. A philosophical buffoonery of the sort found in modern theatre has been performed. . . . The *Act Without Words* closes Beckett's *Endgame*, providing as it were its final interpretation. . . . *Act Without Words* is performed by a clown. The philosophical parable may be interpreted as tragedy or grotesque, but its artistic expression is grotesque only. Gloucester's suicide attempt, too, is merely a circus somersault on an empty stage. Gloucester's and Edgar's situation is tragic, but it has been shown in pantomime, the classic expression of buffoonery. In Shakespeare clowns often ape the gestures of kings and heroes, but only in *King Lear* are great tragic scenes shown through clowning. [31]

Kott's definition of clown is restricted to characters who do not understand the mimetic conventions within which they act. As a result, he sees Gloucester's suicide as clowning and Lear's death as tragic without the need of a clown. Strehler's version is very nearly the reverse of this analysis. He emphasizes the parallel structure of the two plots, turning Lear's death into a true death in opposition to Gloucester's false suicide. Gloucester's suicide is only superficially clowning, precisely because he has no control over the show, which is staged by Edgar, a false madman. Lear, on the other hand, adopts the Fool's poly-valent quality through his induction into clown logic, or to use Kott's terminology, the clown's philosophy. Lear loses the war, but wins the ability to recognize the mimetic conventions of the circus ring in which the entire event has been staged. He and the Fool take charge of the mimetic conventions, whereas Gloucester is only manipulated by them.

Strehler made some unusual decisions concerning the final scene in order to arrive at the effect of Lear's death as a conscious action. Rehearsal diaries indicate that Strehler developed his concept for the final scene over several months of trial and error in which he reversed major decisions up to two weeks from the first public presentations. Finally, he decided to have a seamless sequence through the final battle between Edgar and Edmund and the death of Goneril and Regan all enacted in a separate coral into which Lear would carry the dead Cordelia for a macabre family reunion. Most striking was his decision to leave Lear alone with the dead for his final stage moment rather than surround him with Kent, Edgar, *et al.*, as the text indicates. These characters retire to the dimly lit corners of the stage and the recognition scene between Kent and Lear is omitted. As a result, when Lear says "Pray you, undo this button: thank you, Sir" (*Lear* v.iii.309), there is no one to whom he can direct the line. It is possible that this line refers to a button on Cordelia's costume, but producers almost always give the button to Lear as Marvin Rosenberg has pointed out:

> *Pray you undo this button* may refer to Cordelia's dress; but almost universally it is taken to reflect the constricting of Lear's throat, a last attack of *this mother*, ironically reverberative of a child's appeal to a mother. The release from his last garment—symbolically, from life—recalls visually his first divestment, and both visually and verbally the culmination of that undressing before Edgar in the storm—is there a deep, unspoken impulse to go naked again? go naked to death as he came?[32]

In Strehler's *mise en scène* the entire final scene becomes a soliloquy and these specific lines are reconciled by compounding their contradictions rather than rationalizing a single reading. Strehler's Lear is "like an anciently old baby who has discovered that his favorite toy is broken."[33] For Strehler this moment was Lear's recognition, on some mysterious level that the Fool and Cordelia were one: "Lear's discovery of the possibility of Cordelia and the Fool being one is everything here. It must seem to be a suspicion never resolved. A mysteriously certain uncertainty."[34] It is clear that the "button" line refers directly to the hanged Fool as well as Cordelia. The request to undo the button seems in Strehler's version to be the verbal affirmation of Lear's will to end his life. This intention is given a physical gesture when Lear tears a button from the top of his ragged garment and tosses it to the ground as if he were an orthodox Jew grieving for a dead daughter.[35]

By reminding the audience of the Fool as Lear dies, Strehler also reminds the audience of the central device of his production; the doubling of Cordelia and the Fool and the overall circus atmosphere. Lear purposely lies his head next to Cordelia's and dies seemingly as an act of will. At this moment his white-faced head merges with her whitened head, "bianco bianco," visually uniting them. This is one of the most brightly lit scenes in the play. There is a pool of white light just beyond where the father-daughter couple lie dead. Lear is as close to enlightenment, in the physical and metaphorical sense, as he has ever been in the play. The Fool and Cordelia have been working toward this same objective in their separate roles.

The Fool-Cordelia represents a link with the off stage world beyond the ring. By physically merging Lear with Cordelia-Fool through the placement of the bodies and the lighting of the costumes and acting area, Strehler brings Lear into the same realm as the Fool and Cordelia. Just as she had appeared out of the darkness with the aid of a follow-spot allowing her to defy the scenic convention that trapped the other characters, so Lear, upon his death, transcends the physical stage space by association with his Fool-daughter's body. Just as the Fool led Lear out of darkness into enlightenment metaphorically, by means of his clown logic manifested in Lear as Madness, so the body of the dead Cordelia, the Fool's double and a broken puppet, leads Lear out of the primordial soup that is the setting of Strehler's production. Lear's recognition of the Fool-Cordelia gives him the strength to die, and escape the restrictions of the circus tent, because it is a recapitulation of the clown logic that he learned on the heath. "Never, never, never, never, never" (V.iii.308) becomes a clown-like verbal quibble, reminiscent of Beckett and Grock's repetitious destruction of language, and a cry of despair combined, which leads Lear into pantomime for the button lines and death. This pantomime, however, unlike that of Gloucester's earlier suicide, is not externally manipulated. Gloucester's pantomime saves him from suicide because he misinterprets the mimetic conventions organized by Edgar while remaining within the mimetic conventions of the play as a whole. Lear's pantomime leads to death but his action transcends the mimetic conventions of the circus tent.

We do not know if the world beyond the ring is the "real" world, or heaven, or even if it is any better than the world that Lear inhabits within the audience's view. Although it is fair to say that the implication of enlightenment suggests a better world beyond the mimetic space of the circus ring, definite answers to such questions seem shallow next to the events of the tragedy. Just as it is missing the point to ask who Godot is, so in this Beckettian *Lear*, the concrete answer to how Cordelia and the Fool can be the same person, or how Lear can will himself to die or where they all go at the end remain a mystery. Strehler's story of *Lear* is not about answers so much as the importance of continuing to look for them. In this way, his 1972 production is indeed self-referential. His hiatus from the Piccolo Teatro did not resolve his political identity crisis or send him in a new direction artistically, rather it simply provided him with the strength to broaden his theatrical language. Adding the poetic imagery of Beckettian theater to the Brechtian dialectic approach provided Strehler with richer applications of clown for *Re Lear*.

CLOWN REVISITED AGAIN IN *LA TEMPESTA*

The ending of Strehler's *La Tempesta* (1978) mirrored that of *Re Lear* in that it also had the main character alone on stage. The imagery, however, was in direct contrast to that of *Re Lear*. Prospero, now alone, has come to the end of his voyage of enlightenment, but there is a depressing tone to the resolution of his search; perhaps more depressing than Lear's death. Where the bleak stage environment of *Re Lear* created a longing for the world outside of the mimetic space, the *mise en scène* of *La Tempesta* suggested that the world outside of the mimetic space was far less inviting than Prospero's island with all its imperfections. At the very end of the production Strehler had Prospero break his staff to represent his resolve to leave the island for good. This action was comparable to Lear's tearing off his button. Both actions were physical signs that the central character was making a conscious decision at that moment of the play. When the staff broke, the entire set fell apart as well, putting the scene, which had been lit with increasing brightness throughout the play, into semi-darkness. The final scene was the darkest scene in the production with the possible exception of the storm scene at the beginning. The darkness that was so pervasive in *Re Lear* was always present in *La Tempesta*, but it was always somewhere off stage just beyond the expansive horizon that led away from the island. Conversely, the expansive lightness was always present in *Re Lear*, but only on the other side of the circus tent, blocked off from the characters and the audience. So too, the reversal of light and dark in these two productions seem to correspond metaphorically. Where light seemed to represent spiritual enlightenment always just beyond Lear's living space so the light of Prospero's Island seemed to represent a superior quality to the real world of both Shakespeare and Strehler's Milan.

During the final soliloquy, Strehler had the actor playing Prospero, Tino Carraro, walk out into the audience with his cloak removed and his entire demeanor suggesting Tino Carraro the actor after a long performance asking to go home. When "Carraro" asked the audience to let him return to his dukedom, however, his "Prospero" voice returned and Strehler answered Prospero's request on the audience's behalf by making Prospero return to the stage and having the island return to its former state. Tino Carraro was ostensibly returning to the stage in order to take his curtain call, but the image that Strehler created was also that of Prospero choosing the imaginary world of the island over the circus tent world of his dukedom in Milan. Since the Piccolo Teatro is itself located in Milan, Prospero's final recanting of his decision represents a rejection of the corruption of Milan.

La Tempesta presented a positive vision of theatrical illusion, or at least the fictional world of the stage illusion was a more positive vision than the unseen "real world" of Milan. Prospero is wiser as the magician of the island, than he would be as a duke. The visible fantasy world in La Tempesta is essentially presented as an Utopia or at least a world where Utopia seems ultimately attainable. This is all the more clear when the production is contrasted with Re Lear in which the visible fictional world is the opposite of an Utopia. The circus-world of Re Lear, a dark place of deception and evil, where truth and wisdom lie somewhere outside the compass of the theatre, was directly contrasted in La Tempesta in which the magical world of the island reaffirmed the validity of theatrical expression: "The story of The Tempest was not apart from the place in which we created our show."[36] This one sentence aptly sums up Strehler's view on the relationship of theatre to society during his post exile period. Although Strehler was still committed to a form of theater that was relevant to contemporary society, the merit of the invented world within the walls of the theater was not to be belittled.

Even within the context of the world that Strehler created for La Tempesta he used three different clown traditions for the different characters that were presented in clown motif. One of these, in the person of the displaced monarch Alonso losing his mind, was presented as a White Clown and is a self-referential allusion to Lear. The effect of this reference in La Tempesta is to remind the audience of the previous production, the previous monarch and the previous use of clown imagery for a tragic situation, with the result that his new use of clown became much clearer.

The main clown characters in *La Tempesta* were Trinculo and Stephano who were directly drawn from *commedia dell'arte* and Ariel, also drawn from *commedia* although a distinctly different strand. Trinculo and Stephano hearken back to Strehler's early success with *Arlecchino*, discussed earlier in this chapter, with Stephano portrayed in the style of a conniving Brighella and Trinculo, a simple-minded Arlecchino. As in *Arlecchino*, these two clowns were presented as proletarian characters, one with petit-bourgeois aspirations, the other decidedly lumpen. By contrast, Ariel was presented in a French Pierrot costume in the manner associated with Jean Gaspard "Baptiste" Deburau whose performances at the *Théâtre des Funambules* transformed clown during the early part of the nineteenth century in Paris.

Strehler chose the contrasting clown motifs because he wanted to convey Ariel as a character of dignity, if still a servant. Like Lear's Fool she is a character who is not confined by the mimetic space except that Prospero has caught her and turned her into a puppet. When she asks for freedom she yanks on her clearly visible tether. Even as this tether keeps her as Prospero's servant it is also her means of flying, opening the space vertically while the other characters remain earth bound. By contrasting the stylistic differences of a Deburau-Pierrot to the lumpen characters of Arlecchino and Brighella, Strehler stayed true to the comic spirit of all of these characters while delivering a subtle social and historical message at the same time. The themes of freedom and dignity inherent in Shakespeare's text were expressed with a consistency of motif and comic tone. The audience was encouraged to empathize with the *commedia*-based proletarian clowns even while they laughed at their stupidity and Ariel's flight to freedom was, similarly, associated with the development of the lumpen clowns she outwitted in service to Prospero.

While Ariel evoked Deburau she also reminded the audience of Strehler's Cordelia-Fool especially at the end of *Re Lear*. She was portrayed as feminine, a not uncommon casting choice for Ariel, but of special significance given the Fool-Cordelia doubling. As in the final view of Cordelia she was predominantly white. But most importantly, she represented a free spirit yet is represented as a puppet just as Cordelia is a broken puppet in the final scene of *Re Lear* when she is Cordelia and Fool.

The power of authority is a thematic focus of *La Tempesta*, just as it had been in *Re Lear*, but escape from that authority was equated with maintaining the illusory world of the island, a place that the audience cherishes. We rejoice when Prospero ultimately frees Ariel from her puppet strings because she has attained freedom, but that freedom also means that she can no longer fly! Her flight to freedom was an earth-bound run, although a joyous one, through the stalls. This contradictory image was upstaged a few minutes later by Prospero's return to the island for the curtain call.

STREHLER IN CONTEXT

Strehler used clown as a basic motif of his production again and again because the clown is the theater's most enduring symbol of counter-illusion. Strehler first arrived at this revelation during his rediscovery of *commedia dell'arte* in preparation for *Arlecchino servitore di due padroni*. Counter-illusion becomes, in *Re Lear* a metaphor for counter-authority even while confronting the fact that the play is also about the responsibility of leadership. Just as Strehler, in his earlier production of *Arlecchino*, inserted lines establishing the director's authority over the clown Smeraldina when she oversteps herself through a feminist tirade, so in *Re Lear* the reality of the power of authority is constantly brought to the audience's attention. The only final escape from that authority is to exit the space, as Lear finally does through his death pantomime. Yet in *La Tempesta* he presented the same essential argument with the opposite conclusion, justifying the stage space as a necessary alternate reality to that of the real world beyond the island, and theater.

Strehler comes very close to being an amalgam of the qualities of each of the previous masters. He borrowed from Copeau a respect for the intellectual side of theatrical creativity and looked to the past, specifically *commedia dell'arte* and the academic, historical exploration of this area, to invigorate his company and his productions. Unlike Copeau, however, Strehler managed to avoid the Romantic view of clown as *panacea*, presenting them in a variety of modes, from magically beautiful and wise to class-bound and in need of instruction.

Like Meyerhold, Strehler managed to incorporate the dynamism and showmanship of circus into many of his productions but without developing a codified system or becoming entirely married to ideology. Nevertheless, Strehler remains a political artist and, like Brecht before him, recognizes the metaphoric connection between clowns and power. Just as Brecht incorporated clown logic into his acting technique in order to communicate this way of performing to his company, and

Beckett incorporated clown logic into his texts, Strehler made clown logic a part of his *mise en scène*. But like Beckett, Strehler went beyond the ideologically political application of clown as protagonist and made of his clown surrogates, personal representations of his own doubts, both political and spiritual.

8

Clown as Proletarian Messiah: Dario Fo

DARIO FO (1924–   ) IS A PERFORMER, PLAYWRIGHT, DIRECTOR, AND theorist and, unlike the other artists examined in previous chapters, can also legitimately claim to be a clown himself. Whether wearing the mask of Arlecchino or contorting his elastic, naked face, Fo is instantly recognizable throughout Europe as a descendant of a great tradition of natural clowns. He has made a conscious effort to reinforce this perception in order to forge solidarity with a tradition that has, as he sees it, frequently been the subject of persecution from the state. In this chapter I will show how Fo's dramaturgy developed directly out of his development as a performer. Over the space of his career, he refined his clown technique, focusing more and more on his own transformational skill and the translation of that skill into a dramatic form with which he could express his political message.

Fo's remarkable ability to blend so many talents with popular and populist success has often led to hyperbole on the part of cheerleading critics:

> He is a man of 50—actor, singer, dancer, mime, writer, impresario, chore-
> ographer, political activist, and a personality both feared and opposed, like
> one of the characters in the farces he realizes onstage: opposed by govern-
> ment, politicians, the church, and the petty bourgeois. He is the only actor
> in Italy who can boast of performances attended by 25,000 spectators; the
> only one whose visibility, in the history of postwar Italian theatre, can be
> compared with that of Eduardo DeFilippo and Strehler.[1]

Dario Fo is a clown who needs no white greasepaint or red nose; his own rotund face is mask enough. The agile face; the rounded cheeks and balding pate; the gleeful eyes; the toothy smile that occasionally extends deep into his jaw might be those of a cherub past fifty, his size and repertory of pranks having increased with the passage of time. No ordinary clown, or mime, or satirist or playwright, Fo is all of these, as well as a cultural historian, political activist, stage director, scene and costume designer, and ballad singer.[2]

Fo's wife and partner, actress Franca Rame, has used more sardonic words to describe her husband's attribute as a natural clown. She describes his face as "hopelessly comic."[3]

FO'S INFLUENCES

Fo's first full length stage play was the farce *Gli arcangeli non giocano al flipper* [Archangels don't play pinball] (1959). *Gli arcangeli* had much in common with both Brecht's *Mann ist Mann* and Meyerhold's *Fairground Booth*, but although it included several of the key elements of Fo's later dramaturgy and performance style, it lacked the frightening quality of the models it imitated. The hero of *Gli arcangeli*, Lungo, is a professional fool who has chosen to serve the lowest members of society rather than the elite. Lungo calls himself the poor man's Rigoletto. He is similar to Galy Gay from *Mann ist Mann* in that he is a willing dupe to some small time crooks, except that Lungo is conscious of being used. Lungo's self-conscious identity as a jester to the underclass allows him to play the stooge to his unscrupulous friends. Galy Gay's transformation from stooge to grotesque warrior is a transformation from Auguste to White Clown. Fo's hero, Lungo, remains an Auguste throughout the play although he too transforms in Act II, into a dog! Lungo also resembles Bloody Five from *Mann ist Mann* because he has been castrated during the war, and therefore bears the ironic nickname "Lungo" or "Lungone" [long one] or [really long one]. But here Fo stops short, literally, of putting his hero in the same position as Bloody Five. Lungo has his *osso sacra* [sacrum] shot off rather than his testicles. This comic version of castration still allows for a traditional love relationship between Lungo and his prostitute girlfriend Bionda, played by Fo's wife Franca Rame. Lungo's "real" name is the sentimental *Tempo Sereno* [Fair Weather] and Bionda also has the softer real name Angela, sentimentally corresponding to the archangels of the title.

Gli arcangeli begins with Lungo's mock death in order to con a pastry chef. But where the mock death of Galy Gay transformed Brecht's hero into a frightening character who loses his individuality altogether, Lungo gets the upper hand on his colleagues and the play ends with him and Bionda escaping with a load of cash. Bionda and Lungo are joined in a mock wedding, following the mock death, which they choose to take seriously. In the wedding scene, Bionda is replaced by a grotesque puppet in the same manner as Columbine was in Meyerhold's version of *The Fairground Booth*. But Fo unmasks the puppet Bionda in time for the hero and heroine to out-wit their enemies. *Gli Arcangeli* replaces the bitter tone of *Mann ist Mann* and the all encompassing anarchy of *The Fairground Booth* with an upbeat Socialist fantasy.

In spite of Lungo's identification with a *giullare*, or jester, the first Fo play to adopt a clown motif as its core device was *La signora è da buttare* (1967), [*The Lady's for Throwing Out*].[4] This production used a circus motif, and a cast of clowns to satirize the American government and imply complicity on the part of Lyndon Johnson in the assassination of President John F. Kennedy. *La signora è da buttare* was the last production that Fo would produce through the established theater. Having discovered that a combination of clown and farce was both entertaining and politically effective, Fo made more experiments with this formula after he and Rame founded independent theater companies in the mid 60s. The interjection of clown in his theater coincided with his more assertively political phase, or with the phase in his life in which his political interests and his artistic expression became inextricably united.[5]

It was natural for Fo to turn to Brecht and Meyerhold as models for his own theater because he shares their Marxist ideology. Fo's political mentor is Antonio Gramsci (1891–1937), the founder of the Italian Communist Party. Like Gramsci, Fo is a pragmatist or, in the jargon of left-wing politics, an "open Marxist." Gramsci, a hunchback from Sardinia, championed the marginalized members of society and demanded that their culture be respected. Respect for proletarian culture was of equal importance for Gramsci as economic equality. In fact, the two were viewed by Gramsci as essential elements of the same struggle. He praised Luigi Pirandello (1867–1936) for bringing Sicilian dialect into his plays, an issue also close to Fo's heart.[6] Fo persisted in using dialect in his plays during a period when other communist artists, such as Pier Paolo Pasolini (1922–75),[7] publicly debated its continued use.[8] Despite the fact that Gramsci fell out of favor with left-wing Italians during the 1960s, Fo has taken Gramsci's philosophy as his model and thrown in his lot with the underclass against anyone who dictates to that class whether they be clergy, bosses, politicians, trade unionists or even left wing intellectuals like himself.

Fo and Tragedy (*Umorismo*)

Fo has never strayed too far from clown's comic function, even when putting the laughter associated with clown to a specific political end. He believes that clown is the stage character closest to the proletarian public he wants to reach. Like each of the subjects discussed in the previous chapters, he has used clown to approach modernist tragedy. Yet, while Fo is clearly attracted to the power of tragedy, his comedy is so aggressively comic that the tragic element seems secondary:

> In the days when I was beginning my theatre career, everything to do with clowns was relegated to the level of theatre for minors—in every sense. Faced with this idiotic categorization I was tempted to throw everything up. Personally I did not come into the theatre with any ambition to play Hamlet, but with the aspiration to be the red-nosed comic, the clown . . . but seriously.[9]

On the one hand, Fo is staking his ground in this comment as a comic actor over a tragic actor, but on the other hand, he is also calling for a theater that breaks down *"schematismo imbecille"* [idiotic categories].[10] Fo has even argued that *Hamlet* is a comedy, suggesting that if audiences would look upon Shakespeare's tragedies as comedies, he would be prepared to stage them:

> Yes, I have insisted on several occasions that the structure of *Hamlet* resembles that of a comedy much more than a tragedy precisely because the story is played entirely in *umorismo* , in an ironic key. As is *Romeo and Juliet*.[11]

Fo's choice of the word *umorismo* to describe *Hamlet* is instructive. Luigi Pirandello's theory of theater hinged around his concept of *umorismo* in which the tragic folly of humanity was stressed through abstraction and distancing of the audience. Although most of Pirandello's plays seem closer to the tragic mode than the comic, the use of the term *umorismo* serves a similar purpose in both his and Fo's works. "The complexity of *umorismo* as defined by Pirandello is rooted in its ability to extend beyond one kind of perception to another perception that challenges and modifies the first."[12] Clown is the ideal character for the expression of *umorismo* precisely because of clown's essential quality of bridging (or transgressing) modes of representation.[13] *Umorismo* is an essentially comic view of the world in which comedy is a device to view serious situations in a new way.

Fo used his rhetorical biography of the great Italian clown and film star Totò; *Totò: Manuale dell'attor comico* to reinterpret the anti-comical bias of traditional Italian literary criticism:

> Croce has said, "the concept of the comic does not express anything either of value or lacking value, it creates neither good nor bad, neither useful nor useless, neither beautiful nor ugly, neither true nor false, but it presents a group of facts, and nothing else." *Facts*: and, therefore, events which are consumed by the effectiveness of their action; and that, by illustrating "some aspects of the world of sentiment" they don't express themselves in an artistic manner but as life: Empirically.[14]

Fo uses Croce's words to create an argument for the validity of the comic mode. Croce's comments were, in fact, the *spinta* for Pirandello's essay "*Umorismo*," which was written in defense of comedy and in response to Croce's perceived attack. Fo has described Croce as the greatest disaster in the history of Italian criticism because of his inability to "read" the theater as a physical art form as well as a literary one.[15] Yet Fo manages to take Croce's analysis and harmonize it with his vision of comedy as an "autonomous popular movement."[16] Although *umorismo* was an aesthetic of comedy that arose from the insult to comedy propagated by Croce, Fo is able to embrace *umorismo* and Croce's critique in his own theory of comedy.

Even in his broadest farces and most popular successes, such as *Morte accidentale di un anarchico* [*Accidental Death of an Anarchist*] (1970), Fo continually reminds the audience of the tragic circumstances upon which the play is based. The police execution of an innocent Milanese anarchist, Giuseppe Pinelli, who had been accused of a terrorist bombing formed the basis for the play, and although this event has already occurred before the play begins, that is to say the death of Pinelli is outside of the mimetic space of the play, the reenactment of the crime through a farcical investigation constitutes the main action. In this way, Pinelli's mangled body is never meant to be forgotten even through farcical episodes.

In an earlier play, *Isabella, tre caravelle e un cacciaballe [Isabella, Three Ships and a Con-man]* (1963), Fo expressed the tragic mode in yet a different way. That play was a re-telling of the life of Christopher Columbus, but as performed by an itinerant Renaissance actor trying to keep from the gallows. As the farcical version of Columbus's calamity comes to a close, his doppelgänger, the actor, meets his death by means of the ruthless authority of a different generation. *Anarchist* begins with a tragic death at the hands of the authorities and ends with a revolutionary call to arms, but *Isabella* begins with a stay of execution and ends with a tragic death at the hands of the authorities.

Although Fo often evokes the tragic mode, all of his plays remain comedies in spite of their serious content and political argument. His clowns never apologize for making us laugh because the laughter stems from what Pirandello called "the difference between *comico* and *umoristico*."[17] Whereas the comic, in the traditional or classical sense reduces human behavior, so that it seems less worthy than it is, the "humorous" (*umorismo*) while also invoking laughter, concentrates on conflicts of perception. Initially one laughs because one recognizes an absurdity or as Pirandello says "*avvertimento del contrario*" [awareness of the opposite], but that one's laughter is interrupted or altered when the scene passes to sympathy with the opposite "*sentimento del contrario*."[18] *Umorismo* provides Fo with a workable version of Brecht's theory of estrangement, or *Verfremdung*. *Umorismo* is similar to Brecht's concept in that it changes the audience's perception and actively engages them with the ideas behind the story.

TRUMPETS AND RASPBERRIES

The most telling example of Fo's dedication to clown's function as a purveyor of laughter is the stage history of his only formal attempt at classical tragedy. When the letters of murdered Italian Prime Minister Aldo Moro (1916–78) were made public in 1979, Fo believed that he recognized a similarity between Moro's pleading with his political allies to negotiate with the terrorists and the *agon* found in much Greek Tragedy, in particular in the situation of Sophocles's *Philoctetes*.[19] Inspired by this observation, Fo began work on a play constructed around the Moro letters themselves. Fo consciously imitated the form of Greek Tragedy, so that the audience would make the same connection between the Moro assassination and Greek Tragedy that he had made.

As with so many of his plays, *The Tragedy of Aldo Moro* included a clown in the form of a court-jester, who also provided narration and acted as chorus, while Fo himself took the role of Moro. Fo eventually gave up on the Moro tragedy but came back to the same material when he wrote *Clacson, trombette e pernacchi* [*Trumpets and Raspberries*] in 1981. This play came after Fo's unsuccessful alliance with the Italian Communist Party and as a result contained biting criticism of the party, the labor movement in Italy and, of course, terrorism.

The murder of Aldo Moro served to put an end to the radical left wing movement, as politicians from all parties rallied against the violence of the Red Brigades. Radicals, such as Fo and Rame, were distressed by these developments because in their eyes equally criminal police violence did not receive the same level of attention. Fo's play blamed everyone from the Red Brigades to the police to Moro's cabinet colleagues for the former Prime Minister's death and the subsequent enforcing of status quo politics.[20]

Rather than write a quasi-Greek tragedy to deal with the Moro kidnapping, Fo created an entirely new plot in which a factory worker witnesses the kidnapping of Agnelli, the owner of the Fiat automobile company. The worker and Agnelli are both terribly burned, but through the incompetence of the police and other officials, the two end up trading places. Fo plays both roles, the worker and the capitalist as different clown faces. When he is on as Agnelli, he is the White Face authoritarian clown, although in the unusual situation of having to face the fact that his power has been stripped from him. The Auguste character must hold himself accountable for the results of his humane impulse to save Agnelli from the terrorists.

Trumpets and Raspberries presents two separate tragic ideas. Initially, there is the tragedy of the false death of the worker and the analogy to the national tragedy that was Moro's death, but ultimately, the tragedy becomes the dividing of the individual himself. With both basic clown masks embodied in the same character, Fo's stage persona is clearly identified with both opposing characters and is in a sense torn apart by this opposition. The divided clown that Fo struck upon for *Trumpets and Raspberries* was to become the staple character for the second half of his career. The success of his texts relied more than ever on his talent as a performer and skill as a stage clown. The various characters written down by Fo the author reflect an exploration by Fo the performer of different clown faces.

Fo has devoted much of his life to defining what clown is and to presenting that definition in his written plays and personal presentations. His definition is at once broadly inclusive, encompassing the "clockwork" of Strehler's *Arlecchino*[21] with the loose technique of the *giullari* (medieval buskers or troubadours), and Eduardo De Filippo's (1900–84) civilized version of the modern Neapolitan Pulcinella, with the broad, often vulgar comedy of the cabaret artist and film star Totò.[22] He has always maintained that clown is first and foremost a political performer, a performer who reacts to the power structure of whatever culture he lives in. In this regard Fo is self-consciously aware of the basic clown dichotomy, which he interprets in overtly political terms, making the language of opposing clowns the language of his own dramaturgy:

> Clowns, like minstrels and "comics," always deal with the same problem—hunger, be it hunger for food, for sex, or even for dignity, for identity, for power. The problem they invariably pose is—who's in command, who's the boss? In the world of clowns there are two alternatives: to be dominated, and then we have the eternal underdog, the victim, as in the *commedia dell'arte*, or else to dominate, which gives us the boss, the white clown or Louis, whom we already know. He is in charge of the game, he gives the orders, he issues the insults, he makes and unmakes at will, while various Tonys, the Augustes, the Pagliaccios live on their wits, occasionally rebelling but generally getting by as best they can.[23]

In this quotation, Fo reiterates the basic clown dichotomy using different vocabulary. The basic dichotomy is always allied to the power structure and if Fo thinks his audience might miss this fact he draws their attention to it without worrying about subtlety. Where Beckett, Strehler, and even Brecht used the basic clown dichotomy, knowing that the audience would interpret it as a metaphor of power relationships in the real world, Fo has been less willing to leave any doubt in his audience's mind. The Auguste (Tony) represents proletarian man and anyone who prefers the White Clown (Louis), allies himself with the bosses. This idea of the clown dichotomy as a reflection of class struggle forms the basis for Fo's *Mistero Buffo* (1969).

MISTERO BUFFO

Mistero Buffo traces the role of clown in the spiritual life of the peasantry by reenacting old routines based on religious material. The play is a one man show in which the various episodes are knit together by long narrative introductions. The introductory sections provide the historical context of each episode and allow Fo to make political allusions to contemporary events. *Mistero Buffo*, like *Trumpets*, *Isabella*, and *Anarchist* combines violence, death and suffering with laughter, farce, and clown.

The first scene of *Mistero Buffo*, "Rosa Fresca Aulentissima," is a rereading of a medieval poem identified by De Sanctis[24] as a seminal moment in the development of Italian literary culture.[25] The poem, attributed to Sicilian poet Ciullo d'Alcamo (c. 1280), is a dialogue in which a lover implores a young girl to make love to him and after denying him repeatedly she consents.[26] Fo's version reinterprets the piece, transforming what had been understood as courtly love poetry written by one of King Frederick's courtiers, into a satire about a lord paying fees for the right to rape the daughters of lower families, recited by a minstrel not connected to the court.[27] Fo's version relies on the reading of the piece aloud to transform the meaning. The first line of the poem: *rosa fresca aulentissima ch'apari inver la state* could be interpreted several ways. "Fresh rose smelling so sweet that appears truly (or only) in summer" might be an option, or perhaps, "fresh sweet smelling rose that appears in winter and summer." But Fo reads it so that it means "Fresh rose whose sweet smell appears to defy the state."

This scene serves to set the tone for *Mistero Buffo* in two ways. It introduces the *giullare* character as a political satirist and makes clear that the show will consist of Fo's idiosyncratic readings of ancient texts, reinvesting them with proletarian sensibility that has been expurgated over centuries.

Mistero Buffo, which has been Fo's signature piece for thirty years, is both broadly satirical and pedantic. The clown dichotomy is a key element of *Mistero Buffo* as it is in most of Fo's work. The pseudo-academic voice of "the actor" is Fo's stage identity. The actor is Fo himself as ring-master separating the White Clown characters, primarily God, the high clergy and members of the land owning class, from the Auguste characters, comprised of peasants, clowns, lower clergy, radical monks and Jesus Christ. Fo manages to elide the scholarly actor portrayal of himself with the *giullare*, or minstrel-clown who is the real protagonist of the play. It is the *giullare* who portrays the various characters, while Fo portrays the *giullare*.

Fo's conception of the *giullare* includes all forms of professional players who were free from the purse-strings of a regal or wealthy household. Fo introduced the *giullare* as protagonist with Lungo the hero of his first full length play *Gli arcangeli non giocano al flipper* discussed earlier in this chapter. But Lungo was a contemporary character who imagined himself as a modern incarnation of the *giullare*. In *Mistero Buffo* the *giullare* is portrayed as a medieval character presented by a contemporary performer-author who is imagining himself as a modern incarnation of the *giullare*. In addition to the multi-faceted *giullare*, the one-man *Mistero Buffo* gives Fo an opportunity to play a variety of other clown roles including some uncharacteristic White Clowns.

Fo gives an account of the birth of the *giullare* in *Mistero Buffo*. He introduces the scene by explaining that it is one of the most difficult scenes that he performs suggesting that it will be tough to watch due to its "incredible violence."[28] The story he proceeds to tell is indeed violent. After his expository remarks as "the actor," Fo takes on the persona of the *giullare* :

> Oh people come over here for it's the giullare! I'm the giullare, who jumps, spins and makes you laugh . . . I'll do a little dance, a little song, tell a few jokes! Watch how I twist language! My tongue's like a knife, you try to remember that. But I wasn't always . . . but that's what I want to tell you, how I was born.[29]

He goes on to relate, with no comic relief, how he was originally a peasant who found a bit of land that he worked for himself. When the lord of the valley discovered his success he threatened him and eventually raped his wife who, labeled a whore by the villagers, subsequently wandered off; his children were disgraced, grew ill and died. Distraught, the peasant decides to kill himself at which point Fo's tone changes and what had been stark melodrama transforms into the familiar territory of clown, the comic aspect of which is all the more effective due to the grim nature of the preamble. Like so many of his antecedents, from Arlecchino's "*lazzo* of suicide," to Didi and Gogo in *Waiting for Godot*, the peasant decides to hang himself:

> One night I took a length of rope and made a noose, put it round my neck and said to myself:
> —Fine, I'm going to end it all. Now!
> I was about to end it all, hang myself, when I felt a hand touch my shoulder. I turned and there he was, (I saw him) with a pale face, with big eyes who said to me:

—Could you give me a little to drink?

—But does this seem appropriate to you to come asking for a drink from someone who's about to hang himself?[30]

The man with the big eyes and pale face is Christ, who saves the peasant from death, encourages him to maintain his rage against injustice, and performs a miracle by giving the peasant the power to expose the priests and landlords with his sharp tongue. The miracle is carried out by means of a kiss from Christ to peasant. The peasant, saved from death by Christ, is transformed into the *giullare*, who is committed to the interests of the peasant class.

The transformational quality of the *giullare* is important to the through-line of *Mistero Buffo* because the *giullare* is both introduced as a character and also called upon to portray characters. Meanwhile, the audience is reminded that Fo himself is transforming into the *giullare*. Because the *giullare's* birth was a miracle of transformation, so the scholarly, Marxist actor can miraculously be transformed into the long dead, peasant minstrel. The *giullare* (with his activist clowning) has the sanction of the true Christ, while God the Father is represented as an authoritarian invention of the church, which is at the service of the moneyed class. The basic dichotomy of *Mistero Buffo* is God the Father as White Clown and Christ as Auguste, with all of the subsidiary characters placed in one camp or the other. Fo's portrayal of himself as *giullare* represents a continuous line of activist clowns speaking out against injustice for the good of the working class.

Mistero Buffo is an ongoing project for Fo and as a result there is no definitive, complete text. Nevertheless, a narrative structure does emerge and there is consistency of character in spite of the various episodes being drawn from disparate regions, sources and epochs. *Mistero Buffo* is a selection of pieces from which Fo might draw an assortment of readings depending on the audience for the performance. "The Birth of the *Giullare*" is sometimes performed in Sicilian dialect, for instance, but if Fo thinks that his audience will not be able to follow the story because of the language (dialect) barrier, he will perform it in standard Italian with Sicilian interjections, expletives and asides.

Many of the scenes in *Mistero Buffo* are performed in dialect, but Fo also employs his trademark "grummelot" or "grammelot." *Grammelot* is an amalgam of nonsense words, onomatopoeia, and dialect.[31] According to Fo, Grammelot was developed by persecuted *giullari*, whose scripts had been burned by the censors.[32] He explains the essential technical requirements in the following way:

> To perform a narrative in *grammelot*, it is of decisive importance to have at your disposal a repertoire of the most familiar tonal and sound stereotypes of a language, and to establish clearly the rhythms and cadences of the language to which you wish to refer. . . . First and foremost, it is important to inform the audience of the subject to be discussed.[33]

As well as *grammelot* and use of dialects, Fo's performance style draws widely on direct address to the audience and purely physical characterization. By using these different techniques, he can embody the entire cast of characters in himself without the audience becoming confused. The *giullare* uses broad dialect, made to sound archaic in Fo's mouth. God and the other White Clown characters use more flowery Italian while the narrator, or actor as he is designated in the text, uses modern Italian. As well as these three linguistic modes there is also Fo's use of language in his improvised asides. In these sections he drops the standard Italian used by the academic sounding *Attore*, in favor of a more conversational style peppered with slang.

The genesis of the technique used in *Mistero Buffo* dates to a period well before Fo's political activism or the dramaturgical devices that fill his plays, such as farce, epic style, circus and *commedia*. Fo's first success as a performer came by appearing in revues as a comic story teller. Much of his mime technique was developed in the atmosphere of low cabaret well before he ever met Giorgio Strehler and Jacques Lecoq. Fo's character in these stand-up comic routines became known as Poer Nano. Poer Nano was a non-urban fool who frequently told biblical stories and perversely sided with the wrong character. Poer Nano distorted the common heritage of Catholic Italy through his ignorance of the approved version of the story and his frank, sensual interpretation of the situations surrounding biblical mythology:

> In my town, I was considered as one who had mastered the teachings of the storytellers. Little by little, I had collected many traditional tales, and others I had invented myself. They all had either Biblical motifs or were based on the clichés of a melodramatic tradition or inspired by sensationalist news items of the day, which I obviously rendered in a satirical way. My decision, then to do theatre was not traumatic, instead, it was a natural development. I was a student of architecture and I really started for fun:

first in my home town, Luino, then in Varese; eventually I also did something in Milan.[34]

Fo simply enlarged upon this concept in *Mistero Buffo* by adding pseudo-scholarly commentary from the "real" Dario Fo, complete with slides of visual evidence. Introducing this character at the beginning of *Mistero Buffo*, he opens the play in the following way: " 'Mystery' is a term used during the second and third centuries after Christ to indicate a play, a sacred show."[35] The actor soon explains how *mistero buffo* is a sub-genre of the mystery play: "It was the people who invented the *comic* mystery."[36]

The historical framework for *Mistero Buffo* has drawn criticism from scholars who have challenged Fo's version of medieval popular culture. The most vociferous of these has been Michele Straniero whose book *Giullari e Fo* (1978) pointed out a variety of inaccuracies, misrepresentations and outright fabrications amongst Fo's supposed ancient texts. As well as calling into question the validity of Fo's sources Straniero questions the class-based definition of *giullare* presented in *Mistero Buffo*. Some of Fo's texts are in fact from "bourgeois" sources, asserts Straniero, or from the work of performers who were attached to a court or licensed *commedia* players and therefore Fo's entire premise is based on a lie. Such criticism is valid as an antidote to gullible Fo acolytes who accept all he says on face value but Straniero misses the main point by complaining of Fo's lack of scholarly rigor.

The historian mask is *faux* in *Mistero Buffo* while the *Giullare* mask *is* Fo. This is simply the conceit of the play and should be received as such. Criticism of the pseudo-scholarly mechanism in *Mistero Buffo*, even from friendlier critics than Straniero, such as Fo's first biographer, Valentini, prompted him to underplay this element in performance replacing it with more and more analogous contemporary stories.[37]

Fo's idiosyncratic account of the lives of the minstrel heritage and their connection to the spiritual life of Italy and Europe is carefully designed to incorporate his own persona as the living embodiment of the tradition he is explicating. By replacing Poer Nano with Dario Fo, he frees himself to make direct connections between these farcical religious-historical stories and the contemporary political scene. In "La nascita del villano" Fo explains that God created the *villano* to do the dirty work that man no longer wanted to do. After creating the *villano* God proclaims how he shall live:

Actor: (*in God's voice*) Since he has been born naked, give him a bit of rough canvas, the kind used for holding fish, so he can make himself a nice pair of trousers. Breeches, which must have an opening down the middle, and with no laces, so that he doesn't waste too much time when he pisses.

We could almost be dealing with today's employers here! As I go round Italy doing these shows, I often find myself brought up against these cruder facts of life. For example we were performing in Verona one time, and some girls turned up in the theatre with posters that they hung around the walls. They were on strike. They were on strike because their employer had banned them from going to the toilet. [38]

This digression continues for another three minutes becoming more and more outrageously lewd, leading finally to Fo miming a worker trying to use the toilet within the allotted time (2 minutes, 35 seconds) prescribed by management.

Such specific commentary would have been impossible for the naive Poer Nano but is a natural extension of the irrepressible political activist Dario Fo. Not only does the Dario persona allow him to make these discursive comments in the middle of an otherwise unrelated story, it lends credence to the digression. The digression is not the result of one character on-stage interrupting another character, as Fo was wont to do during performances of *Anarchist*, but rather it is presented as Dario Fo having just thought of a related point drawn from his experience, even though the digression is thoroughly rehearsed.

Fo designs his performances to specifically frustrate the illusion that he is playing a different character when telling his stories. He will ostentatiously enter from the audience creating the image of someone simply carrying on a conversation with a member of the crowd, then stepping on-stage to engage the whole group in conversation:

> By using the prologue to establish an intimacy with the audience, by employ-ing metanarratorial devices, and by manipulating the performance setting, he succeeds in transforming the bourgeois theater into a piazza, with spec-tators and *giullare* sharing the same space. [39]

On the face of it, this style of performance, as Scuderi points out, diminishes barriers between performer and audience, but it is also part of an elaborate effort to create the illusion that the off-stage Fo and Fo the performer are the same character.

Although *Mistero Buffo* dispensed with the alter-ego of Poer Nano the performance technique remained essentially the same. Fo's ability to switch from character to character, to divide himself into different, frequently opposing, voices is the central performance device. A good example of this is again from "La Nascita del villano," where Fo switches between himself as narrator to the voices of God, man, and Adam. God asks Adam for another rib so that he can make a new creature to alleviate man's working misery. But Adam cries and does not want to give up any more ribs. Fo continues the story as narrator:

> Just then a donkey passed, and God the Father was struck by an idea; He's a volcano when it comes to those! He motioned towards the ass and suddenly it swelled up. Nine months passed, the beast's belly got so big it was ready to explode . . . a loud noise was heard, the ass gave a tremendous fart, and with that jumped out the stinking *villano*.
> "Oh what a lovely nativity!"
> "Shut up, you!"[40]

The asides at the end of this series both belong to the narrator, are separate from any of the other identifiable characters of this section, and yet they are also in conflict. Even within the context of a single character, Fo argues with himself vocally and physically.

Fo's approach to physical acting stems from his early experience as a mime and cabaret performer as well as his later training with Lecoq.[41] His introduction to "The Resurrection of Lazarus" from *Mistero Buffo* gives some idea of Fo's physical technique, in this case completely divorced from his verbal "tricks."

> This piece was regarded as the ultimate showstopper among virtuosi, because in it the Giullare needs to portray something like fifteen or sixteen different characters in succession, without using anything but the body to differentiate the characters: not even varying his voice; with gestures only.[42]

Fo utilizes the kind of physical dexterity and "measure" or "moderation" that he describes as typical of Totò in the final episode of *Mistero Buffo*. "Bonifacio VIII" usually follows "The resurrection of Lazarus" episode that Fo calls "un cavallo di battaglia" because of the number of characters the actor must portray. *Mistero Buffo* is designed in such a way that Fo must divide himself more and more as the evening progresses. The only way he can "top" this demonstration is to reduce it to a single mask. In "Bonifacio VIII" Fo portrays the pope only. Other characters talk to the Pope, but unlike the earlier episodes, we must infer what is said by Bonifacio's lines and reactions. The narrative voice does not intervene to add commentary or clarify the story.

Bonifacio dresses for a procession in Rome where he comes across Christ bearing his cross. Despite being revolted by Christ's beggar-like appearance he decides it would be politic to be seen with him in his martyrdom. He tries to remove the rings and baubles with which he has just had himself adorned. Christ does not acknowledge the Pope and instead accuses Bonifacio of a variety of crimes, chiefly executing monks sympathetic to the peasantry. Finally, Christ kicks Bonifacio around the stage and Bonifacio reveals his genuine opinion of Christ to Christ:

> You listen to me. I'm not afraid to tell you that it would give me great pleasure to see you nailed up: that day of all days I'm getting drunk, I'm giving myself the pleasure of dancing . . . Dancing! Going to a whorehouse! Because I'm Bonifacio, I'm the Prince I am![43]

In this way, Fo ends *Mistero Buffo* not playing the Auguste character, Christ, but only miming the result of his actions on the White Clown—Pope Bonifacio VIII. Fo forces the audience to imagine Christ, and by doing so, to identify with him as part of them. Having spent most of the episodes conjuring the idea that he is a reincarnation of the *giullare*, granted his power through the kiss of Christ, Fo passes the miracle of transformation to the world of the audience in the finale as if to suggest a form of Marxist communion. This "communion" is similar to the catharsis of tragedy although more positive. As in Medieval theater, the death of Christ is an event worth celebrating, but Fo's Christ does not die for our sins so that we may enter the Kingdom of Heaven. His martyrdom offers a different kind of salvation, born of class consciousness rather than spiritual awareness.

AUTONOMOUS CLOWN

Several scholars have suggested that Fo's career was marginalized in Italy where he never enjoyed the special status of licensed mischief maker that clowns appear to have in other cultures. Ron Jenkins, who has worked closely with Fo and Rame as a simultaneous English translator, has made this same point, comparing Fo to the clowns of Bali with whom Jenkins has also worked. The Balinese clowns, unlike the marginalized Fo, speak for the entire community with the sanction of the authorities. Antonio Scuderi picks up this cue from Jenkins:

> If the giullare-clown role Fo has taken on were accepted and tolerated, it would serve the same function it does in many cultures, wherein clown-figures use humor and their privileged position-which allows them to perform outside the boundaries of social control—as a vehicle to provide disruptive, saturnalian energy; an opposing critical viewpoint; or social reprimand. [44]

Is this position what Fo actually sought during his career, or is it rather what he scrupulously avoided? Is it possible to "perform outside the boundaries of social control" if the clown is made an integral part of social control by means of a state sponsored "privilege?" Is it likely that a clown who was "accepted and tolerated" would mete out a "social reprimand" to those who have accepted him?[45] Fo has answered these questions himself. On the state sponsored theatre of the former Soviet Union he had this to say:

> If you go to Russia today you notice there's not a single satirical play on there. Not a single one. I've been to Moscow, I've been to Kiev and Stalingrad, I've been right up to the North and I've never seen one. But do you know what I did see? Pisshouse theatre. If you can only believe in the revolution by keeping a straight face, with no irony, no grotesqueness, then I don't believe in it. [46]

Fo is a gadfly. Were he to be co-opted by a tolerant state, as Jenkins and Scuderi propose, Fo would be de-clowned. He would sooner occupy a vacant theater, as he did when his *La Comune* moved into the *Palazzina Liberty*, an abandoned Milan theater in 1974, than lobby for government grants that would marry his art to the establishment. Fo believes that artists should have *autonomia* [independence] which for him goes hand in hand with self-sufficiency. [47] At the Italian Communist party's conference on theater in 1976 Fo conflicted with the party's official policy of increased government subsidy for theater: "Autonomy is the opposite of the idea of culture understood as a government service, (thanks to Paolo Grassi), It was he who reinvented this term."[48] Fo proposes poor theater for the poor in which theater tickets are subsidized rather than theater companies. [49] Fo would "even go naked" rather than depend upon subsidies and lose his independence. [50]

Christ's magical kiss, which Fo metaphorically passes to the world of the audience in the finale of *Mistero Buffo*, has been accepted by a new generation of potential *giullari*. In the next chapter, several of the current clowns who have been inspired by, or worked directly with Fo are examined. Fo's method of creating viable social satire through the recreation of past clown forms has been especially effective in America, where a great tradition of stage clowning has recently begun to be rediscovered, offsetting the *ennui* of the Broadway theater scene.

9

Clown as Protagonist in the Heartland of Popular Culture

AMERICAN POPULAR CULTURE, ESPECIALLY THE FILMS OF CHAPLIN, Keaton, and the Marx Brothers, provided inspiration for European modernists, but American theater did not adopt its own popular tradition as an integral element of its high culture in the same way. Post-war American theater was mostly concerned with exploring the American experience through realism, and offered little space for grotesque characters.[1] As a result, clown in the American theater has developed primarily through the efforts of the performers themselves, rather than through a body of dramatic literature or approaches to *mise en scène*, inspired by popular forms, as in Europe.

This chapter concentrates on American performers who have borrowed the ideas and experiments of the European masters and endeavored to apply these principles back in America. This process presents an interesting example of cross-cultural influence, in which the contemporary American clowns imitate versions of their own popular tradition as seen through the eyes of European modernists. Along with this revision of American clown has come a definition of popular culture with a political component. The current generation of American clowns has consciously accepted the "Fo-giullare" concept of clown as an apostle of popular culture with a social mission. But how does this idea translate to the American context, where political expression is rarely acknowledged as an appropriate element of the performing arts, and popular culture is defined in commercial terms and associated with the star system?

The reinterpretation of American popular culture through the filter of European high art began in earnest with R. G. Davis, founder of the San Francisco Mime Troupe. Davis set out to carry on the traditions of Decroux, Beckett, Strehler, Brecht, and Fo in America, when he formed the San Francisco Mime Troupe in 1959, but he soon rejected those aspects of the European tradition that had become associated with high culture and strove to develop a style that reflected the American experience more directly.

SAN FRANCISCO MIME TROUPE

Davis received a Fulbright Scholarship in 1957 to study mime with Étienne Decroux in Paris for six months.[2] Upon returning to the U. S., he became an associate director of The San Francisco Actor's Workshop, which had recently been founded by Herb Blau as an alternative theater. Davis recruited performers from The Actor's Workshop for his own group and presented Beckett's *Act Without Words* I and II to accompany The Actor's Workshop production of *Endgame*.

Davis's ensemble, The R. G. Davis Mime Troupe, performed a collection of original mimes entitled *Games—3 Sets* at the San Francisco Art Institute in 1959. This presentation gave the new group a foothold in the avant-garde scene, which they followed up with *The 11th Hour Mime Show*, "the avant-garde event of the season," at the Encore Theatre, the home of The Actor's Workshop.[3] This production was followed by *Krapp's Last Tape* in 1961. Despite a seemingly harmonious relationship, Davis severed all ties with the Actor's Workshop in January 1963. He felt that what had been a progressive endeavor was becoming corrupted through grant affiliations, particularly from the Ford Foundation.[4] Like Dario Fo, Davis was willing to "go naked," rather than become affiliated with the establishment through subsidies. Upon leaving the security of an established theater, he was forced to begin from scratch.

Davis's approach became much more intensely political after his experience with the Actor's Workshop. He became a committed Marxist and determined to engage in a more direct form of political theater targeted at a less elite audience. Davis "helped the company to take seriously the ideas of Marx and the Chinese cultural Revolution."[5] The intensifying of Davis's political identity led him to change the name of the company to the San Francisco Mime Troupe in order to emphasize the collective rather than its founding director. Although he retained the word mime in the name of his new company, the troupe moved away from the style of French mime Davis had learned in Paris, and the avant-garde repertoire which, in his mind, were elitist forms that excluded the audience he wanted to reach.

Davis redefines mime as a clown form with direct connections to Epic Theatre. He distinguishes between mime and pantomime, calling Marceau a pantomimist and Chaplin a mime. Pantomimists like Marceau are less clown-like, and less comic, than mimes like Chaplin. In order to explain this difference, Davis paraphrases Brecht's table comparing the dramatic and the epic theater.[6]

The Pantomimist	The Mime
Closer to dance	Closer to drama
Usually masked and mute	Can speak and sing
Moves to music	Moves to act
Using	*Using*
"Nothing there"	Tangible props
he must communicate his prop	he exhorts and manipulates their
to tell his story	symbolism to comment on the story
Charmed	*Stimulated*
the viewer guesses	the viewer thinks
"what does he have there?"	"what does what he has there mean?"[7]

In the place of mime, the San Francisco Mime Troupe adopted *commedia dell'arte* as its basic style. They performed scenarios that could be adapted into original works, invigorated with contemporary comedy, and used to satirize such issues as the U. S. government's involvement in Vietnam.[8] The Mime Troupe's experiments with *commedia* taught them how to contradict text through physical action in a manner similar to Brechtian *Gestus*, but, although *commedia* was more clearly a popular form than mime, it was still derived from a European model and, therefore, not ideally suited to American social issues.

The desire to develop a style based on an American form led to research on the blackface minstrel show. This wholly American genre was a clown-centered form with music that included a built-in political relevance.[9] Davis revived the minstrel show in 1965 with *A Minstrel Show or: Civil Rights in a Cracker Barrel* as a critique of both American racism and the white-liberal values of the civil rights movement:

> The element that made the show particularly American and in part an American commedia, was that it was based upon the many years of minstrel show history in the collective theatrical history of the United States.

> Minstrel types were imbedded in white unconsciousness: we saw the show's
> stereotypes in oppressed ghetto characters. Whereas our commedia poked
> holes in American stuffiness, the minstrel show up-chucked the unmelted
> pieces from the melting pot. [10]

The Mime Troupe's minstrel show was created without a script
per se, but from the group's research of traditional minstrel shows,
which was applied to demystify contemporary attitudes about race
and civil rights. [11] Rather than shrinking from the stereotyped clowns
of the minstrel show, Davis embraced them in order to embarrass the
audience and to satirize the revised stereotypes that mid-1960s America
was developing: [12]

> Uncle Tom, it turns out, was not as horrible as I imagined. The minstrel
> darkie is a variation of a Tom, either slow drawl outside and quick witted
> inside, or the snappy urban dude . . .
> In struggling to leap out of slavish obedience to racist America, civil rights
> lambasted the Uncle Tom, however, not in this show. We raised him to smart
> alec, to wise conniver, to brute threat to white man's existence, and learned
> to respect him. [13]

As in the traditional blackface form, the key clowns of The Mime
Troupe's minstrel show were the end-men, Mr. Bones and Mr. Tambo
(renamed Inkspot in their version). The Interlocutor, a ringmaster
character, was named Gimme. In one particularly striking scene the
relationship between these characters is made crudely clear. The White
Clown (with a black face in this instance) and Auguste dichotomy is
translated into American racial terms with the addition of the white
interlocutor representing the ringmaster figure whose rules must be
interpreted and misinterpreted by the black clowns. Bones enters with
a placard on him labeled "nigger," Inkspot enters labeled "Negro,"
and Gimme enters labeled "White." Rather than depict the white
interlocutor as a racist bigot, he was portrayed as a centrist liberal. The
premise for the scene is that the three each need to use the toilet and get
into a convoluted routine to determine who should go first. The White
Clown "Negro" insists that the white man go first. The interlocutor
"white" man protests that the Negro was first in line. The Negro protests
"after you, I insist." etc. The Auguste "nigger" stands watching them
argue politely, then moves ahead of them exclaiming with contempt:
"After me! Shit, you goin' to stand there and debate who is going to
take de first piss?" [14]

With *A Minstrel Show* Davis had succeeded in presenting an entirely American clown form that directly addressed one of the most pressing social questions of the day, but minstrelsy could not serve as a basic style for the company unless they confined themselves to racial issues. The fact was that the roots of popular culture in America were racist in nature, and the minstrel clowns could not function as apostles of popular culture with a proletarian social mission in the "Fo-giullare" sense. After the minstrel experiment the Mime troupe returned to *commedia* as its dominant style until R. G. Davis finally left the company in 1969.

Davis adopted a popular style for his company as an extension of a Marxist political philosophy after having experimented with high art forms:

Every progressive-minded populist and/or Marxist would agree that the use of popular forms or non-elite means is important in both sustaining new material under discussion and reaching out to those who are exploited, abused, or oppressed. Yet the mere use of popular forms, like the mere fact of being born into the working class, does not guarantee progressiveness. [15]

Davis's motive in adopting a popular style for his company had been as a tool in a political argument not because of the intrinsic value of the form itself:

Just because workers do it, or oppressed peoples believe it or have "always" done it, does not mean that it is beneficial to them, or needed once they are in power. In newly liberated countries the problem is both more apparent and more intricate, especially where there has been a series of colonial oppressors and different cultural codes have been absorbed by the colonized. Which of the inherited popular forms shall be discarded? Which shall be deemed progressive Socialist? [16]

Davis implied that a post-revolutionary culture would select appropriate forms and dispense those to the people for their social betterment. [17] He distinguished between "populist" forms, which are beneficial, and "popular" forms, which, although they stem from the working class, are as tainted as elite culture because of America's consumer culture which turns art into a product.

Davis ended up leaving the Mime Troupe because of frustration with the training level of the participants. After guiding the company away from "elitist" forms of theatre in favor of *commedia* and minstrelsy, he found he could no longer collaborate with performers who did not

share his high level of expertise gained, ironically, from the elite schools
of mime in France:

> As distinctions between expertise and will dissolved due to pressure from
> participatory democracy and idealistic fantasy, the antagonism between
> professional performer and amateur participating member increased. [18]

In spite of his own departure from the Mime Troupe, R. G. Davis' work
with the company spawned a generation of artists who took Davis's idea
of popular activist theater and molded it to suit their own talents and
individual vision.

Although he shares Davis's view of popular culture, clown Bill Irwin
has maintained ties with the elite culture rejected by Davis. Irwin has
managed to carve out a space for popular culture as a critical element
of high art, especially modern dance and postmodern performance
art. In doing so he has garnered a wide audience, critical acclaim and
maintained the populist goal of popular culture typified by the "Fo-
giullare" and the Mime Troupe.

BILL IRWIN

Bill Irwin studied theatre at U C L A and Cal Arts, where he met
Herb Blau. Irwin followed Blau to Oberlin College where he became
part of Blau's experimental group Kraken. [19] While at Oberlin, Irwin
met his future wife and choreographer Kimi Okada then working with
The Oberlin Dance Cooperative. Okada was a major influence on
Irwin, who combined clown sense with his dancing skill to create comic
versions of modern dance repertoire. Irwin's experiments with clown
and dance, begun during his Oberlin period, paralleled Cocteau's use
of the Fratellini brothers in *Le Boeuf sur le toit* in 1920. [20] What Cocteau
and the Fratellini did to modern dance, that is deflate its pomposity
through the energy of popular entertainment, Irwin was to do to
postmodern dance in the 1980s. Although their marriage of six years
ended, Kimi Okada has continued to act as principal choreographer
for Irwin's successful Broadway shows. [21]

After Irwin's theater training at university, he enrolled at Ringling
Brothers, Barnum & Bailey Clown College in Venice, Florida. After
graduation Irwin decided not to join "The Greatest Show on Earth,"
but traveled instead to San Francisco, where he worked the street and

performed at renaissance festivals until joining the Pickle Family Circus. While with the Pickle Family, Irwin became part of a remarkable clown team with Englishman Geoff Hoyle and Pickle founder Larry Pisoni.[22] Together, the three produced entrées along the lines of the Fratellini Brothers. Like the Fratellini, the team was made up of three elemental clowns with Irwin representing air, Hoyle fire and Pisoni earth.[23] With a small scale circus, Irwin honed his craft in a populist form based on the model of the Mime troupe, but without the overt political argument. The Pickle Family Circus did not present political issues as part of its spectacle as the San Francisco Mime Troupe had done, but Pisoni did conceive of the company as a socially committed enterprise.[24] For Irwin, life after the Pickle Family led to Broadway fame and a Macarthur genius grant in 1984.

Irwin moved from being a populist clown to a star performer when Mike Nichols hired him to play Lucky (opposite Steve Martin and Robin Williams) in the highly publicized New York production of *Waiting for Godot* in 1988. Although not all reviewers were enamored with Irwin's portrayal of Lucky in Nichols's "Yuppie *Godot*," it provided a key step in Irwin's career, simply because he shared the stage with two of the country's most famous clowns in a modern classic. Despite the mixed reviews that *Waiting for Godot* received, the production led to another Beckett project for Irwin, this time with Joseph Chaikin (1935–) directing, based on Beckett's prose works entitled *Texts for Nothing*.[25] Mel Gussow said of the performance:

> With Mr. Irwin alone with Beckett's words and thoughts, the play is an eloquent 65 minutes, saying more about man's misfortunes than many plays do in double or triple the time. The performance offers an acting lesson in how Beckett's prose can be transformed into theater.[26]

The critical success of the Chaikin collaboration established Irwin as a popular clown who could cross over into the legitimate repertoire. Irwin's New York successes created a celebrity image for him that added to his already proven ability to handle major roles in the classical and modern canon as well as continuing to present his own shows.[27] An important collaborator during this period was David Shiner, the star clown of the Cirque de Soleil, with whom he performed the silent show *Fool Moon* in 1993.[28] David Shiner's description of his clown persona reiterates the tragic clown face as defined by Paul Margueritte at the turn of the century: "My clown is tragic, neurotic, and at the same time

he makes you laugh with his jacket sleeves and pant legs that are just
a little bit too short. He can never be a face in the crowd even though
he tries."[29] Both Irwin and Shiner inherited the tragic subtext of clown
from the European modernist tradition. Yet at the same time, they
evoked the Broadway clowns from the past. In his review of *Fool Moon*,
critic Frank Rich explained how Shiner and Irwin complemented each
other:

> The hard angles of Mr. Shiner, whose extraordinarily quick witted humor
> is peppered with urban angst and aggression, adds the spice needed to
> balance Mr. Irwin, whose sweet comic personality is one of gentle, almost
> bland bemusement. Just as the dark and intense Mr. Shiner can look like
> the conniving Chico Marx in his fool's cap, so the blond and pacific Mr.
> Irwin looks like Harpo in his.[30]

By intermittently clowning in original creations and legitimate roles
in Beckett, Brecht, Molière, and Shakespeare, Irwin paralleled the
careers of the great Broadway clowns of the 1930s and 1940s, such as
Victor Moore (1876–1962), Ed Wynn (1886–1966), Bobby Clark (1888–
1960), and especially Bert Lahr (1895–1967),[31] all of whom performed
in vaudeville and burlesque while also playing Congreve, Shakespeare,
Molière, and Beckett.[32] Unlike these earlier popular performers, who
worked their way up through the star system with little or no formal
education, Irwin self-consciously designed his career to bridge high
and low culture.

Irwin was also fascinated by film clowns and began experimenting
with mixing theater and video in performance. Beginning with *Largely
New York* in 1989, he included modern technology as a comic partner.
He taped himself and included his video image in his live performances.
In this way he could enter as the live clown and pass into a different
mode and out again.[33] The illusion created is that the video cameras
capture and distort his image, trapping him and forcing him to deal
with a foreign techno-environment from which he eventually escapes.
In these performances, Irwin explores clown's inherent ability to bridge
mimetic modes and stage spaces. Like the great clowns of the silent
film era Irwin presents a contemporary Auguste against whom modern
technology conspires:

> Alone on stage with a video monitor and camera, Irwin still comes out on
> the losing end of the battle against technology, but the vulnerability of the

live performer is more compelling, and the virtuosity with which he tries to defend himself raises the struggle to the level of high art. [34]

This relationship to technology changed when Irwin accepted an opportunity to reach the largest audience for a clown act in history by taking part in the closing ceremonies of the Olympic games in Atlanta in 1996. His performance at this event included several of his standard devices as well as providing a neat macrocosm of the Clown-Auguste dichotomy. He presented himself as a marching band leader, leading a real marching band, which promptly refused to follow his directions. Upon realizing that he had been "leading" a band that was not following, he frantically tried to reassert control. After several minutes of intricate choreography designed to look like chaos, Irwin managed to get his image displayed on the giant video screen that dominated the Olympic stadium. His imposing video image succeeded in restoring order where his tiny human body could only fail. Bill Irwin, in a monstrous reincarnation of his White Clown, with technology as an ally rather than a foe, asserted his authority before a billion or so viewers. The place of technology in Irwin's performance had entirely reversed itself. While at one time his presence seemed to provide a critique of the technological age, his reliance on video and above all his performance at the Olympics seem to cede his once defiant clown presence to the screen's power. Vaudeville comedian Red Buttons said of his rise to Hollywood fame; "The good time is the small time, the big time is the hard time;"[35] for Irwin, the small time is the good clown (Auguste), the big time is the hard clown (Ringmaster).

The big time, on Irwin's Olympic scale, has eluded Irwin's onetime pickle partner, Geoff Hoyle. As a result Hoyle has remained closer to the ideological definition of popular culture inherited from the San Francisco Mime Troupe, Brecht, and Fo.

GEOFF HOYLE

Geoff Hoyle, originally from England, was encouraged while studying theater at Birmingham University in 1967 to go to the source of physical theater, which in those days meant Paris and Étienne Decroux. [36] According to Hoyle, Decroux had a great sense of humor and a respect for low comedians, whom he encouraged his students to go and study. "I never imitated him (Decroux); I knew I would take what

I learned and use it in my own way."[37] Hoyle insists that there is no difference between mime and clown because, for him, "it's all acting . . . it's all about character and situation." Hoyle compares his technique to Brecht's epic acting:

> It is something like Brecht's description of the narration of a street accident—a perfect example of the solo performer's ability to recount dramatically, play all the parts and still remain quite clearly himself. As a storyteller and pantomime (in the original sense of "imitator of everything") I try to transform myself to evoke events, objects and people by using a kind of "body wit." Honing the "body wit" is an important constituent of the work since it provides an element of social commentary expressed through a comic world-view. I sometimes call it the "questioning mirror." It requires the continuing development of the mimetic eye and ear.[38]

Hoyle's "questioning mirror" is his way of expressing the clown logical approach that he has developed throughout his career.

Geoff Hoyle's post-Pickle experience has meant a reunion with Irwin to perform Brecht's *Mann ist Mann* at La Jolla playhouse, a stint with Montreal's Cirque de Soleil and an ongoing relationship with the Berkeley Rep. where he appeared in *The Servant of Two Masters*, *Volpone*, *Endgame*, and *Act Without Words*. Hoyle, like Irwin, has had success playing Beckett, Fo and Brecht, but less success at conquering Broadway. Nevertheless he, like Irwin, has self-consciously tried to recreate the Broadway clown tradition.[39] Hoyle has developed performance pieces and acted classic and modern clown roles but has not had contemporary American texts to showcase his clown logical style. In an effort to provide such a text, Henry Miller's short novel: *The Smile at the Foot of the Ladder* (1958) was adapted as a vehicle for Hoyle.

THE CLOWN WHO WASN'T TRAGIC ENOUGH

The dramatization of Miller's quirky novella was the brainchild of Joel Schechter who organized "The Congress of Clowns," an interdisciplinary conference on clowns at San Francisco State University, where *Smile* was staged in 1994. In many ways, the task of dramatizing Miller's story was an easy one for Hoyle and for Pisoni, who directed, because the subject matter was so familiar to the both of them. "This is reliving old material for us," Pisoni said to me during a break in rehearsals.[40]

Miller's story is about a great clown named Auguste who becomes obsessed with clown's transformational quality, with his ability to visit the moon, with himself as an avenue to God and the purpose of life. "The great favorite had many tricks up his sleeve but this one was inimitable. Never before had a buffoon thought to depict the miracle of ascension."[41] With this discovery, Auguste becomes so enamored that he ceases to make audiences laugh and eventually loses his job. After traveling the country alone for awhile, he meets up again with his old circus friends and begins to travel with them doing general labor. When the star clown, Antoine, is too ill to perform, Auguste goes on in his place. Auguste impersonates the White Clown, Antoine, a mediocre performer. Auguste explains to Antoine that he will give his career the boost it needs and then disappear. In the ring he imagines how he will teach Antoine the new routine:

> As he proceeded to perfect the turn from one phase to the next, Auguste made mental notes to explain how to reproduce the effects he was achieving. He was hopping about like three different beings at once: Auguste the master, Auguste as Antoine, and Antoine as Auguste.[42]

During the rehearsal process Hoyle, a born Auguste, had a difficult time playing Antoine. He could imitate the White Clown character, as an actor, but tended to revert to his Auguste persona when improvising.

Although Hoyle had self doubts in rehearsal over this problem, it solved itself in an interesting way in performance. The role required that he "top" himself as Antoine and give a magnificent performance that "the papers were full of the next day." Hoyle simply discarded the pretext of the show entirely at this point and went out into the real audience and improvised freely, dropping the mask of both Antoine and Auguste at that point, and interacting directly with the theater crowd as his own clown persona.

Despite the effectiveness of the improvised portions of the show, having no real script to work with proved to be a major stumbling block. Most of the dialogue was taken directly from the story as written by Miller, but early on in rehearsals Pisoni confided in me that he had no idea how to end the play. "Miller doesn't give us much to work with. I'll have to think of something." But, Miller does in fact have a clown logical ending to his novella, if written in an obfuscatory, stream of consciousness style. Having just woken up from a nap on a park bench the psychological torment that Auguste has been living with seems to have disappeared:

> The earth was swooning now in that deep violet which ushers in twilight. Auguste reeled in ecstasy. "At last. At last!" he shouted, or thought he shouted, for in reality his cry was but a faint reverberation of the immense joy which rocked him. A man was coming towards him. A man in uniform and armed with a club. To Auguste he appeared as the angel of deliverance. Auguste was about to throw himself into the arms of his deliverer when a cloud of darkness felled him like a hammer blow. He crumpled at the officer's feet without a sound. Two bystanders who had witnessed the scene came running up. They knelt down and turned Auguste over on his back. To their amazement he was smiling. It was a broad, seraphic smile from which the blood bubbled and trickled. The eyes were wide open, gazing with a candor unbelievable at the thin sliver of a moon which had just become visible in the heavens. [43]

Although this ending is ecstatic, the fact remains that Miller has Auguste beaten to death by a policeman. But Pisoni rejected the ending as too pessimistic and focused instead on the transfiguration aspect of Auguste's last minute epiphany. Pisoni opted for a strongly spiritual ending in which Geoff climbed a rope ladder to the top of the theatre and essentially levitated in a crucifixion pose, but with an ecstatic expression on his face. [44] The illusion was created that Auguste conquered gravity, but the earthly bludgeoning by the policeman was entirely omitted, directly contradicting Miller's nihilist narrative. Pisoni based his ending on Miller's commentary in which he said of Auguste's character and death:

> A clown is a poet in action. He *is* the story which he enacts. It is the same story over and over—adoration, devotion, crucifixion. "A Rosy Crucifixion," *bien entendu*. I wanted my protagonist, Auguste, to go out like a light. But not in death! I wanted his death to illumine the way. I saw it not as an end but as a beginning. When Auguste becomes himself life begins—and not just for Auguste but for all mankind. [45]

Pisoni's *mise en scène* skipped directly to Miller's "Rosy Crucifixion" sub-text, passing entirely over the tragic action. In rehearsal, Pisoni had referred to *Smile* as "a drama of initiation and martyrdom," but in performance it was impossible for the audience to understand that the martyr had been sacrificed.

Pisoni's decision to stress the ecstatic and regenerative aspect of Auguste's story reflects a contradictory tendency begun with The San Francisco Mime Troupe. On the one hand, most of the artists from this tradition want to merge clowning and serious theater, but on the other hand, they tend to stress a positive message at the expense of the tragic mode. The tragic mode is rejected because it contradicts their commitment to popular culture as defined by the ideological base, which stems mainly from Fo and Brecht. As in Fo's *Mistero Buffo*, the emphasis is placed on Auguste's transformational potential. Even if he dies, another clown will carry on his struggle.

WILLIAMS AND MARTIN STAR IN *WAITING FOR GODOT*

Irwin, Hoyle, and the Mime Troupe, all share a concept of popular culture as an ameliorative social force. But popular culture can also be defined as that which appeals to the broadest possible group or to people generally. Two clowns who fulfill this wider definition of popular culture are Robin Williams and Steve Martin. These two clowns share many of the values and background of the other performers examined in this chapter, but their television and film star status make them special cases in which the two concepts of popular culture collide, presenting a new dilemma for the clowns.

Since the 1970s, Steve Martin and Robin Williams have been the most consistent and high profile examples of the clown dichotomy in a widely popular idiom.[46] Robin Williams is the contemporary American Auguste. After a brief period working as a street mime in New York City, Williams became a successful stand-up comic. He soon landed a job in television and then began a successful film career.[47] His television role as a space-alien allowed Williams to use his stand-up comedy persona, that of a hyper-kinetic commentator on contemporary culture, in a context that was marketable to a wide audience. The alien did not understand the basic aspects of American culture and the comedy was rooted in his efforts to learn these cultural codes.[48]

The White Clown equivalent to Robin Williams's anarchic and irrational Auguste was Steve Martin. Like Williams, Martin was also a veteran of the stand-up comedy scene who had a varied background as magician, musician, dancer and writer.[49] Where Williams typified hyper energy and an Auguste-like inability to grasp social norms, Martin was a caricature of the "ordinary guy" who, in keeping with the tradition of the White Clown, over-interprets these norms in his struggle to remain "ordinary." Martin and Williams had never worked together on stage or screen, but they shared a desire to return to the stage and perform in work that would challenge their acting skills.[50] They were able to exercise the expressive potential of their clown characters when they joined forces to present Beckett's *Waiting for Godot*, directed by yet another veteran of stand-up comedy who became successful in Hollywood, Mike Nichols (1931–).[51]

Bill Irwin as Lucky and the always serious F. Murray Abraham as Pozzo joined Williams as Gogo and Martin as Didi for a limited engagement of *Waiting for Godot* in 1988. The results of this collaboration of the most notorious talents in popular culture were mixed. A planned Broadway run of the show was canceled due to film commitments for Williams and Martin. Reviews were mostly hostile either to the overly comic presentation, to Beckett's play itself, or to both.

If the production demonstrated anything, it showed that Beckett's play had not lost any of its ability to rankle and confuse. Thirty years after the first Broadway production of *Godot*, American critics still could not grasp the clown logic at the core of Beckett's esoteric drama. Mimi Kramer gave the production a scathing review in which she damned the director, performers and Beckett equally. Nevertheless, her critique has an ironic resonance with the basic clown dichotomy. Explaining why Martin and Williams were wrong for the roles of Vladimir and Estragon she complained:

> What can have been the point of casting two such idiosyncratic performers in roles created to embody universality and anonymity? Robin Williams is the guy who makes us laugh by assuming an oddness of manner—by talking too fast or in a funny voice. His signature role is that of an alien—the Russian émigré or the non-conformist d.j. so zany he appears to be from outer space. Martin, meanwhile, has made a career of sending up universality. What the outward elements of his style—the aura of colossal oafishness and ineptitude, the nasal monotone, the squint, the seemingly unmanageable frame—add up to is a portrait of the average American male as a grotesque.[52]

Kramer's description of the two performers is quite accurate and also effectively describes the White Clown—Auguste split in a contemporary American context. This description underscores the fact that these two performers were ideal for their roles, but Kramer can't accept such popular performers as Martin and Williams in the roles of Didi and Gogo because she has a notion that Beckett's characters must be anonymous and universal. Kramer's logic stems from the odd fact that the naturalist bias of American popular culture assumes that performers and their characters are essentially the same. If we know Martin and Williams from their films, we know who they are. But, as Kramer's own review attests, they are the classic White Face and Auguste clowns represented in Beckett's play.

Williams and Martin represent an extreme example of the dilemma facing many American performers. Success stamps them with preconceptions in the audience's mind, which then hamper their creativity or continued development as serious artists or, in this case, clowns. With success comes acceptance of their comic identities which, ironically, normalizes them and makes them unable to function as clowns except when they obfuscate their identity in some naturalistic way.[53] With his screen persona mired in a naturalistic "over-fit" of character and his attempt at acting in a modern masterpiece rejected by the critics, Martin has turned to writing plays for the stage himself.

THE MASTERS' VOICE?

The performer-driven nature of the American clown scene has developed its own unique voice that is tied directly to the individual styles and talents of the clowns. While this accounts for the charm of their shows it has also led to two related difficulties. When the American clowns appear in modern classics from the European canon, such as Williams and Martin in *Godot*, they are criticized for insinuating their uniquely American voice into the foreign text. In the case of Hoyle and Pisoni's production of *Smile*, they chose an American text that was set in Europe with French characters and Hoyle literally changed his voice, using a mock-French accent throughout the performance. When they create their own shows, such as Irwin's Broadway productions and Hoyle's one-man shows, the texts are expressions of their idiosyncratic stage personae and do not add to an American canon that a subsequent generation of clowns are likely to explore. Where Dario Fo, also an idiosyncratic clown, writes plays that then become part of the international repertoire, the star system links the American clown performers with the texts they create, and does not let them go.

10

Conclusion: The Return of the Film Clown

THIS BOOK HAS EXPLORED THE USE OF CLOWN IN TWENTIETH-CENTURY theater, using five masters of modernism as primary examples. Now that the century has come to a close the values and foci of modernism are being reevaluated. By reviewing the attraction of clown to modernism, and considering the current state of theater, some prognostication on the future of clown can be made.

While much of the theatrical activity of the twentieth century was preoccupied with dispensing with previous forms of drama, in effect declaring that tragedy and comedy were irrelevant formal distinctions, the impulse toward tragedy remained a strong motivating force. The very audacity of clown's non-tragic status made him an attractive candidate for tragic hero in the modern theater. This incongruity allowed twentieth-century artists to evoke the tradition of tragedy while contradicting the expectations of that genre at the same time. In this way, clown was used as a kind of testing ground for modern tragedy.

In each of the examples from the previous chapters, clown was used to contradict previous notions about theater, and some connection to the tragic mode seemed to offer the most effective means of framing this implied critique. Margueritte's Pierrot made naturalists reevaluate their approach to representation, while Cocteau's experiments helped create modern dance. Meyerhold satirized Russian Symbolism and naturalism before replacing these forms with equally rigid aesthetic criteria. Brecht developed a contradictory acting style based on clown logic, but applicable to any character in any situation. Beckett applied clown logic to create dramatic texts with a poetic action distinct from previously understood ideas of dramatic language or narrative. Strehler demonstrated that Brecht and Beckett's innovations could be applied to texts from earlier eras, creating modernist presentations of classic plays. Fo presented clowning as a counter-authoritarian way of life, implying that the main job of clown was outside of the theater. In each case where clown was used to indicate a formal innovation, or to reframe an existing form, clown was also presented as a hero of tragic stature.

Each of the five masters examined in the core chapters of this book staged a clown death that can be compared to Harlequin's "*lazzo* of suicide" from *Harlequin Empereur dans la lune* and Margueritte's *Pierrot assassin de sa femme*. In each case, the clown cheats death in some way, but that cheating of death has a different significance with each example.

In Meyerhold's *Fairground Booth*, there are two deaths. The first one is the death of Clown, who suffers a bloody bludgeoning and the second one is Columbine's transformation into the essence of death, but both Clown and Columbine transform out of their death-like states, corrupting the narrative flow of the play. Meyerhold's clowns cheat death at the expense of theatrical representation. In Brecht's *Mann ist Mann*, Galy Gay also escapes death through transformation, but his transformed self is more frightening to the audience than the death he has avoided. The mime in Beckett's *Act Without Words* considers taking his own life, but when he realizes that his efforts are only encouraging his off-stage tormentor, he chooses not to participate, thereby cheating both death and the audience, whose desire to see his dilemma resolved is frustrated by the mime's stasis. In Strehler's *Re Lear*, Gloucester transforms mimetic space from potentially frightening to pathetically comic through his false suicide. Lear, on the other hand, transcends mimetic space in his death scene having already transformed into a clown under the Fool's tutelage on the heath. Fo's protagonist in *Mistero Buffo*, the "Christ-giullare," dies over and over again but, by struggling to overcome oppression, is resurrected in a new generation of class-conscious clowns.

In the same way that the formal and tragic uses of clown became curiously intertwined in modernist applications of clown, so too were the political and popular aspects of clown closely connected. Clown as political metaphor had special credence because of the roots of clown in popular culture, but the more clown was adopted by self-conscious intellectuals, the harder it became to justify its status as popular culture. Although some artists have redefined popular culture, giving it a political significance beyond its mass appeal, even this revolutionary definition has been made redundant by the late-twentieth century aesthetic of postmodernism.

Dismayed with the "shenanigans" of postmodern theater, Enoch Brater has suggested that a play with "a beginning, middle and end" will appear refreshing in the next generation, "especially if it is one of the more realistic sort from when walls were walls and men were men."[1] Is it necessary for theater to return to a more conservative model to continue as a valid social experience that gives joy to an audience? While such nostalgia for a theatrical innocence of the past is naive, clown, who was used as a means of disrupting theatrical representation during the modernist period, can in Brater's words "appear refreshing" in the postmodern age.

Postmodern director Robert Wilson has attempted to explain the ultra-slow motion and shocking tempo changes that characterize his productions as adaptations of the style of clowns and vaudeville co-medians. He uses Jack Benny and Red Skelton as prototypes of the gesture language that he transmits to the performers in his shows.[2] Wilson offers Benny's slow burn, followed by the equally slow physical reaction in which he raises one hand to his cheek, as a model for effec-tive stage movement. Similarly, Red Skelton pauses for more time than any traditional actor would before giving an exaggerated reaction to a line or action. Despite Wilson's claim that clown movement is at the core of his theater there is little evidence of clown logic in his produc-tions. This is because all of the movement is choreographed equally. No single character ever stands out as different or in contrast to the rest. In fact, if the real Jack Benny or Red Skelton were to enter a Robert Wilson production they would appear to demystify Wilson's elaborate creations, much as Bill Irwin does in *Regard of Flight* and *Largely New York*.

Although postmodern artists, such as Wilson, have co-opted clown's disruptive quality as a generalized performance style, clown remains a distinct and vital part of the contemporary theater scene. Clown is as popular today as it has been at any time of the century. A new breed of clowns has grown up with a self-conscious awareness of the blend between high art and low comedy. Irwin, Hoyle, Martin, Williams, and a host of like-minded performers are using this self-awareness to create new genres in which clown can continue to provide a vital contribution to theatrical aesthetics and theater's social function. As the short list of contemporary clowns above indicates, the most exciting area for clowning at the turn of our century is the same medium that prompted so much clown-energy at the beginning of the century: the movies.

Rebirth of the Film Clown

Film clowns are more popular and significant now than they have been since the silent era. This was illustrated by the fact that Roberto Begnini and Robin Williams won successive best-actor awards at the annual Academy Awards ceremony. Unfortunately, Robin Williams won for one of his least clown-derived performances, cementing his already demonstrated predilection for melodrama. Nevertheless, the stamp of official Hollywood approval gave him license to return to his clown persona, although in a modified form, in his next two features. It has long seemed that comic actors were frozen out when serious consideration of acting was considered. None of the great film comics ever won best-actor Oscars although Chaplin, Keaton, Bob Hope, and Woody Allen all won either special awards or awards in other categories. The anti-comic bias that dominated most of the century would seem to have run its course as a spate of clown-centered films have succeeded both at the box-office and with critics in the 1990s.

The film that launched the sub-genre that allowed the serious film clown to thrive again was Marc Caro's 1991 *Delicatessen*. This film, perhaps more than any other, most clearly demonstrates the nature of this recent genre. *Delicatessen* is set in a post-apocalyptic France in which no meat exists and the French culture that revolves around shopping at the butcher shop is made redundant, unless the local delicatessen switches to human sandwiches. The vision is at once a nightmare of the future and a nostalgic lament for a lost culture. The film depicts cannibalism in a suburban apartment building in which the hero is a vegetarian clown who takes a job as handyman in the building. From his first entrance the hero is marked as clown by his overly-long, clown shoes. We soon learn that he lost his best friend, a trained monkey, while performing in the ring. The meat-starved audience ate him on the stage. In early scenes of the film the hero, played by Dominique Pinon, uses clown-logical strategies to solve simple problems connected with his supposed job as the building handyman, such as hanging by his suspenders in order to paint the hallway. Eventually, his clown abilities are stretched to the limit when the tyranny of the cannibals is overthrown in an orgy of violence. Ultimately, the horror is replaced with music and sunshine.

This cult hit is one of the most graphically violent and deeply disturbing films in recent memory, yet it is relentlessly comic, true to its clown-logical structure and oddly beautiful as well. The death and violence that appear so frequently in mainstream film so as to dull the audience's senses, prompting producers to outdo themselves with each release, seem to have their corollary in these clown reflections.

The most significant film in the new wave of tragic clowns is Roberto Benigni's *Life is Beautiful* (1997) winner of the Academy Award for best foreign film in 1999 as well as best actor for its star. Despite its enormous success, *Life* sparked a controversy because it is partly set in a Nazi death camp. American critics lodged an outright assault on the film, accusing it of trivializing the Holocaust. Some critics went so far as to call *Life* an obscene travesty once it began winning European film awards, gathering popular acclaim, and was seemingly bound for more glory at the Oscars.[3] Still other critics became equally passionate advocates for the film.

The film's supporters have compared Benigni to Chaplin, and heralded *Life* as a breakthrough film for Benigni. The most reasoned defense of the film has come from Maurizio Viano in *Film Quarterly* who lauded *Life* for its ability to bridge popular culture and strict intellectual argument by means of a deeply spiritual core, but no critic in either the pro- or anti-Benigni camps have pointed out that the film is part of a recent trend in film clowning. All of the controversy has centered on the perceived commercialization of the holocaust in recent years as if the trend that began with Spielberg's *Schindler's List* (1993) had simply taken the logical next step by following a successful melodrama with comedy. But *Life* conforms to Benigni's established pattern as a writer, director and star in which he has carefully constructed a clown persona who confronts our worst nightmares. His two previous hits were also set against a grisly background. Benigni played both a ruthless gangster and his harmless Doppelgänger in *Johnny Stecchino* (1991). His double role in *Johnny Stecchino* was an homage to Chaplin's Barber/Hitler from *The Great Dictator* applied to the Italian Mafia and its macho mythology rather than German Fascism.

The Monster (1994) is, if anything, more disturbing than *Life*, because it leads the audience to believe that the comic protagonist is a sexually perverted serial killer. While we laugh at Benigni's fringe character in *The Monster* we are not sure, initially if he will turn out to be guilty or not. The grisly reality of rapist-murderers in contemporary society does not hold the same forbidden position, however, as the historical fact of the Nazi holocaust. As Viano has said "to many, of course, the Holocaust allows for no artistic license: its depiction must obey the rules of tragic realism-the only mode/mood commonly held fit for fictions on a reality that vastly surpassed fiction."[4] In each of these films, Benigni upped the stakes a little more, putting his character in increasingly frightening circumstances with increasingly tragic overtones. The passionate response to *Life* whether positive or negative underscores the fact that clown as a device for serious storytelling has not lost its effectiveness.

The Success of *Life* proved to be somewhat of a curse for Robin Williams when he released his own Holocaust film, *Jakob the Liar* in 1999. Where hostile critics attacked, but ultimately failed to affect the success of *Life*, public reaction to *Jakob the Liar* seemed to be in agreement with the critics who unreasonably damned *Jakob*. *Jakob* is not nearly as bad a film as its critical reaction would lead us to believe, but it suffered by comparison to Benigni's *Life*. *Jakob* provided the critics who believe that the holocaust is an impossible topic to treat through comedy, an avenue to vent their spleen, cheerfully knowing that this "tear-jerking funnyman" would not reap the same awards as Benigni.[5]

Why did Robin Williams fail where Benigni succeeded? The simple answer is that *Life* is a better movie, but Williams, as I argued in the previous chapter, is a gifted actor, a true clown, and should have been able to make it work. *Jakob* failed because Williams treated the subject with too much verisimilitude, something critics attacked *Life* for avoiding, while the central character lacked the unpredictable clown logic that Benigni applied. Benigni never apologizes for being a clown, whereas Williams continues to compensate for his clown-tendencies with earnest sentimentality. In other words, he aborts clown logic in favor of bourgeois sensibility, or in this case by attempting to portray ghetto life, and Nazi atrocities naturalistically. The most poignant example of the contrast between the two approaches to similar material comes with the death of the clowns themselves.

Jakob is a much more violent film than *Life*, opting in scene after scene for verisimilitude over clown logic. An early scene *in Jakob* in which Jakob convinces his friend, a barber, not to hang himself pays homage to the *lazzo* of suicide. Jakob must improvise in order to keep his friend alive. The gallows humor inherent in the scene has a long tradition, but Williams underplays it to such an extent that only a clown scholar would recognize that the suicide lazzo is a classic clown situation. In keeping with the relentlessly depressing tone of this film the audience is treated to the spectacle of the barber swinging at the end of his rope near the end of the film. Where *Godot* gives Didi and

Gogo a reprieve, *Jakob* implies that there is no escape from misery. In the last scene of the film, Jakob is shot by the Nazis in front of the assembled ghetto who are about to be transported to the death camps. The last shot of Jakob is an aerial view in which the dead body looks up to heaven, blood streaming out of the mouth and smearing the nose. The image is clearly Robin Williams as a dead clown, but the clown in this character was sacrificed on the altar of naturalism before the film began. By contrast, the death of Benigni's character happens off camera. We never see how, exactly, he meets his death other than that he keeps clowning by doing a silly walk off camera. Benigni's character is not heroic because he does some un-clownlike activity, such as refusing to give in to torture as Jakob does, but rather he is heroic because he maintains his clown's view of the world, established in the first half of the film, through the impossible to imagine second half in the concentration camp.

Both *Jakob* and *Life* thrust the clown into the role of tragic hero, but more than that, they thrust the clown into the most incomprehensible and frightening situation of the twentieth century: the holocaust. Where Williams decided to repress his clown persona in deference to such sensitive material, Benigni used clown to tap into his audience's repressed feelings on that same material. Audiences seem prepared to accept clown as a spokesman for the most difficult subject matter even where critics balk. There is clearly a need in contemporary culture for a theatrical mode besides naturalism that can confront the subject matter we fear the most. Graphic violence and morose naturalism, which seem to be close relatives in contemporary culture, are not, by themselves, adequate reflections of the complex problems of the modern world, nor the complexities of our history.

Modernism spent the twentieth century establishing the tragic subtext of clown, down playing the clown's comic function in doing so. Now that this subtext has been established to the point where even popular audiences take it for granted, audiences seem prepared to accept the combination of laughter and fear as a necessary alternative genre to the predominant realist mode. The recent clown films are akin to the Satyr plays of ancient theatre because they function as an alternate genre to the grim realism of such films as *Schindler's List* in the same way that Satyr plays provided a balance to tragedy. By returning to mainstream popular culture (i.e., film) clown has reemerged with new options for theatrical form.

The laughter this new generation of clowns provoke is of an elemental kind, different from that produced by standard comedy. It is similar to the laughter of very young children who laugh when an adult throws a towel over his or her head. A nine-month old is never completely sure if the world that has disappeared will be recovered again. The baby's laughter at "peek-a-boo" is always colored with terror, just as the audience at the end of *Endgame* is not certain whether Hamm will ever have the handkerchief removed from his face. Clown laughter is, by nature, closely associated with this elemental terror and exciting sense of discovery. Clown is not clown because he is funny, he is funny because he is clown. No Kidding!

Notes

Chapter 1. Introduction

1. Dario Fo, *Tricks of the Trade*, trans. Joe Farrell (New York: Routledge, 1991), 178.

2. Enid Weslford, *The Fool: His Social and Literary History* (London: Faber and Faber, 1935), 320.

3. Otto Griebling, for instance, performed a routine in which he roamed the circus audience, while the other acts were performing, as a mailman trying to deliver a ludicrous package such as a huge block of ice that would get smaller each time he appeared or a potted plant that would grow. He would accost members of the audience desperate to find the owner of the package.

4. *Shrew*, IV, ii 214–15.

5. On one occasion, a great Russian clown, Anatole Durov, appeared in the audience during a performance of his competitors (the Fratellini Brothers) after having spread a rumor that he had died, so as to upstage their show with his resurrection.

6. See Chapter 8.

7. Fo, *Tricks*, 172.

8. Paul Bouissac, *Circus and Culture* (Bloomington: Indiana University Press, 1976), 164–65.

Chapter 2. Clown as Focus of Agon

1. This was also true of other aspects of *commedia*, such as music, stage combat and even dramatic recitation. If a performer or troupe had a reputation for good stage fights or fine singing they would work these thoroughly rehearsed elements into each show without regard to narrative.

2. The *lazzi* of suicide are associated with two Harlequins of the seventeenth century, Biancolelli (1637–88) and Gherardi (1663–1700), both of whom were celebrated Italian players in Paris. Later, it appeared in written form, published as an episode in the play *Harlequin Empereur dans la lune* (1684) and was kept as part of Aphra Behn's English version of the same play, *The Emperor of the Moon* (1687). Carlo Goldoni contributed his own version with *Il Mondo Della Luna* (1743), subsequently an enormously popular opera set by both Galuppi and Haydn.

3. *Harlequin Empereur dans la lune* (my translation), this version taken from *Le Theatre Italien de Gherardi* (Amsterdam: 1721).

4. Anya Peterson Royce, *Movement and Meaning* (Bloomington: Indiana University Press, 1984), 166.

5. Daniel Gerould, "Paul Margueritte and *Pierrot Assassin of His Wife*," *The Drama Review* 23 (March 1979): 103–19.

6. Margueritte's piece presents a special problem because he published it as a prose narrative, but performed it as a silent pantomime.

7. He also included elements of *Grand Guignol* for dramatic effect such as flames at the end of *Pierrot assassin*.

8. Paul Margueritte, *Le Printemps tourmente* (Paris: Plon Nourrit, 1902), 179.

9. Margueritte and Mallarmé had a close relationship for some years but it ended when Margueritte expressed his desire to marry the poet's daughter. Mallarmé's admiration for Margueritte did not extend to admitting him into the family.

10. Alfred Jarry's *Ubu Roi* was first performed in Paris that same year, making 1888 a convenient beginning to clowns as protagonists in modern theater.

11. A detailed account of the image of clown in fine art can be found in Naomi Ritter, *Art as Spectacle* (London: University of Missouri Press, 1989).

12. Arlecchino's curtain speech is similar to the introductory monologue from I *Pagliacci* (1893), by Ruggiero Leoncavallo (1858–1919).

13. Aside from being one of the great pianists and critics of his day, Busoni was an adventurous composer and an influential teacher. Among his prodigious crop of young students was Kurt Weill, collaborator with Bertolt Brecht on The *Three Penny Opera*, *Mahagonny*, and *Mann ist Mann*.

14. *L'Histoire du soldat* has stayed in the clown and mime repertoire ever since, with noted productions by Jacques Copeau, Marcel Marceau, and Dario Fo.

15. Glenn Watkins, *Pyramids at the Louvre* (London: Bellknap Press, 1994), 238.

Chapter 3. Chasing and Gagging Clown

1. Footit, an Englishman named Theodore Hall (1864–1921), was the most famous White Clown of the early twentieth century. Along with his partner, Chocolat, a Cuban named Raphael Padilla (1868?-1917), he helped establish the authoritarian nature of the White Clown by abusing his Negro partner. Antonet came directly prior to Footit. His Auguste partner was Beby. Clown lore claims that the two never spoke off-stage, carrying their Clown-Auguste aggression into their real lives.

2. The Fratellini never appeared with animals during their hey-dey at the *Cirque Medrano*.

3. Laurence Senelick, *Cavalcade of Clowns* (Santa Barbara: Bellerophon, 1985), 43.

4. Gordon Craig, *Gordon Craig on Movement and Dance* (London: Dance Books, 1977), 37–57.

5. Frank Ries, *The Dance Theatre of Jean Cocteau* (Ann Arbor: UMI Press, 1986), 62.

6. *La Piazza: Spettacoli Popolari Italiani* (Milano: Gallo Grande, 1959). My translation.

7. Tristan Remy, *Les Clowns* (Paris: Bernard Grasset, 1945), 147–213.

8. Pierre Mariel, *Les Fratellini: Histoire de trois clowns* (Paris: Socièté Anonyme, 1923), 189–93.

9. The other five composers were Arthur Honegger, Francis Poulenc, Georges Auric, Germaine Taillefer, and Louis Durey.

10. Darius Milhaud, *Ma Vie Heureuse*, trans. D. Evans, G. Hall, and C. Palmer (New York: Marion Boyars, 1987), 88.

11. Ibid., 87.

12. Ibid.

13. Frank Ries, *The Dance Theatre of Jean Cocteau* (Ann Arbor, MI: UMI Research Press, 1986), 68.

14. *Musical Standard* (17 July 1920), 20.

15. For more on Artaud's opinion of Copeau see "Le theatre Français cherche un mythe," *El Nacional Revolucionario* (28 June 1936). Reprinted in Gallimard VIII, 254–56.

16. "A School for Dramatic Art." *World Theatre* 4 (Winter 1954): 37–49.

17. An excellent example of an entire modernist play based on this aspect of clown is *Kaspar* (1968) by Austrian playwright Peter Handke (1942–).

18. Jacques Copeau, *Registres* IV (Paris: Gallimard, 1974), 156.

19. *Registres* IV, 156.

20. Jean Dorcy, *The Mime* (London: White Lion, 1961), 48.

21. Ibid., 87.

22. Ibid., 50.

23. Ibid., xvii.

24. Étienne Decroux, *Paroles sur le mime* (Paris: Gallimard, 1963).

25. Jacques Lecoq, the most important exponent of French mime after Decroux, is also a product of the Copeau family, having trained with Copeau's daughter, Marie-Hélène Copeau and her husband Jean Dasté whose company he joined in 1945. Later, he founded the *École Jacques Lecoq* where he trained a generation of mimes.

26. Most clowns today are trained in mime, either at theatre schools which include mime in their curriculum, or at the three French schools still operating in Paris, the École Jacques Lecoq, the Marceau Studio or the Decroux school which carries on under the direction of his son Miximilian.

27. The issue becomes further complicated when we consider performances of *Act Without Words* by clowns with traditional mime training such as Geoff Hoyle's acclaimed 1994 production at The Berkeley Rep. (See Chapter 8).

Chapter 4. Meyerhold's Transformation

1. After the Soviet Union adopted Socialist Realism as its official artistic platform, Meyerhold fell out of favor, was arrested, tortured, and died in prison. In 1955, Meyerhold was "rehabilitated," his concepts were made acceptable and many of his old productions were restaged.

2. Edward Braun, *Meyerhold: A Revolution in Theatre* (London: Methuen, 1995), 19–20.

3. Meyerhold followed his debut as Treplev with Tusenbach in *The Three Sisters*. After leaving the Art Theatre he recreated these roles, and added Astrov from *Uncle Vanya* with his own company, The Company of Russian Dramatic Artists, situated in the provincial town of Kherson.

4. The characters and spirit of the Russian *Skomorokhi*, Russian minstrels, much like the Italian *commedia dell'arte*, were passed on to the puppet theatre after the older form died out. Unlike the gradual evolution of *commedia*, however, the *Skomorokhi* were abruptly extinguished by Czar Aleksei who outlawed the minstrels in 1648. The persistence of the puppet theatre, which had adopted the traditional *Skomorokhi*

characters, was assured during the nineteenth century due to the patronage of Peter the Great.

5. No completely satisfactory English equivalent to the term *Balaganchik* exists. The play is often referred to as *The Puppet Show* or *The Puppet Booth* although the most direct translation of *Balaganchik* is *Little Show Booth*.

6. Meyerhold produced *The Fairground Booth* within the first year of his becoming director at the theatre of Russia's most celebrated actress of the period, Vera Komissarzhevskaya (1864–1910). The collaboration between Meyerhold and Komissarzhevskaya was short-lived. The two parted company after only one year.

7. The first important influence in Blok's life was the Russian mystic philosopher Vladimir Soloviev. Soloviev espoused a kind of Goddess cult in which the ideal of eternal wisdom was personified in Sophia. Blok in turn glorified his own wife Lyubov Dmitrevna as the living reincarnation of the mythical Sophia. At the age of 20, Blok wrote a volume of poems *Stikhi o prekranoi dame* [*The Verses About the Beautiful Lady*] (1905), which became the focus of this cultic movement. The philosophy was an extreme form of Romanticism combined with Russian mysticism.

8. Vsevolod Meyerhold, *Meyerhold on Theatre*, trans. Edward Braun (New York: Hill and Wang, 1969), 141.

9. *Russian Symbolist Theatre*, trans. Michael Green (Ann Arbor: Ardis, 1986), 51.

10. Meyerhold, *Meyerhold on Theatre*, 70–71.

11. Vladimir Durov is frequently confused with his brother Anatoly in accounts of the Russian circus during this period. The two brothers performed together from time to time and used many of the same devices. They were both interested in training animals, especially animals normally thought incompatible, to perform trivial activities associated with bourgeois life such as a dog and a cat serving tea to a rat and a mouse.

12. Both Meyerhold and Blok had spent time in Paris and we know that Meyerhold witnessed much of the Paris cabaret scene which undoubtedly influenced *The Fairground Booth*.

13. *Russian Symbolist Theatre*, trans. Michael Green (Ann Arbor: Ardis, 1986), 55.

14. Ibid., 56.

15. Ibid.

16. "On Drama," *Russian Dramatic Theory* (Austin: University of Texas Press, 1981), 131.

17. Meyerhold, *Meyerhold on Theatre*, 138–39.

18. Ibid., 115.

19. Yevgeny Znosko-Borovsky, "*Russky teatr nachala*" in Braun, *Meyerhold*, 97.

20. "Kapellmeister" is an antique word meaning orchestra conductor or conductor of a private orchestra. At one time it was an official title carrying some prestige as was the case when J. S. Bach was appointed to the position of Kapellmeister to Prince Ernst of Kothen in 1717. In the context of *Columbine's Scarf* the connotation is of an old fashioned authoritarian conductor. See *Harvard Concise Dictionary of Music*, ed. Don Michael Randel (Cambridge, Mass: The Belknap Press, 1978), 249.

21. Braun, *Meyerhold*, 98.

22. *Carnival* was written by Schumann in 1835 as a piece of program music on the subject of Harlequin and Pierrot.

23. Both *Carnival* and *Columbine's Scarf* were presented at The House of Interludes in Petersbourg.

24. *Carnival* was adventurous in its audience-performer relationship as well. The entire piece was only a part of a larger masquerade. Fokine had painter Leon Bakst (1866–1924) to help him realize his concept which placed the main theatrical event in a greater masquerade, creating an environmental, or site specific, form of theater.

25. Meyerhold, *Meyerhold on Theatre*, 144.

26. Ibid., 117.

27. Ibid., 147.

28. Ibid., 198.

29. Nikolai Pesochinski, "The Biomechanical Actor in Meyerhold's Theory and Workshop," lecture-demonstration, The International Federation for Theatre Research, l'Université du Quebec à Montréal, 1995.

30. Herbert Marshall, *The Pictorial History of the Russian Theatre* (New York: Crown Publishers, 1977), 126.

31. Heinrich von Kleist, *Samtliche Werke* (Munich, 1912), 884.

32. Bavarian clown Karl Valentin made use of his extreme height and slim body to exaggerate the illusion of a character who seemed always about to topple.

33. Eurhythmics was developed by Émile Jacques-Dalcroze (1865–1950) to teach music through gestures. It became a worldwide movement after Dalcroze established institutes in Germany and Switzerland, widely used as a method of teaching interpretive, semi-improvised dance. Usually applied to music, it has also been used with poetry and dramatic text as an abstract method of movement.

34. Mime is based on the concept of *contre-poids*, a regulation of the body's weight so that the appearance of external force, or objects, can be created even though the mime is restricted to the use of his or her own body. Eurhythmics encourages the performer to allow his or her center of gravity to be dictated by the music, or spoken text which is part of nature and therefore more perfect. The human performer, also part of nature, can learn to tap into this Rhythmic pulse and reflect it through the body. Biomechanical actors work to achieve perfect balance within prescribed expressive poses and move outwards from this perfected stillness.

35. Jacques-Dalcroze, the inventor of Eurhythmics, was also inspired by Gordon Craig's concept of the Über-marionette. He invited Craig to witness an exhibit of Eurhythmics set to poetry, but Craig protested that this form of "dance" was not what he meant by Über-marionette.

36. Toc is the exact moment in a physical action when the center of gravity shifts from one part of the body to another. Mimes teach themselves to internalize these points by hesitating slightly before continuing the motion. In performance, the overall motion may appear fluid, but each toc is still present in the mime's score.

37. Nikolai Pesochinski, Instructor in Biomechanics at St. Petersbourg Academy of Theatre Arts (personal communication).

38. Torben Jetsmark, *The Dramatic Body* (Winnipeg: Blizzard Press, 1992).

39. Mel Gordon, Meyerhold, Eisenstein and Biomechanics: Actor Training in Revolutionary Russia (London: McFarland & Co., 1996), p. 38.

40. Mel Gordon, "Meyerhold's Biomechanics," *Drama Review* 18, no. 3 (September 1974).

Chapter 5. Clown in Brecht's Theory of Acting

1. Sergei Tretiakov (1892–1930) worked closely with Meyerhold on *Earth Rampant* (1923) and *Roar China!* (1926).

2. Katherine Bliss Eaton has stressed Brecht's indebtedness to Russian theater, and Meyerhold in particular in *The Theatre of Meyerhold and Brecht* (London: Greenwood Press, 1985.) Russian historian Konstantin Rudnitsky has acknowledged some cross fertilization but concluded that the German Brecht lacked the emotional vitality of a Russian like Meyerhold! Konstantin Rudnitsky, "The Lessons Learned from Brecht," *Theatre Research International* 6, no. 1 (1980–81): 62–72.

3. John Willett, *The Theatre of Bertolt Brecht* (New York: New Directions, 1959), 168.

4. "As a blueprint for the future they [the theoretical writings] are only likely to mislead . . . The theory may illuminate his own methods of production, but it is a bad guide, easily leading the producer into affectation or tedium." Willett, *Theatre of Brecht*, 187.

5. The most complete account of Brecht's strategy in defending himself from artistic enemies who should have been political allies, is given in Klaus Völker, *Brecht: A Biography*, trans. John Nowell (New York: Seabury Press, 1978), 239–57.

6. Bertolt Brecht, *Brecht on Theatre*, trans. John Willett (New York: Hill and Wang, 1964), 37.

7. Brecht, *Brecht on Theatre*, 138.

8. Bertolt Brecht, "The Question of Criteria for Judging Acting," in *The Collected Plays*, vol. 2, pt. 1, ed. John Willett and Ralph Mannheim, trans. Gerhard Nellhaus (London: Methuen, 1979), 107.

9. Although the exact order of scenes is not entirely certain, because Büchner never left a final draft, an early scene takes place at a carnival where a Barker announces the central theme of the play in proto-Brechtian fashion, "with his wife in trousers and a monkey dressed as a man," the Barker calls out: "Roll up, ladies and gentlemen. Examine this beast as God made him. Nothing to him, you see? Then observe the effect of art: he walks upright and has a coat and trousers. Also a sword. The monkey's a soldier." Georg Büchner, *Woyzeck*, trans. Victor Price (Oxford: Oxford University Press, 1971), 111–12.

10. Contemporary French composer and conductor, Pierre Boulez (1925–), once asserted that the failure of modern opera could have been prevented had Brecht and Stravinsky collaborated. See Vera Stegmann, "An Opera for Three Pennies, a Violin for Ten Francs: Brecht's and Stravinsky's Approaches to Epic Music Theater," *Brecht Unbound* (London: Associated University Press, 1992), 119.

11. Copeau produced the original French production, taking the role of the narrator himself. Since then there have been several important productions which have stressed clown elements by Marcel Marceau, Igor Kipnis, Giorgio Strehler and Dario Fo.

12. John Fuegi, *Brecht and Company: Sex, Politics, and the Making of Modern Drama* (New York: Grove Press, 1994), 43–44.

13. Joel Schechter, "Brecht's Clowns: Man is Man and After," *The Cambridge Companion to Brecht*, ed. Peter Thomson and Glendyr Sacks (Cambridge: Cambridge University Press, 1994), 76.

14. Sometimes such ridicule could be dangerous for the clowns if Spanish soldiers happened to be in the audience. On one occasion Spaniards beat Pulcinella to death for satirizing them. Katherine Lea, *Italian Popular Comedy* (New York: Russell & Russell, 1934), 51.

15. One of Chaplin's most important films, *The Great Dictator* (1939), came several years after the original productions of *Mann ist Mann*.

16. Bertolt Brecht, *Diaries 1920–22*, trans. John Willett (New York: St. Martin's Press, 1979), 140–41.

17. From Portuguese *bonzo*, signifying a Chinese or Japanese, Buddhist monk.

18. Brecht, *Collected Plays* 2: 23.

19. The patriarch of the Fratellini family, Gustave Fratellini, was a medical assistant to Garibaldi during Italy's war of independence. He supposedly entertained prisoners when he was captured by the Austrians.

20. Pierre Mariel, *Histoire de Trois Clowns* (Paris: Societé Anonyme, 1923), 183 (my translation).

21. A similar routine was a staple at the Black Cat club in Paris during the 1890s, in which the elephant was presented in a shadow play. Harold Segel, *Turn of the Century Cabaret* (New York: Columbia University, 1987), 69.

22. The biography of the Fratellini, quoted above, was published in 1923 when Brecht was completing the first version of *Mann ist Mann*.

23. Bertolt Brecht, *A Man's a Man*, trans. Eric Bentley (New York: Grove Press, 1961), 164.

24. Brecht, *Collected Plays* 2: 46.

25. Joel Schechter, *Durov's Pig* (New York: Theatre Communications Group, 1985), 29.

26. Denis Calandra, "Karl Valentin and Bertolt Brecht," *Drama Review* 18, no. 1 (March 1974): 93.

27. Ibid.

28. Brecht, *Collected Plays* 2: 51.

29. Ibid., 54.

30. Ibid.

31. Ibid., 86.

32. Willett, *Theatre of Brecht*, 144–50.

33. Calandra, "Valentin and Brecht," 96.

34. Bertolt Brecht, *The Messingkauf Dialogues*, trans. John Willett (London: Methuen, 1963), 69.

35. Bertolt Brecht, *Poems*, ed. and trans. John Willett and Ralph Mannheim (London: Methuen, 1976), 55.

36. Brecht, *Collected Plays* 2: 46.

37. Ibid., 46.

38. Brecht may have gotten the idea of referring to himself from a couple of other sources. George Bernard Shaw (1856–1950), whom he admired, used this device in *The Doctor's Dilemma* (1905) and German playwright Christian Dietrich Grabbe (1801–36) also used it in his bizarre play *Jokes, Satire and Deeper Meaning* (1822).

39. Brecht, *Collected Plays* 2: 38.

40. Brecht, *Brecht on Theatre*, 140.

41. Brecht, *Collected Plays* 2: 60–61.

42. Ibid., 68–69.

43. Buster Keaton's *The General* (1927), set during the American Civil War, includes a scene, which has an interesting counterpart in Brecht's *Mann ist Mann*. Keaton plays a train engineer who cannot fight in the Rebel army because he is deemed too valuable in his regular job. Nevertheless, he gets involved in the battle when his girl is kidnapped by the Union army. He chases the union soldiers, who are escaping in one train, with his own engine. At one point, he captures a cannon and attempts to aim it at the train carrying the enemy. He knows nothing about how to make the cannon work. At first, he puts too little gunpowder in, and the cannon ball only travels a few feet, landing next to him in the engine. Then he uses too much powder and succeeds in annihilating the enemy train.

44. Eric Bentley has called *Edward II* (1924) Brecht's only tragedy, but several of Brecht's plays, especially in his early period, approach tragedy. *Baal* is a tragedy, albeit an episodic one. Brecht's adaptation of Marlowe's *Edward II* grew out of his hands-on direction of the play. He directly enlisted Karl Valentin's assistance in working with the actors. Calandra, "Valentin and Brecht," 86.

45. Klaus Völker, *Brecht: A Biography*, trans. John Nowell (New York: Seabury Press, 1978), 121.

46. "Today one could go so far as to compile an aesthetics of the exact sciences. Galileo spoke of the elegance of certain formulae and the point of an experiment; Einstein suggests that the sense of beauty has a part to play in the making of scientific discoveries; while the atomic physicist Robert Oppenheimer praises the scientific attitude, which 'has its own kind of beauty and seems to suit mankind's position on earth." Bertolt Brecht, "A Short Organum for the Theatre," trans. Eric Bentley, *Playwrights on Playwriting* (New York: Hill and Wang, 1961), p. 74.

47. Bertolt Brecht, *Collected Plays*, vol. 3, part 2, ed. John Willett, trans. Geoffrey Skelton (London: Methuen, 1997), p. 27.

48. Ibid., 31.

49. David Wiles, *Greek Theatre in Performance* (Cambridge: Cambridge University Press, 2000), 28.

50. A similar transformation from Auguste to White Clown occurs in *The Great Dictator* (1939). Chaplin utilized the physical similarity between his tramp character and Adolf Hitler. Chaplin plays Hitler as the essential opposite of his tramp character, but he also includes a version of his familiar tramp character by playing a Jewish barber. Chaplin's Hinkel is a clown and his Barber is a clown. Just like Galy Gay before and after his transformation, Hinkel and the barber are the two extremes of the clown dichotomy, White Clown and Auguste. The performance is further complicated when the barber is mistaken for Hinkel and in this sense is transformed into Hinkel during a scene recalling the Nuremberg Rally. Standing in front of a microphone, with all of Europe listening, Chaplin, in the role of tramp, seizes the power of the dictator to convey a message of peace and tolerance. The tramp's transformation into Hitler is necessary in order to counteract the menace.

51. Brecht, *Collected Plays* 2: 106.

Chapter 6. Clown in Beckett's Theater

1. Beckett began work on *En Attendant Godot* in French in 1948. The French version was published in 1952 and first performed in 1953; Beckett began to write the English version that same year. The first English language production was in 1955.

2. Much criticism of Beckett's theater has centered on the perceived apolitical nature of his vision. Kenneth Tynan was typical of European critics who made little distinction between theatrical aesthetics and political alliances: "The theater, in particular the European theater, was drawn up in battle formation. On the one hand Sartre and Brecht, on the other Beckett and Ionesco." Kathleen Tynan, *The Life of Kenneth Tynan* (New York: William Morrow and Company, 1987), 253.

3. Hans Mayer, "Dogs, Brecht and Beckett," trans. Jack Zipes, *Essays on Brecht: Theater and Politics* (Chapel Hill: University of North Carolina Press, 1974), 71–78.

4. Mayer suggests that such a play would have been repeating his earlier *Puntilla and his Man Matti* (1940), but this play was itself a reworking of a play by Finnish playwright Hella Wuolijoki at whose villa Brecht spent the summer of 1940 as a guest.

5. Even those in the "Beckett camp" tended to acquiesce with the Brechtians on this point: "Brecht and Beckett are often viewed as polar opposites-Brecht the propagandist of social change and Beckett the poet of individual anguish. Not surprisingly, then, Brecht casts his audience in a role of social significance, whereas Beckett demands only their witness." Ruby Cohn, " 'Theatrum Mundi' and Contemporary Theater," *Comparative Drama* 1 (Spring 1967): 30.

6. Joel Schechter, *Durov's Pig: Clowns, Politics and Theatre* (New York: Theatre Communications Group, 1985).

7. Samuel Beckett, *Waiting for Godot* (New York: Grove Press, 1954), 47.

8. As explicated in Chapter 2, Harlequin turns to the audience for advice, even assistance in helping him to kill himself. The clowns from *Mann ist Mann* each vie for the audience's approval. They are, as Schechter rightly points out, all aware of themselves as characters in a play, but it is also clear that the audience is meant to choose between a variety of presented world views by the end of the play.

9. As explained in Chapter 5, Brecht and Lorre chose to portray Gay with a whiteface when confronted with the horror of continued life.

10. Richard Seaver, *I Can't Go On, I'll Go On* (New York: Grove Press, Inc. 1976), ix.

11. *Beckett at 80*, ed. Enoch Brater (Oxford: Oxford University Press, 1986), 49.

12. Beckett, *Godot*, 23.

13. Beckett probably changed the name to Gogo in order to avoid just such a simplistic decoding of his play.

14. John Lahr, *Notes on a Cowardly Lion* (New York: Limelight, 1969), 273.

15. Seaver (1976), xxxviii.

16. Beckett, *Godot*, 15.

17. See Chapter 5.

18. See Chapter 3.

19. Grock was fluent in French, German, Italian, Spanish, and English.

20. John Towsen, *Clowns*, (New York: Hawthorne Books, 1976), 232.

21. Beckett, *Godot*, 9.

22. It is impossible for Beckett to have witnessed the original Bim and Bom because F. Kortezzi (who was Bom) died nine years before Beckett was born. Nevertheless, the team of Bim and Bom either in the flesh, through a performance by a different pairing, or through clown mythology, recurs several times in Beckett's writing spanning three decades.

23. Ruby Cohn, *Just Play: Beckett's Theater* (Princeton: Princeton University Press, 1980), 177.

24. Ibid. 176.

25. Beckett, *Godot*, 49.

26. *The Cambridge Companion to Beckett*, ed. John Pilling (Cambridge: Cambridge University Press, 1994), 67.

27. Beckett may have been inspired by Sean O'Casey (1884–1964) whose *Juno and the Paycock* (1924) features a pair of clowns, Captain Boyle and his sidekick Joxer, who also conform to the basic dichotomy. In 1934, Beckett referred to O'Casey as: "A master of knockabout in this very serious and honourable sense—that he discerns the principle of disintegration in even the most complacent solitudes." If Hamm and Clov are Didi and Gogo at a later time, perhaps Didi and Gogo are Boyle and Joxer at a later date. Deirdre Bair, *Samuel Beckett A Biography* (New York: Harcourt Brace Jovanovich, 1978,) 183.

28. Seaver, *Can't Go On*, 480–81.

29. Beckett, *Godot*, 41.

30. Samuel Beckett, *Endgame* (New York: Grove Press, 1958), 22.

31. Later, Beckett added *Act Without Words II* in which a pair of characters are introduced, although, unlike their more demonstrative predecessors, Didi and Gogo, the mimes of *Act Without Words II* do not engage each other on any communicative level.

32. Beckett's political opinions were solidly developed by the time he left Trinity College Dublin. His tutor there, Thomas Rudmose-Brown was, in Beckett's own words, a "free thinker" on religious and political issues equally who, therefore, declared to be "neither Fascist nor Communist, Imperialist or Socialist." James Knowlson, *Damned to Fame: The Life of Samuel Beckett* (New York: Simon and Shuster, 1996), 66.

33. John Russell Brown pointed out the self contained nature of Beckett's dramaturgy: "*Waiting for Godot* is mainly about a state of being, that cannot be defined except by the play, but which seems to relate from time to time to many notions about what life is and might be . . . Beckett has shown that theatrical illusion can communicate, by its hidden structure, the unifying and creative vision of its author, which never speaks directly." *Theatre Language* (New York: Taplinger, 1972), 246.

34. *Act Without Words* I, II, 100–22.

35. Kelly claimed to have invented this entrée although it is generally attributed to another American clown whose stage name was Shorty Flemm.

36. See Chapter 4.

37. Denis Calandra, "Karl Valentin and Bertolt Brecht," *Drama Review* 18, no. 1 (March 1974): 95.

38. Samuel Beckett, *Act Without Words* I (New York: Grove Press, 1958), ll. 1–14.

39. Ibid., ll. 15–28.

40. Ibid., ll. 29–31.

41. An account of this early draft of *Endgame* can be found in Ruby Cohn, "The Play That Was Rewritten: *Fin de Partie*," in *Just Play: Beckett's Theater* (Princeton: Princeton University Press, 1980), 173–186.

42. Beckett took an active role in the French resistance during the war, for which he was awarded the *Croix de Guerre* in 1945. After the fall of France, Beckett initially left Paris for the safety of unoccupied southern France, but soon returned to join a Resistance cell code-named Gloria. Almost all of the group's members were killed during the war including Beckett's close friend, Alfred Peron. Regarding his experience during the war, Beckett said: "I was fighting against the Germans who were making life hell for my friends and not for the French nation." See Alan Simpson, *Beckett and Behan and a Theatre in Dublin* (London: Routledge, 1962), 64.

43. Bair, *Samuel Beckett*, 513.

44. Christian Prigent, "A Descent From Clowns," *Journal of Beckett Studies* 3, no. 1 (Autumn 1993): 4.

45. "While it is certain that the space described, time beaten, the being staged, are those of tragedy, the characters are unhappy fools, buffoons who know nothing. Beckett himself makes a clown of himself, dusts the tragic with the powder of farce, with the stuff of sentences perforated by a deadpan humor. He exposes his clownish truth, exposes the truth of invariable descent as a clown from a clown, decked out in a language grotesque and stirring, a language of artifice stubbornly unready to be naturalized, repaired, rectified, purified, or reeducated." Prigent, "Descent," 13.

46. Bair, *Samuel Beckett*, 574.

47. Samuel Beckett, *The Complete Collected Shorter Plays* (New York: Grove-Weidenfeld, 1984), 163.

48. Ibid., 163.

49. Beckett, *Godot*, 37.

50. Normand Berlin, *Beckett at 80*, ed. Enoch Brater (Oxford: Oxford University Press, 1986), 57.

51. Bertolt Brecht, "The Street Scene," in *The Theory of the Modern Stage*, ed. Eric Bentley (New York: Penguin, 1986), 96.

52. Berliner Ensemble company member, actor and director Herbert Olshock, explained the use of this song to me during several personal conversations (1990–91). The dog song is used as an all purpose text to which actors must supply action and character. This exercise helps the actors to divorce their portrayal of character and action from the text.

Chapter 7. Clown in Giorgio Strehler's Theater

1. Strehler's first foray into "absurdist" theater was a production of *Le Balcon* by Jean Genet (1910–86) in 1976.

2. Giorgio Strehler, *Per un teatro umano* (Milano: Feltrinelli, 1974), 47–48, (my translation).

3. Strehler's *Faust Project*, consisting of both parts of Goethe's massive text, continued his self-referential approach to *mise en scène*. It was produced in several fragmentary stages from 1989 through 1992.

4. Giogio Strehler, news conference at University of Toronto, 1991.

5. Strehler, *Teatro Umano*, 289.

6. Ibid., 13.

7. Giorgio Strehler, *Incontro* (Toronto: Istituto Italiano di Cultura, 1989), 58.

8. Strehler, *Teatro Umano*, 14.

9. John Rudlin, *Commedia Dell'Arte: An Actor's Handbook* (New York: Routledge, 1994), 192.

10. Strehler, *Teatro Umano*, 94.

11. Pierre Duchartre, *The Italian Comedy* (New York: Dover, 1929), 48.

12. *Servitore di due padroni*, Act II, viii (my translation).

13. Strehler, *Teatro Umano*, 134.

14. Kott established this basic definition of clown erroneously, stating that Arlecchino was the first clown. What he may have meant was that Arlecchino is the first clown that comes to mind. If so it would appear to be a result of Strehler's production.

15. Strehler, *Teatro Umano*, 51.

16. In order to help create a fresh approach to the play, Strehler commissioned a brand new Italian translation from Angelo Dallagiacoma and Luigi Lunari who, together with the director and some input from the acting company, continued to work on the Italian text throughout the period of rehearsals and previews.

17. Beckettian *geste* is examined in Chap. 6.

18. Agostino Lombardo worked closely with Strehler on *Lear*, *I Giochi di Potenti* (Strehler's version of Shakespeare's Henry cycle), and *La Tempesta* which he translated from English especially for that production.

19. Agostino Lombardo, *Il Re Lear di Shakespeare* (Verona: Bertani, 1973), 266.

20. Strehler's *mise en scène* differs here from one of Brecht's directorial tenets. Brecht believed that the stage should never be too obscured by darkness because the audience would be more inclined to view the stage as a fantasy world cut off from reality. As with many other of Brecht's specific aesthetic preferences Strehler does not slavishly follow his master on this point.

21. Lombardo, *Re Lear*, 264 (my translation).

22. Ibid., 30.

23. Giorgio Strehler, "Appunti per la Regia," in *Il Re Lear di Shakespeare* (Verona: Bertani, 1973), 31 (my translation).

24. Giorgio Strehler, *Inscenare Shakespeare* (Roma: Bulzoni, 1992), 94–95 (my translation).

25. Strehler, "Appunti," 40.

26. Ibid.

27. Ibid., 44.

28. Ernesto Rossi, "Le prove di *Re Lear*," in *Il Re Lear di Shakespeare* (Verona: Bertani, 1973), 217.

29. Strehler, "Appunti," 44–45.

30. Jan Kott, *Shakespeare Our Contemporary* (London: Methuen, 1964), 168.

31. Ibid., 147–48.

32. Marvin Rosenberg, *The Masks of King Lear* (London: Associated University Press, 1972), 319.

33. Strehler, "Appunti," 40.

34. Strehler, *Inscenare Shakespeare*, 86.

35. In Jonathan Miller's 1970 production of *The Merchant of Venice*, Laurence Olivier used a similar gesture on the lines "I would my daughter were dead at my foot, and the jewels in her ear." (III.i.87).

36. Strehler, *Inscenare Shakespeare*, 104.

Chapter 8. Clown as Proleterian Messiah

1. Luigi Ballerini and Giuseppe Risso, "Dario Fo Explains: An Interview," *The Drama Review* 22, no.1 (March 1978): 34.

2. Joel Schechter, "Dario Fo's Obscene Fables," *Theater* 14, no. 1 (Winter 1982): 87.

3. Rame made this remark at a lecture demonstration at the University of Toronto in 1995.

4. Fo's first important piece of political satire, *Il dito nell'occhio*, [*A finger in the eye*], which was produced at the Piccolo Teatro in 1953, drew mainly on French farces such as those of Feydeau (1862–1921) and Labiche (1815–1888) rather than circus or *commedia* clowning. Both *Il dito nell'occhio* and Fo's first mainstream hit *Gli arcangeli* maintained much of the basic elements of French farce, such as mistaken identities, infidelity, fast-paced action, and characters endlessly entering and exiting from separate doors.

5. At the beginning of his career, Fo worked within the context of a generalized leftist artistic *milieu*. He worked at the Piccolo Teatro where he met and studied mime with Jacques Lecoq. Together Fo and Lecoq presented *Il dito nell'occhio* (1953) at the Piccolo. Fo learned a great deal from Giorgio Strehler and the exciting atmosphere of the Piccolo Teatro. "There we were able to create a rapport between literary and grassroots theatre. My experience at Il Piccolo was very important. Above all because of the mimes I worked with. I remember Strehler used to come and lend us a hand with the lights. He always came to our rehearsals—he would hide among the seats not to disturb us. It was a meaningful working relationship." See Ballerini and Risso, "Dario Fo Explains," 44.

6. Dante Germino, *Antonio Gramsci: Architect of a New Politics* (Baton Rouge: Louisiana State University Press, 1990), 254.

7. Pasolini initially wrote in his native Friulian dialect and also greatly admired Gramsci. One of his first important poems, *Le ceneri di Gramsci* ["Gramsci's ashes"] (1955), was written in dialect.

8. Pietro Frassica, *Immagini del novecento italiano* (New York: MacMillan, 1987), 125.

9. Dario Fo, *Tricks of the Trade*, trans. Joe Farrell (New York: Routledge, 1991), 84.

10. Dario Fo, *Manuale minimo dell'attore* (Torino: Einaudi, 1987), 112.

11. Dario Fo with Luigi Allegri, *Dario Fo: dialogo provocatorio sul comico, il tragico, la follia e la ragione* (Roma: Laterza, 1990), 50 (my translation).

12. Roger Oliver, *Dreams of Passion: The Theatre of Luigi Pirandello* (New York: New York University Press, 1979), 167.

13. Just as Brecht had been schooled and inspired by Karl Valentin, so Pirandello worked closely with Sicilian clown Angelo Musco for whom he wrote *Liolà* (1916) and *Beretto a sonagli* [Cap and Bells] (1917).

14. Dario Fo, *Totò, Manuale dell'attor comico* (Torino: Adelph, 1991), 99.

15. Fo, *Dialogo provocatorio*, 135.

16. Dario Fo, *Atti del Convegno sul teatro del Partito Comunista Italiano* (Roma: Bulzoni, 1977), 145.

17. Fo, *Totò*, 93.

18. Ibid.

19. The title character in *Philoctetes* is punished despite being entirely innocent and only elevated to a higher plane through the intervention of Heracles so that he can help the Greeks in their struggle with Troy. Philoctetes is, therefore, an archetypal symbol of the political pawn. Fo's inspiration to write a modern version of *Philoctetes* partly came from a similar re-working of the Sophocles original, *Philoktet* by Heiner Müller (1929–96) at the Volksbühne theater of Berlin in 1968.

20. This play has been interpreted as an apology for terrorism and used in the United States as evidence to prevent Fo from appearing in person to perform his plays.

21. Although Fo developed into a more aggressively political artist than Strehler or Lecoq, declaring that he did not want to continue "playing jester to the bourgeoisie," he did not therefore condemn the research into *commedia* of his previous collaborators at the Piccolo Teatro. "The objection I most commonly hear advanced about this work [*Arlecchino*] is that it has little of the savour of improvisation, but rather that it goes like clockwork, like a comic mechanism with pre-programmed timing, or alternatively that it has too much precision and too little liberty of imagination." See Fo, *Tricks*, 27–29.

22. Antonio De Curtis (1898–1967) alias Totò, Neapolitan variety comedian and film star. Fo considered Totò to be the twentieth-century Arlecchino.

23. Fo, *Tricks*, 172.

24. Francesco De Sanctis (1817–83) was Benedetto Croce's teacher, a fellow Neapolitan, literary historian and liberal political philosopher.

25. This entire scene is left out of the English language translations of *Mistero Buffo*. Fo never gives the traditional rendering of the poem because most of his Italian audience would have learnt it at school. Without reference to this knowledge the episode makes little sense.

26. De Sanctis suggests that the early poets were all called Sicilians because they were drawn to Palermo by Frederick II, King of Sicily and Emperor of Germany (referred to by Dante as "the great clerk.") See Francesco De Sanctis, *History of Italian Literature*, Vol. 1, trans. Joan Redfern, (New York: Basic Books, 1931), 3.

27. Ibid., 8. Fo tends to exaggerate De Sanctis and Croce's effort to hide the identity of Ciullo d'Alcamo. De Sanctis admits that "the language of Ciullo is not Sicilian dialect, but the vulgar tongue of the Italian troubadours, still very rough material and containing a large mixture of local expressions."

28. Dario Fo, in *Le Commedia di Dario Fo*, vol. 5, *Mistero Buffo* (Torino: Einaudi 1977), 71.

29. Ibid., 72.

30. Ibid., 80.

31. Fo's play *Quasi per caso una donna: Elisabetta*, [*Elizabeth: almost accidentally a woman*] about Elizabeth I of England, had an entire major character, performed by Fo in grammelot (and drag). Although Fo does not speak English, he often performs grammelot in an English style in order to satirize American and British politicians.

32. Fo, *Tricks*, 61–62.

33. Ibid., 57–58.

34. Ballerini and Risso, "Dario Fo Explains," 37.

35. Fo, *Mistero Buffo*, 5.

36. Ibid., 5.

37. Chiara Valentini dismissed Fo's account of his sources in *La Storia di Dario Fo* (Milano: Feltrinelli, 1977).

38. Dario Fo, *Mistero Buffo*, trans. Ed Emery (London: Methuen, 1988), 58.

39. Antonio Scuderi, "Framing and Improvisation in Dario Fo's *Johan Padan*," *Theater Annual: A Journal of Performance Studies*, (1996): 89.

40. Fo, *Mistero Buffo*, 85 (my translation).

41. His prototype for performance was again Totò whose development of the physical approach to comedy he described in the following way: Totò invented an extraordinary mask from the reworking of various Commedia dell'Arte prototypes, and also dedicated much study to the disarticulated movements of puppets. From these elements he forged sequences of dance step actions, at times mincing about, at times leaping forward with giant strides, all the while flailing his arms in the air and contorting the whole upper part of his body into bizarre formations, to irresistible comic effect." See Fo, *Tricks*, 24.

42. Fo, *Mistero Buffo*, 96.

43. Ibid., 118.

44. Antonio Scuderi, "Subverting Religious Authority: Dario Fo and Folk Laughter," *Text and Performance Quarterly* 16, no. 3 (July 1996): 224.

45. Fo was awarded the ultimate symbol of "acceptance and tolerance," the Nobel Prize for literature in 1997.

46. Tony Mitchell, "Dario Fo's *Mistero Buffo*: Popular Theatre, the Giullari, and the Grotesque," *Theatre Quarterly* 9, no. 35 (Autumn, 1979): 16.

47. Fo, in *Atti*, 305.

48. Fo, *Atti*, 145.

49. Ibid., 297.

50. Ibid., 149.

Chapter 9. Clown as Protagonist in the Heartland

1. One notable exception that proves the rule is *J. B.* (1958) by Archibald Macleish (1892–1982). In this play the biblical story of Job is told as a modern American tragedy enacted in a circus ring with God and the Devil as competing clowns. Despite being honored with the Pulitzer Prize for drama, the play did not start a trend of verse plays or plays with grotesque protagonists.

2. Davis had studied dance at Ohio University, University of New Mexico and Connecticut College and worked in modern dance companies before becoming interested in mime. His first formal study of mime was with Paul Curtis at the American Mime Theater where he also became part of the performing company.

3. Blau wrote the program notes for this production in which he compared the goals of the young company with Copeau's efforts at theatrical renovation. "When Jacques Copeau, one of the great innovators of the modern theatre, resigned from the Comedie Fraçaise, he went literally to the country, to go back to the soil of his art." See R. G.

Davis, *San Francisco Mime Troupe: The First Ten Years* (Palo Alto: Ramparts Press, 1975), 19.

4. In later years he was to accuse Blau of having been a C. I. A. operative.

5. Davis, *San Francisco Mime Troupe*, 11.

6. See Becht, *Brecht on Theatre*, 37.

7. R.G. Davis, "Method in Mime," *Tulane Drama Review* 6, no. 4 (Summer 1963): 63.

8. Carlo Mazzone, an Italian actor who had played Brighella in Giorgio Strehler's production of *Arlecchino, servitore di due padroni*, instructed the actors in *commedia* technique and provided the troupe with eight leather masks made by master mask-maker Amleto Sartori. In this way The Mime Troupe had a direct connection with Strehler's research into *commedia dell'arte.*

9. The blackface minstrel show was the dominant form of popular entertainment during the nineteenth century and lasted well into the twentieth century. Minstrelsy was enjoyed by both black and white audiences and presented by both black and white troupes. Blackface troupes comprising all-white casts would perform for white audiences and blackface troupes with African Americans performed mostly for black audiences although they had some success with white audiences as well. Never, however, did black and white minstrel performers "black up" to appear together.

10. R. G. Davis (1975), 52.

11. Davis had first thought to stage *The Blacks: A Clown Show* (1959) by Jean Genet (1910–86), as a means of tackling racism, but decided, instead, to avoid European, avant-garde models, and explore America's own popular tradition.

12. Desegregation spelled a softening of black clown tradition. What was acceptable as comedy among blacks was not viewed as funny once white audiences were included, and if transformed into bitter social satire, as with the comedy of Dick Gregory, it was too threatening to be popular with white audiences.

13. R. G. Davis (1975), 52.

14. Ibid., 62.

15. R. G. Davis, "A Playwrights' Polemic: A Shortage of Themes," *West Coast Plays* 10 (Fall 1981): 94.

16. Ibid.

17. The Cultural Revolution in China illustrates what actually happens when cultural forms are selected and "discarded." Davis called openly for a cultural revolution in America, yet Chinese drama after such a revolution was forced to conform to the whims of Mao Tse-tung's third wife Jiang Qing (1914–), a former movie actress who purged theatre of "ancient" elements. All but one of the working playwrights of the day in China were unable to produce their work, many of them were imprisoned. See William Dolby, *A History of Chinese Drama* (New York: Barnes and Noble, 1976).

18. Davis, *San Francisco Mime Troupe*, 125.

19. Blau formed Kraken after leaving The Actor's Workshop in San Francisco.

20. See Chapter 3.

21. The two were married while they were both performing with The Pickle Family Circus.

22. Pisoni had been drawn to San Francisco specifically to work with the Mime Troupe with whom he worked for three and a half years and introduced juggling as a staple of Mime Troupe performance. Longing to form a genuine circus, Pisoni and

another Mime Troupe veteran, Peggy Snider, left in 1974 to form a new company, The Pickle Family Circus, in which he, his wife and children all performed.

23. Terry Lorant, Jon Carroll, *The Pickle Family Circus: Years of Greatness, Times of Glory* (San Francisco: Pickle Press, 1986), 18–42.

24. The circus was used as a vehicle for fund-raising and the distribution of pamphlets on such subjects as pro-choice, day-care, housing and improved conditions for the elderly.

25. Joseph Chaikin is a former member of the Living Theater who established the Open Theater in New York in 1963 and has been one of America's most influential avant-garde directors since that time.

26. Mel Gussow, *New York Times* (2 November 1992), C3.

27. Irwin played Galy Gay in Brecht's *Mann ist Mann* at La Jolla Playhouse in 1985, Laertes opposite Kevin Kline's Hamlet for The New York Shakespeare Festival in 1990 and later appeared in Molière's *Scapin* in a version adapted by himself along with collaborator Mark O'Donnell in 1994.

28. Shiner studied theatre at college in Virginia and began doing mime in the style of Marcel Marceau. He traveled to Europe where he worked as a street mime. By his own admission, he was a poor performer during this period, "I was very bad. I got sick of that whole mime routine. I just wanted to be hysterically funny. Then one night I stopped a police car and made the cop get out, and I frisked him, and I soon had a big crowd. It was really guerrilla theater. I would take over the pit in front of the Beaubourg in Paris, pick fights with motorcycle gangs. I'd do anything." *New York Times* (21 February 1993), H5.

29. Cirque de Soleil Program (1990), 39.

30. Frank Rich, *New York Times* (26 February 1993), C1.

31. Irwin's play *The Courtroom* was partly a recreation of a routine Bobby Clark performed in Burlesque.

32. The Broadway stage had a great clown tradition, but with the decline of burlesque and vaudeville, clown moved off of theatrical boards and onto television and film screens. The first two decades of television provided an outlet for the Broadway clown in the form of variety shows in which the standard vaudeville program was packaged for the small screen. Milton Berle, Jerry Lewis and Bob Hope, all of whom had appeared on Broadway or in Vaudeville, left the theatre for film and television.

33. His efforts were reminiscent of Czech scenic designer Josef Svoboda (1920) and his "Laterna Magika." Svoboda's work was initially with film rather than video since video was much clumsier in the 1960s when Svoboda began his experiments, but the idea of integrating live action and film was much the same. Svoboda too used clown in his work most notably in *The Magic Circus* (1977).

34. Ron Jenkins, *Acrobats of the Soul* (New York: Theatre Communications Group, 1988), 158.

35. Quoted in Michael Bristol, *Big-time Shakespeare* (London: Routledge, 1996), 3.

36. Hoyle did some of his routines for the French officials in charge of granting funds for study at French cultural institutions. "They didn't seem to think it was funny when I mimed stepping in horse shit, but they gave me the money!" This led to three years of training with Decroux and one year at the Gymnase du Cirque, Paris (personal communication, 1994).

37. Personal communication, 1994.

38. Geoff Hoyle, Artistic Statement, National Endowment for the Arts, 1993.

39. He has developed original performance pieces that, like Irwin's, are historically-conscious clown shows. *The Fool Show* premiered at La Jolla Playhouse in 1988 and had a short run in New York in 1990. The second of his solo shows was *The Convict's Return* which drew its title from an old sketch by the legendary Broadway clown Bobby Clark (1888–1960).

40. When first Irwin, and then Hoyle left the Pickle Family, the clown characters changed. Originally, Irwin was physically very much a White Clown with full white make-up. Hoyle's character was named Auguste, so naturally he was the Auguste while Pisoni was an intentionally ineffectual ring master. After Irwin left, the dynamic between the clowns had to change. Pisoni and Hoyle had to compensate for the loss of Bill Irwin's grotesque yet elegant White Clown. Hoyle became Mr. Sniff, a much more grotesque Auguste than his old, subtler character. While Hoyle's original character wore almost no make-up, Mr. Sniff had an enormous bobbling nose (personal communication, 1994).

41. Henry Miller, *The Smile at the Foot of the Ladder* (New York: New Directions, 1958), 3.

42. Ibid., 27.

43. Ibid., 40.

44. This was accomplished by fixing a safety rope to the back of his belt and having him let go of the rope ladder he had used to climb to the ceiling spreading his arms out in a Christ-like pose with no visible means of support.

45. Miller (1958), 46.

46. Robin Williams, one of the most dynamic and successful clowns of the past three decades, was educated at the Juilliard School where clown technique was taught by John Towsen. Despite revealing his considerable talent to Towsen, John Houseman (1902–88), head of the Drama program from 1968–76, did not ask Williams to return.

47. After appearing as an alien on the television sit-com *Happy days*, the network produced the hit series *Mork & Mindy* (1978–82), specifically as a vehicle for Williams's Auguste clown.

48. His first film role was as another other-worldly Auguste, derived from comic strips. In *Popeye* (1980) directed by Robert Altman, Williams was joined by many of his friends from the clown world including Geoff Hoyle, Bill Irwin, Larry Pisoni, and Hovey Burgess. The film was a daring attempt to use clowns to bridge the mimetic conventions of action with the mimetic conventions of cartoons. Unfortunately, *Popeye* was a major disappointment financially. Partly as a result of this failure Williams's film roles have tended to be less rooted in clown in his later career.

49. Martin was a comedy writer for television at 22 years of age.

50. Williams has tried to satisfy his talent by taking on dramatic film and television roles outside of his clown personality. Martin attempted to merge his comic identity with a semi-tragic performance in the formalist film *Pennies from Heaven* (1981). This film was remarkable because it attempted to portray different levels of mimetic performance, a realistic and fantasy depression era America, and blurred the boundaries between the images. Unfortunately, *Pennies* was a financial failure and Martin has avoided playing so dark a film role ever since. Martin Followed *Pennies* with another film that experimented with mimetic space, *Dead Men Don't Wear Plaid* (1982), this

time with an unambiguously comic through-line, but it only did marginally better than the tragic *Pennies*.

51. Nichols had been a successful night club comic with partner Elaine May who also became a Hollywood director and comic actress.

52. Mimi Kramer, *New Yorker* (21 November 1988), 135.

53. Martin's most successful screen performance, for instance, is as a contemporary Cyrano in his *Roxanne* (1987) where the giant nose served as a clown mask through which Martin's contemporary character could still resonate. Williams attempted to merge his clown skill with a serious role in *Jakob the Liar* (1999) with mixed results.

Chapter 10. Conclusion

1. Enoch Brater, "After the Absurd," *Around the Absurd: Essays on Modern and Postmodern Drama*, ed. Enoch Brater and Ruby Cohn (Ann Arbor: The University of Michigan Press, 1990), 300.

2. Robert Wilson, lecture demonstration, University of Toronto, 1995.

3. For the best examples of these scathing reviews of *Life* see S. Kaufmann *New Republic*. 23 November 1998, 26–27, G. Peary, *Boston Phoenix*. Arts Section, October 30, 1998, 9, and J. Hoberman, *Sight and Sound*. February, 1999, 20–23.

4. M. Viano, "*Life is Beautiful:* Reception, Allegory, and Holocaust Laughter." *Film Quarterly* 53, no.1, (Fall 1999): 26–34.

5. Jeffrey Wachs in his review of *Jakob the Liar* wondered if Williams might be jealous that, "Roberto Benigni stole his crown as film's top tearjerkin' funnyman."

Bibliography

Althusser, Louis. *For Marx*. Trans. Ben Brewster. London: Verso, 1977.

And, Metin. *Drama at the Crossroads*. Istanbul: Isis Press, 1991.

Armin, Robert. *A Shakespeare Jestbook, Robert Armin's "Foole upon Foole (1600)*. Ed. H. F. Lippincott. Salzburg: Umiversotat Salzburg, 1973.

Artese, Ermina. *Dario Fo parla di Dario Fo: Intervista e saggio introduttivo di Ermina Artes*. Cosenza: Lerici, 1977.

Bair, Deirdre. *Samuel Beckett: A Biography*. New York: Harcourt Brace Jovanovich, 1978.

Bakhtin, Mikhail. *The Dialogic Imagination*. Trans. Michael Holquist and Caryl Emerson. Austin: University of Texas Press, 1981.

———. *Rabelais and his World*. Trans. Helene Iswolski. Cambridge: M. I. T. Press, 1968.

Ballerini, Luigi, and Giuseppe Risso. "Dario Fo Explains: An Interview." *The Drama Review* 22, no. 1 (March 1978): 33–48.

Barrault, Jean-Louis. *Reflections on the Theatre*. Trans. Barbara Wall. London: Rockliff, 1951.

Barthes, Roland. "Style and its Image," in *Literary Styles: A Symposium*. London: Oxford University Press, 1971.

Battistini, Fabio. *Gli Spazi dell'incanto*. Milano: Silvana Editoriale, 1987.

Beckett, Samuel. *Waiting for Godot*. Vol. 1 of *The Theatrical Notebooks of Samuel Beckett*. Ed. Douglas Macmillan and James Knowlson. London: Faber and Faber, 1993.

———. *The Complete Dramatic Works*. London: Faber and Faber, 1986.

Bentley, Eric. *The Brecht Memoir*. Forward by Martin Esslin. Evanston, Ill.: Northwestern University Press, 1985.

———. "Man's a Man." In *Brecht Commentaries*. New York: Grove Press, 1980.

———. *A Man's a Man and The Elephant Calf by Bertolt Brecht*. New York: Grove Press, 1964.

———. *In Search of Theater*. New York: Atheneum, 1948.

Berlin, Normand. "The Tragic Pleasure of *Waiting for Godot*." In *Beckett at 80/Beckett in Context*, ed. Enoch Brater. New York: Oxford University Press, 1986.

Berrong, Richard, M. *Rabelais and Bakhtin*. Lincoln: University of Nebraska Press, 1986.

Berson, Misha. "Flirting with Farce." *American Theatre* (July/August 1995): 8–9.

Biely, Andrei. "Reminiscences of A. Blok." Trans. Vera Dixon. In *Novy Mir 1925–1967*, ed. Michael Glenny, 57–93. London: Jonathan Cape, 1972.

Billington, Sandra. *A Social History of the Fool*. New York: St. Martin's Press, 1984.

Binni, Lanfranco. *Dario Fo*. Firence: La Nuova Italia, 1977.

Blok, Aleksandre. "On Drama." Trans. Laurence Senelick. In *Russian Dramatic Theory*. Austin: University of Texas Press, 1981.

Blumenthal, Eileen. "For Laughs, Bill Irwin Does Dancing Shoes." *New York Times*, 8 May 1988, 26.

Booker, Keith, and Dubravka Juraga. *Bakhtin, Stalin, and Modern Russian Fiction: Carnival, Dialogism, and History*. London: Greenwood Press, 1995.

Bouissac, Paul. *Circus and Culture: A Semiotic Approach*. Bloomington: Indiana University Press, 1976.

Brater, Enoch. *The Drama in the Text: Beckett's Late Fiction*. New York: Oxford University Press, 1994.

————. *Why Beckett*. London: Thames and Hudson, 1989.

————. *Beyond Minimalism: Beckett's Late Style in the Theater*. New York: Oxford University Press, 1987.

————. *Beckett at 80/Beckett in Context*. New York: Oxford University Press, 1986.

Braun, Edward. *Meyerhold: A Revolution in Theatre*. London: Methuen, 1995.

————. *The Theatre of Meyerhold*. New York: Drama Book Specialists, 1979.

————. *Meyerhold on Theatre*. London: Methuen, 1969.

Bray, Barbara. "The New Beckett." *Observer* (16 June 1963): 29.

Brecht, Bertolt. *Diaries, 1920–1922*. Ed. Herta Ramthun. Trans. John Willett. New York: St. Martin's Press, 1979.

————. *Collected Plays*. Vol 2. Trans. John Willet and Ralph Manheim. New York: Vintage Books, 1977.

————. *Bertolt Brecht Poems*. Ed. John Willet and Ralph Manheim. London: Eyre Methuen, 1976.

————. *A Man's a Man and The Elephant Calf*. Ed. and trans. Eric Bentley. New York: Grove Press, 1964.

Bristol, Michael D. *Carnival and Theater: Plebeian Culture and the Structure of Authority in Renaissance England*. New York: Routledge, 1985.

Brown, Frederick. *Theatre and Revolution: The Culture of the French Stage*. New York: Viking Press, 1980.

Brown, John Russell. "Beckett and the Art of the Nonplus." In *Beckett at 80/Beckett in Context*, ed. Enoch Brater. New York: Oxford University Press, 1986.

Brustein, Robert. "Exploding an Anarchist Play." *The New Republic*, 17 (December 1984): 25–26.

Burgess, Hovey. "The Classification of Circus Techniques." *Drama Review* 18, no. 1 (March, 1974): 65–70.

Busby, Olive Mary. *Studies in the Development of the Fool*. London: Oxford University Press, 1923.

Busoni, Ferruccio. *Selected Letters*. Ed. and Trans. Antony Beaumont. London: Faber and Faber, 1987.

Cairns, Christopher. "Dario Fo and the Commedia dell' Arte." In *Studies in the Commedia dell' Arte*, ed. David G. George and Christopher J. Gossip. Cardiff: University of Wales Press, 1993.

————. *The Commedia dell'Arte from the Renaissance to Dario Fo*. Lewiston, N.Y.: Edwin Mellon Press, 1988.

Calandra, Denis. "Karl Valentin and Bertolt Brecht." *Drama Review* 18, no. 1 (March 1974): 86–98.

Campbell, William. *Villi the Clown*. London: Faber and Faber, 1981.

Caputi, Anthony. *Buffo: The Genius of Vulgar Comedy*. Detroit: Wayne State University Press, 1978.

Carlson, Marvin. *Theatre Semiotics: Signs of Life*. Bloomington: Indiana University Press, 1991.

Cecchi, Umberto. *L'Arlecchino del Re Sole: La vita e il teatro di Evaristo Gherardi*. Prato: Edizioni del Palazzo, 1986.

Cervellati, Alessandro. *Questa Sera Grande Spettacolo: storia del circo italiano*. Milano: Mondo Popolare, 1961.

Chansky, Dorothy. "Largely Bill Irwin." *TheaterWeek* (15 May 1989): 8–14.

————. Review of *A Man's a Man* by Bertolt Brecht (La Jolla Playhouse, California). *Village Voice* (13 August 1985): 86.

Charney, Maurice, ed. *"Bad" Shakespeare: Revaluations of the Shakespeare Canon*. Madison, N.J.: Farleigh Dickinson University Press, 1988.

Chukovsky, Kornei. *Alexandre Blok as Man and Poet*. Ed. and trans. Diana Burgin and Katherine O'Connor. Ann Arbor: Ardis, 1982.

Cocteau, Jean. *Cocteau's World*. Ed. and trans. Margaret Crosland. London: Peter Owen, 1972.

Cohen, Derek. *Shakespeare's Culture of Violence*. London: St. Martin's Press, 1993.

Cohn, Ruby. *Casebook on Waiting for Godot*. New York: Grove Press, 1967.

————. " 'Theatrum Mundi' and Contemporary Theater," *Comparative Drama* 1 (Spring 1967): 30–38.

————. *Samuel Beckett: the Comic Gamut*. New Brunswick: Rutgers University Press, 1962.

Copeau, Jacques. *Texts on Theatre*. Ed. and Trans. John Rudlin and Norman H. Paul. London and New York: Routledge, 1990.

————. *Les Registres du Vieux Columbier*. I: *Appels*. Paris: Gallimard, 1974. II: *Moliere*. Paris: Gallimard, 1976. III: *Les Registres du Vieux Columbier*. Paris: Gallimard, 1979. IV: *Les Registres du Vieux Columbier*. Paris: Gallimard, 1984.

Craig, Gordon. "The Actor and the Über-Marionette," In *Gordon Craig on Movement and Dance*, ed. Arnold Rood. New York: Dance Horizons, 1977.

Croce, Benedetto. *Ariosto, Shakespeare and Corneille*. Trans. Douglas Ainslie. London: George Allen and Unwin, 1922.

Cruciani, Fabrizio. *Jacques Copeau o le aporie del teatro moderno*. Roma: Mario Bulzoni, 1971.

Davis, Jessica Milner. *Farce*. London: Methuen, 1978.

Davis, R. G. *San Francisco Mime Troupe: The First Ten Years*. Palo Alto: Ramparts Press, 1975.

de Curtis, Liliana. *Totò a prescindere*. Milan: Arnoldo Mondadori, 1992.

De Sanctis, Francesco. *History of Italian Literature*. With an introduction by Benedetto Croce. Trans. Joan Redfern. New York: Basic Books, 1931.

Deak, Frantisek. "The Agitprop and Circus Plays of Vladimir Mayakovsky." *The Drama Review* 57 (March 1973): 46–53.

Decroux, Etienne. *Paroles sur la mime*. Paris: Gallimard, 1963.

Decroux, Maximilien. *Ecrits sur Pantomime, Mime Expression Corporelle*. Paris: TEMP, Theatre Ecole Mouvement et Pensee, 1975.

Derrida, Jacques. *Dissemination*. Trans. Barabara Johnson. Chicago: University of Chicago Press, 1981.

Dick, Kay. *Pierrot*. London: Hutchison and Co., 1960.

Dickens, Charles. *Memoirs of Joseph Grimaldi*. Ed. Richard Findlater. London: MacGibbon and Kee Ltd., 1968.

Dietl, Eduard. *Clowns*. München: Markus Verlag, 1967.

Disher, Maurice Willson. *Clowns and Pantomimes*. London: Constable, 1925.

Disher, Maurice Willson. *Greatest Show on Earth*. New York: Benjamin Blom, 1969.

Dolby, William. *A History of Chinese Drama*. New York: Barnes and Noble, 1976.

Donahue, Thomas. *Structures of Meaning: A Semiotic Approach to the Play Text*. Madison, N.J.: Farleigh Dickinson University Press, 1993.

Dorcy, Jean. *The Mime*. Trans. Robert Speller Jr. and Marcel Marceau. London: White Lion Publishers Ltd., 1961.

Drew, David. *Kurt Weill: A Handbook*. Berkeley: University of California Press, 1987.

Duchartre, Pierre. *The Italian Comedy*. New York: Dover, 1965.

Durov, Vladimir. *My Circus Animals*. Boston: Houghton Mifflin, 1936.

Eaton, Katherin Bliss. *The Theater of Meyerhold and Brecht*. London: Greenwood Press, 1985.

Elam, Keir. *The Semiotics of Theatre and Drama*. London: Methuen and Company, 1980.

Emery, Ed. "Dario Fo's Trumpets and Raspberries and the Tradition of Commedia." In *The Commedia dell' Arte from the Renaissance to Dario Fo*, ed. Christopher Cairns. Lewiston, N.Y.: Edwin Mellen Press, 1989.

Enters, Angna. *On Mime*. Middletown, CT: Wesleyan University Press, 1965.

Esslin, Martin, et al. "Playwrights' Polemic: A Shortage of Themes." *West Coast Plays* 10 (Fall 1981): 73–100.

———. *Bertolt Brecht*. New York: Columbia University Press, 1969.

———. *The Theatre of the Absurd*. New York: Anchor Books, 1961.

Ewen, Frederic. *Bertolt Brecht: His Life his Art and his Times*. New York: Citadel Press, 1967.

Farrell, Joseph. "Dario Fo: Zanni and Giullare." In *The Commedia dell'Arte from the Renaissance to Dario Fo*, ed. Christopher Cairns. Lewiston, N.Y.: Edwin Mellen Press, 1989.

Fellini, Federico. *I Clowns*. Bologna: Cappelli, 1970.

Felner, Mira. *Apostles of Silence: The Modern French Mimes*. Madison, N.J.: Fairleigh Dickinson University Press, 1985.

Fisher, Seymour and Rhoda. *Pretend the World is Funny and Forever: A Psychological Analysis of Comedians, Clowns and Actors*. Hillsdale, N.J.: LEA, 1981.

Fo, Dario. *Dario Fo Plays*. Vol. 1, *Mistero Buffo, Accidental Death of an Anarchist, Trumpets and Raspberries, The Virtuous Burglar, One Was Nude and One Wore Tails*. Ed. Stuart Hood. Trans. Ed Emery, et al. London: Methuen Drama, 1992.

———. *Totò: Manuale dell' attor comico*. Turin: Aleph, 1991.

———. *The Tricks of the Trade*. Ed. Stuart Hood. Trans. Joe Farrell. New York: Routledge, 1991.

———. *Dialogo Provocatorio sul comico, il tragico, la follia e la ragione: con Luigi Allegri*. Rome: Laterza, 1990.

———. *Mistero Buffo: Comic Mysteries*. Ed. Stuart Hood. Trans. Ed Emery. London: Methuen, 1988.

———. *Archangels Don't Play Pinball*. Ed. Stuart Hood. Trans. R. C. McAvoy and A-M. Giugni. London: Methuen, 1987.

———. *Manuale minimo dell' attore*. Turin: Einaudi, 1987.

———. *Le commedie di Dario Fo*. Vol. 6, *La Marcolfa, Gli imbianchini non hanno ricordi, I tre bravi, Non tutti ladri vengono per nuocere, Un morto da vendere, I cadaveri si spediscono e le donne si spogliano, L'uomo nudo e l'uomo in frak, Canzoni e ballate*. Turin: Einaudi, 1984.

———. *Dario Fo and Franca Rame: Theatre Workshops at Riverside Studios, London: April 28th, May 5th, 12th, 19th, 1983*. London: Red Notes, 1983.

———. "Popular Culture: A Speech by Dario Fo." Trans. Tony Mitchell. *Theater* 14, no. 3 (Summer/Fall 1983): 50–54.

———. *Storia della tigre*. Milan: La Comune, 1980.

———. *Le commedie di Dario Fo*. Vol. 5, *Mistero buffo, Ci Ragiono e canto*. Turin: Einaudi, 1977.

———. *La signora é da buttare*. Turin: Einaudi, 1976.

———. *Le commedie di Dario Fo: Gli arcangeli non giocano a flipper, Aveva due pistole con gli occhi bianchi e neri, Chi ruba un piede é fortunato in amore*. Turin: Einaudi, 1966.

Foakes, R. A. *Hamlet Versus Lear: Cultural Politics and Shakespeare's Art*. Cambridge: Cambridge University Press, 1993.

Fry, Northrop. *Anatomy of Criticism*. Princeton: Princeton University Press, 1957.

Fuegi, John. *Brecht and Company: Sex, Politics and the Making of the Modern Drama*. New York: Grove Press, 1994.

Garfein, Herschel and Mel Gordon. "The Adriani Lazzi of the Commedia dell' Arte." *The Drama Review* 22, no. 1 (March 1978): 3–12.

Geduld, Harry M. *Chapliana Vol 1: The Keystone Films*. Bloomington: Indiana University Press, 1987.

Germino, Dante. *Antonio Gramsci: Architect of a New Politics*. Baton Rouge: Louisiana State University Press, 1990.

Gerould, Daniel, ed. and trans. *Gallant and Libertine: Eighteenth-Century French Divertissements and Parades*. New York: Performing Arts Journal Publications, 1983.

——, ed. and trans. *Twentieth Century Polish Avant-garde Drama*. Ithaca: Cornell University Press, 1977.

Gilman, Richard. *The Making of the Modern Drama: A Study of Büchner, Ibsen, Strindberg, Chekhov, Pirandello, Brecht, Beckett, Handke*. New York: Farrar, Strauss, 1974.

Gilman, Susan. "Bill Irwin: Not Just Clowning Around." *West Side Spirit* (12 June 1988): 4.

Gladkov, A. "Meyerhold Speaks." Trans. Olive Stevens. In *Novy Mir 1925–1967*, edited by Michael Glenny. London: Jonathan Cape, 1972.

Gopnik, Adam. "Steve Martin: The Late Period." *New Yorker* (29 November 1993): 98–113

Gordon, Mel, and Alma Law. *Meyerhold, Eisenstein and Biomechanics: Actor Training in Revolutionary Russia*. Jefferson, N.C.: McFarland, 1996.

Gordon, Mel. "Meyerhold's Biomechanics." *Drama Review* 18, no. 3, (September 1974): 73–88.

Grant, Steve, and Tony Mitchell. "An Interview with Dario Fo and Franca Rame." *Theater* 14, no. 3 (Summer/Fall 1983): 43–49.

Grassi, Paolo. *Piccolo Teatro*. Milano: Nicola Moneta Editore, 1958.

Gray, Ronald. *Brecht the Dramatist*. Cambridge: Cambridge University Press, 1976.

Green, Michael, ed. and trans. *The Russian Symbolist Theatre: An Anthology of Plays and Critical Texts*. Ann Arbor: Ardis, 1986.

Green, Stanley. *The Great Clowns of Broadway*. New York: Oxford University Press, 1984.

Grossvogel, David. *Four Playwrights and a Postscript: Brecht, Ionesco, Beckett, Genet*. Ithaca, N.Y.: Cornell University Press, 1962.

——. *The Self-Conscious Stage in Modern French Drama*. New York: Columbia University Press, 1958.

Guazzotti, Giorgio. *Teoria e realtà del Piccolo Teatro di Milano*. Torino: Giulio Einaudi Editore, 1965.

Gussow, Mel. "Beckett's Short Lesson in Lifelong Misfortunes." *New York Times*, 2 November 1992, C13.

——. "Bill Irwin's Adventures as a Post-Modern Hoofer," *New York Times*, 17 May 1988, C15.

——. "Profiles: Bill Irwin." *New Yorker* (11 November 1985): 51–87.

Hassan, Ihab. *The Literature of Silence: Henry Miller and Samuel Beckett*. New York: Alfred A. Knopf, 1967.

Hawkes, Terrence. *Structuralism and Semiotics*. Berkeley: University of California Press, 1977.

Helbo, Andre. *Approaching Theatre. Under the direction of Andre Helbo, J. Dines Johansen, Patrice Pavis, Anne Ubersfeld.* Bloomington: Indiana University Press, 1991.

Hilton, Julian. *Performance.* London: Macmillan, 1987.

Hirst, David. *Dario Fo and Franca Rame.* London: Macmillan, 1989.

Hoover, Marjorie L. *Meyerhold and His Set Designers.* New York: Peter Lang, 1988.

———. *Meyerhold: The Art of Conscious Theater.* Boston: University of Massachusetts Press, 1974.

Hotson, Leslie. *Shakespeare's Motley.* New York: Oxford University Press, 1952.

Hoyle, Geoff. "Why the Sitcom of the Renaissance Still Entertains." *New York Times,* 8 April 1990, Section 2, 1, 35.

Hurwitt, Robert. "Minimalist Comedy, Maximalist Quality." *San Francisco Examiner,* 5 November 1993, D9.

Issacharoff, Michael. "Drama and the Reader," *Poetics Today* 2, no. 3 (1981): 255–263.

———. "Space and Reference in Drama," *Poetics Today* 2, no. 3, (1981): 211–24.

Jenkins, Ron. *Subversive Laughter: The Liberating Power of Comedy.* New York: Free Press, 1994.

———. *Acrobats of the Soul.* New York: Theatre Communications Group, 1988.

Jetsmark, Torben. *The Dramatic Body.* Ed. and trans. Per Brask. Winnipeg: Blizzard Publishing, 1992.

Jones, Louisa E. *Sad Clowns and Pale Pierrots: Literature and the Popular Comic Arts in 19th-Century France.* Lexington, Ky.: French Forum Publishers, 1984.

Jones, Welton. "He'd Rather Be a Clown." *San Diego Union,* 21 July 1985, E1–E5.

Kalb, Jonathan. *Beckett in Performance.* Cambridge: Cambridge University Press, 1989.

Kamin, Dan. *Charlie Chaplin's One Man Show.* Forward by Marcel Marceau. London: Scarecrow Press, 1984.

Kennard, Joseph Spencer. *The Italian Theatre.* New York: Benjamin Blom, 1964.

Kern, Edith. "Beckett and the Spirit of the Commedia dell'Arte." *Modern Drama* 9 (December 1966): 260–67.

———. "Concretization of Metaphor in the Commedia dell'Arte and the Modern Theatre." *Proceedings of the Fourth Congress of the International Comparative Literature Association.* Ed. Francois Jost. The Hague: Mouton, 1966.

———. "Drama Stripped for Inaction: Beckett's Godot." *Yale French Studies* 14 (Winter 1954): 41–47.

Kipnis, Claude. *The Mime Book.* Colorado Springs: Meriwether Publishing, 1974.

Kirstein, Lincoln. *Movement and Metaphor: Four Centuries of Ballet.* New York: Praeger Publishers, 1970.

Kleberg, Lars. *Theatre as Action: Soviet Russian Avant-Garde Aesthetics.* Trans. Charles Rougle. London: Macmillan, 1993.

Knapp, Bettina. *The Reign of the Theatrical Director: French Theatre: 1887–1924*. New York: Whitson, 1988.

Knowlson, James. *Damned to Fame: The Life of Samuel Beckett*. New York: Simon and Schuster, 1996.

Kogan, Norman. *A Political History of Italy: The Postwar Years*. New York: Praeger, 1983.

Kott, Jan. *The Bottom Translation: Marlowe and Shakespeare and the Carnival Traditions*. Trans. Daniela Miedzyrzecka and Lillian Vallee. Evanston, Ill.: Northwestern University Press, 1987.

———. *The Theater of Essence and Other Essays*. Evanston, Ill.: Northwestern University Press, 1984.

———. *Shakespeare our Contemporary*. Trans. Boleslaw Taborski. New York: Norton, 1964.

Kowalke, Kim H. *A New Orpheus: Essays on Kurt Weill*. New Haven: Yale University Press, 1986.

Kramer, Mimi. Review of *Waiting for Godot*, by Samuel Beckett (Mike Nichols, director, New York). *New Yorker* (21 November 1988): 135–36.

Lahr, John. *Notes on a Cowardly Lion*. New York: Limelight Editions, 1969.

Lamont, Rosette C. "Giorgio Strehler's Faust II," *West European Stages* (Fall 1991): 5–10.

Lawson, Joan. *Mime: The Theory and Practice of Expressive Gesture with a Description of its Historical Development*. New York: Dance Horizons, 1957.

Lea, K. M. *Italian Popular Comedy*. 2 vols. Oxford: Clarendon Press, 1934.

Leach, Robert. *Vsevolod Meyerhold*. Cambridge: Cambridge University Press, 1989.

Leydi, Roberto. "I Fratellini." In *La Piazza: Spettacoli populari italiani*. Milan: Gallo Grande, 1959.

Lorant, Terry, and Jon Carroll. *The Pickle Family Circus: Years of Greatness, Times of Glory*. San Francisco: Pickle Press, 1986.

Machotka, Hana. *The Magic Ring: A Year with the Big Apple Circus*. New York: William Morrow and Company, 1988.

Manea, Norman. *On Clowns: The Dictator and the Artist*. New York: Grove Weidenfeld, 1992.

Mariel, Pierre. *Les Fratellini: Histoire de trois clowns*. Paris: Societé Anonyme d'Editions, 1923.

Martin, Steve. *Picasso at the Lapin Agile and Other Plays*. New York: Grove Press, 1996.

Mayer, Hans. "Dogs, Brecht and Beckett," Trans. Jack Zipes. In *Essays on Brecht: Theatre and Politics*, ed. Siegfried Mews and Herbert Knust. Chapel Hill: University of North Carolina Press, 1974.

McMillan, Dougald, and Martha Fehsenfeld. *Beckett in the Theatre: The Author as Practical Playwright and Director*. Vol. 1. London: Riverrun Press, 1988.

Meyerhold, Vsevolod. *Meyerhold on Theatre*. Trans. Edward Braun. New York: Hill and Wang, 1969.

Mignon, Paul-Louis. *Jacques Copeau ou le mythe du Vieux-Columbier*. Paris: Editions Julliard, 1993.

Milhaud, Darius. *My Happy Life*. Trans. Donald Evans, George Hall and Christopher Palmer. New York: Marion Boyars, 1987.

Miller, Henry. *The Smile at the Foot of the Ladder*. New York: New Directions Books, 1948.

Millner, Cork. "Steve Martin Wild and Serious Guy." *Saturday Evening Post* (November/December 1989): 54.

Mitchell, Tony. *Dario Fo: People's Court Jester*. London: Methuen, 1985.

———. "Open House with Dario Fo and Franca Rame." *Theater* 15, no. 3 (Summer/Fall 1984): 65–68.

———. "Dario Fo's 'Mistero Buffo': Popular Theatre, the Guillari, and the Grotesque." *Theatre Quarterly* 9, no. 35 (Autumn 1979): 3–16.

Morera, Esteve. *Gramsci's Historicism: A Realist Interpretation*. London: Routledge, 1990.

Nicoll, Allardyce. *Masks, Mimes and Miracles*. New York: Cooper Square, 1963.

———. *The World of Harlequin: A Critical Study of the Commedia dell'Arte*. Cambridge: Cambridge University Press, 1963.

Pagnini, Marcello. *The Pragmatics of Literature*. Trans. Nancy Jones-Henry. Bloomington: Indiana University Press, 1987.

Pearce, Richard. *Stages of the Clown: Perspectives on Modern Fiction from Dostoyevsky to Beckett*. Carbondale: Southern Illinois University Press, 1970.

Pertile, Lino. "Dario Fo." In *Writers and Society in Contemporary Italy: A Collection of Essays*, ed. Michael Caesar and Peter Hainsworth. New York: St. Martin's Press, 1984.

Pietropaolo, Domenico. *Science of Buffonery: Theory and History of the Commedia dell'Arte*. Toronto: Dovehouse Editions, 1989.

Pilling, John, ed. *The Cambridge Companion to Beckett*. Cambridge: Cambridge University Press, 1994.

Prigent Christian, "A Descent from Clowns," *Journal of Beckett Studies* 3, no. 1 (Autumn 1993): 4.

Prosperi, Mario. "Contemporary Italian Theatre." *The Drama Review* 22, no. 1 (March 1978): 17–32.

Radcliffe-Umstead, Douglas. *The Birth of Modern Comedy in Renaissance Italy*. Chicago: University of Chicago Press, 1969.

Rame, Franca, and Dario Fo. *Parliamo di donne: Due atti unici di Franca Rame e Dario Fo*. Milan: Kaos Edizioni, 1992.

———. *A Woman Alone and Other Plays*. Trans. Gillian Hanna, Ed Emery, and Christopher Cairns. London: Methuen Drama, 1991.

Rasi, Luigi. *I comici italiani: Biografia, bibliografia, iconografia*. 3 vols. Florence: Fratelli Bosca, 1987.

Remy, Tristan. *Entrées Clownesques*. Paris: L'Arche, 1962.

———. *Jean-Gaspard Deburau*. Paris: L'Arche, 1954.

————. *Les Clowns*. Paris: Bernard Grasset, 1945.

Rich, Frank. " 'Fool Moon': A Giant Step for Clownkind." *New York Times*, 26 February 1993, C1.

————. "Theater: Bill Irwin's 'Courtroom'." *New York Times*, 10 May 1985, C7.

Richard, Lionel. *Cabaret, Cabarets: Origines et decadence*. Paris: Plon, 1991.

Richards, David. "A Post-Industrial Didi and Gogo on the Open Road." *New York Times*, 21 February 1993, H5.

Ries, Frank W. D. *The Dance Theatre of Jean Cocteau*. Ann Arbor: UMI Research Press, 1986.

Ritter, Naomi. *Art as Spectacle: Images of the Entertainer since Romanticism*. Columbia: University of Missouri Press, 1989.

Rolfe, Bari. *Mimes on Miming: Writings on the Art of Mime*. Ed. with historical notes by Bari Rolfe. Los Angeles: Panjandrum Books, 1978.

Rosen, Richard. "When It Hurts to Laugh." *New York Times*, 1 November 1992, B5.

Rosenberg, Marvin. *The Masks of King Lear*. Newark: University of Delaware Press, 1972.

Royce, Anya Peterson. *Movement and Meaning: Creativity and Interpretation in Ballet and Mime*. Bloomington: Indiana University Press, 1984.

Rudlin, John. *Commedia dell'Arte: An Actor's Handbook*. London: Routledge, 1994.

————. *Jacques Copeau*. Cambridge: Cambridge University Press, 1986.

Rudnitsky, Konstantin. "The Lessons Learned from Brecht," *Theatre Research International* 6, no. 1 (Winter 1980–81): 62–72.

————. *Meyerhold the Director*. Trans. Sydney Shultze. Ann Arbor: Ardis, 1981.

Saint-Denis, Michel. *Theatre, The Rediscovery of Style*. London, 1960.

————. "A School for Dramatic Art." *World Theatre* 4 (Winter 1954): 37–49.

San Francisco Mime Troupe. *By Popular Demand: Plays and Other Works*. San Francisco: The Troupe, 1980.

Scala, Flaminio. *Scenarios of the Commedia dell'Arte*. Trans. and ed. Henry F. Salerno. New York: New York University Press, 1967.

Schechner, Richard. *Essays on Performance Theory: 1970–1976*. New York: Drama Book Specialists, 1977.

Schechter, Joel. "Brecht's Clowns: *Man is Man* and after." *The Cambridge Companion to Brecht*, ed. Peter Thomson and Glendyr Sacks. Cambridge: Cambridge University Press, 1994.

————. *Satiric Impersonations*. Carbondale: Southern Illinois University Press, 1994.

————. *Durov's Pig: Clowns, Politics and Theatre*. New York: Theatre Communications Group, 1985.

————. "Dario Fo's Obscene Fables." *Theater* 8, no. 1 (Winter 1982): 87–90.

Schmidt, Paul. *Meyerhold at Work*. Austin: University of Texas Press, 1980.

Scott, Virginia. *The Commedia dell'Arte in Paris 1644–1697*. Charlottesville: University of Virginia Press, 1990.

Scuderi, Antonio. "Framing and Improvisation in Dario Fo's *Johan Padan*." *Theatre Annual* 49 (1996): 76–91.

———. "Subverting Religious Authority: Dario Fo and Folk Laughter." *Text and Performance Quarterly* 16, no. 3 (July 1996): 216–32.

Seaver, Richard W., ed. *Samuel Beckett, I Can't Go On, I'll Go On: A Selection from Samuel Beckett's Work*. New York: Grove Press, 1976.

Segel, Harold B. *Turn of the Century Cabaret*. New York: Columbia University Press, 1987.

Senelick, Laurence, ed. *Russian Dramatic Theory*. Austin: University of Texas Press, 1981.

Shapiro, Laura. "Send in the Clown." *Newsweek* (15 May 1989), 76–77.

Short, Randall. "He'll Never Stop Clowning Around: Interview with Bill Irwin." *Newsday* (30 April 1987): 89.

Simon, John. Review of *Waiting for Godot*, by Samuel Beckett (Mike Nichols director, New York). *New York Magazine* (21 November 1988): 134.

Smith, Winifred. *The Commedia dell'Arte*. New York: Benjamin Blom, 1964.

Souriau, Etienne. *Les deux cent mille situations dramatiques*. Paris: Flammarion, 1950

Speirs, Ronald. *Brecht's Early Plays*. London: Macmillan Press, 1982.

Stone, Laurie. "Fool Hardy." *Village Voice* (24 April 1990): 104.

Storey, Robert. *Pierrots on the Stage of Desire*. Princeton: Princeton University Press, 1985.

———. *Pierrot: A Critical History of a Mask*. Princeton: Princeton University Press, 1978.

Strehler, Giorgio. *Incontro*. Toronto: Istituto Italiano di Cultura, 1989.

———. *Appunti per Re Lear*. Milano: G. and R. Associati, 1977.

———. *Per un teatro umano*. Milano: Feltrinelli, 1974.

———. *Il Re Lear di Shakespeare: Appendice: Irrappresentabile o Illeggibile? di Agistino Lombardo*. Verona: Bertani, 1973.

Taylor, Ronald. *Kurt Weill: Composer in a Divided World*. New York: Simon and Schuster, 1991.

Thetard, Henry. *La Mervailleuse Histoire du Cirque*. Vol. 3. Paris: Prisma, 1947.

Toll, Robert, C. *Blacking Up: The Minstrel Show in Nineteenth-Century America*. New York: Oxford University Press, 1974.

Toole-Stott, R. *Circus and Allied Arts: A World Bibliography*. 4 vols. Derby, England: Harpur and Sons, 1958–71.

Towsen, John. "Molière 'a l'Italienne:' Dario Fo at the Comédie Française." *Theater Magazine* (Summer/Fall 1992): 52–61.

———. *Clowns*. New York: Hawthorn Books, 1976.

Valentin, Karl. *Gesammelte Werke*. Munich: R. Piper, 1961.

Valentini, C. *La Storia di Dario Fo*. Milan: Feltrinelli, 1977.

Van Erven, Eugene. *Radical People's Theatre*. Bloomington: Indiana University Press, 1988.

Vaughan, David. "The Silent Treatment, in this Case Speaks Volumes." *New York Times*, 21 February 1993, H5.

Vial, Veronique, and Hélène Dufresne, eds. *Cirque du Soleil*. Montreal: Productions du Cirque Du Soleil, 1993.

Volker, Klaus. *Brecht: A Biography*. Trans. John Nowell. New York: The Seabury Press, 1978.

Walker, Katherine Sorley. *Eyes on Mime: Language without Speech*. New York: John Day Company, 1969.

Watkins, Glenn. *Pyramids at the Louvre: Music, Culture, and Collage from Stravinsky to the Postmodernists*. Cambridge: Harvard University Press, Belknap Press, 1994.

———. *Soundings: Music in the Twentieth Century*. New York: Schirmer Books, 1988.

Weber, Bruce. "Just Clowning around with Intellect." *New York Times*, 3 March 1993, C1.

Welsford, Enid. *The Fool: His Social and Literary History*. London: Faber and Faber, 1935.

Wettach, Adrian. "Grock's Entrée." Trans. John Towsen. *Mime, Mask and Movement* 1, no. 1 (Spring 1978): 25–40.

———. *Grock, King of Clowns*. Trans. Basil Creighton. London: Methuen, 1957.

Wilde, Larry. *The Great Comedians Talk about Comedy*. New York: Citadel Press, 1968.

Wiles, David. *Greek Theatre in Performance*. Cambridge: Cambridge University Press, 2000.

———. *The Masks of Menander*. Cambridge: Cambridge University Press, 1991.

———. "Taking Farce Seriously: Recent Critical Approaches to Plautus." In *Themes in Drama*. Cambridge: Cambridge University Press, 1988.

———. *Shakespeare's Clown*. Cambridge: Cambridge University Press, 1987.

Willeford, William. *The Fool and his Scepter: A Study in Clowns and Jesters and their Audience*. Evanston, Ill.: Northwestern University Press, 1969.

Willett, John. *The Theatre of Bertolt Brecht*. New York: New Directions, 1959.

Winkler, Elizabeth Hale. *The Clown in Modern Anglo-Irish Drama*. Bern: Peter Lang, 1977.

Winn, Stephen. "The Berkeley Rep's Beckett." *San Francisco Chronicle*, 5 November 1993, C5.

———. "The Clown Who Can Fly—Almost." *Connoisseur* (September 1982): 141–144.

Worton, Michael. "*Waiting for Godot* and *Endgame*: Theatre as Text." In *The Cambridge Companion to Beckett*, ed. John Pilling. Cambridge: Cambridge University Press, 1994.

Yacowar, Maurice. *Loser Take All: The Comic Art of Woody Allen*. New York: Frederick Ungar, 1979.

Zeif, Sasha. "My Night at the Palace." *Theater* 14, no. 2 (Spring 1983): 48–54.

Zguta, Russell. *Russian Minstrels: A History of the Skomorokhi*. Philadelphia: University of Pennsylvania Press, 1978.

Index